Faulkner

and the

Thoroughly Modern Novel

Faulkner

and the

Thoroughly Modern Novel

∘ Virginia V. James Hlavsa ∘

University Press of Virginia
Charlottesville and London

THE UNIVERSITY PRESS OF VIRGINIA
Copyright © 1991 by the Rector and Visitors
of the University of Virginia

First published 1991

Library of Congress Cataloging-in-Publication Data

Hlavsa, Virginia V. James, 1933–
    Faulkner and the thoroughly modern novel / Virginia v. James
Hlavsa.
        p.   cm.
    Includes bibliographical references.
    ISBN 0–8139–1311–X (cloth).
    1. Faulkner, William, 1897–1962—Criticism and interpretation.
    2. Modernism (Literature)—United States. I. Title.
    PS3511.A86Z788   1991
    813'.52—dc20   90–19688
                                                          CIP

Printed in the United States of America

Contents

To Dick and David

Acknowledgments

P RAISE BE FOR the many workers in these fields! My professors, John Thompson at SUNY Stony Brook and Ruth Vande Kieft at CUNY Queens College both challenged me with useful measures of skepticism before they believed. Kathryn Lukoski, Melda Duhun, Sue Nicholas, Helen Cutner, Ken Kaiser, and my former colleagues at Queens College, Bette Weidman, Mitzi Hamovitch, and Rosemary and Leonard Deen, all suffered through early drafts, each in their varied ways raising crucial questions. Patty Mondragon began and my sister, Mary Krauthamel, finished the onerous task of compiling a concordance for *Light in August*. My brother, Keen James, edited many of my manuscripts. My best friends, Jeannette Jansky and my husband, Richard, sustained me in my battles with the nay-sayers. I am proudest of my son, David, who grew up hearing about Faulkner, and then, reading my manuscripts, taught me.

I am grateful for permission to quote from *Light in August* and from *Absalom, Absalom!* by William Faulkner, reprinted by permission of the publisher, Random House Inc.

For permission to quote from and reproduce manuscript materials I thank the Manuscripts Division, Special Collections Department, University of Virginia Library, William Faulkner Collections (#6074), of which Faulkner's autograph manuscript of *Light in August* is a part; and to the Knight Library, University of Oregon, which holds the manuscript fragment from chapter 15 of *Light in August*.

Permission to quote from both manuscripts has been kindly granted by W. W. Norton & Company, Inc.

Portions of this study appeared in *Novel* as "The Vision of the Advocate in *Absalom, Absalom!*"; in the *Bulletin of Research in the Humanities* as "St. John and Frazer in *Light in August*: Biblical Form and Mythic Function"; in *Faulkner and Humor: Faulkner and Yoknapatawpha, 1984* as "The Levity of *Light in August*"; in *American Literature* (reprinted by Duke University Press in *On Faulkner: The Best from American Literature*) as "The Mirror, the Lamp and the Bed: Faulkner and the Modernists"; in *Katallagete* as "Beginning with the Word: Faulkner's Use of the Fourth Gospel"; and in *Faulkner and Religion*, forthcoming from the University of Mississippi Press, as "The Crucifixion in *Light in August*: Suspending Rules at the Post." All are reprinted with the permission of those publishers.

The drawing on the title page and on the jacket is by William Faulkner (from *Ole Miss*, 1919–20) and is used by permission of the University of Mississippi, Department of Archives and Special Collections.

PART ONE

Faulkner the Modernist

CHAPTER I

The Mirror, the Lamp, and the Bed

Mr. Faulkner, did you intend any Christ symbolism in Joe Christ-mas?

No, that's a matter of reaching into the lumber room.

"Well," said Sherlock Holmes, "I say . . . that a man should keep his little brain-attic stocked with all the furniture that he is likely to use, and the rest he can put away in the lumber-room of his library, where he can get it if he wants it."

The Five Orange Pips

IMAGINE THAT we had a book entitled *A Day in the Life of Leopold Bloom*. Its author, a poorly educated Dubliner named Joyce, gave out that it was simply a collection of yarns gathered from local folk. Surely the response would be mixed. Even as they acknowledged his genius, critics would complain of the book's confusion of styles; the repetition and density of the diction; the odd obsessions; the clichés in the Gerty MacDowell chapter; the literary survey at the hospital; the headlines in the newsroom.

Because early readers of Faulkner thought that he was an unedu-
cated country boy, far from the main currents of modernism, they
were unaware that he, like Joyce, was organizing his works according to external structures. Looking for simple stories, critics discovered problems of style, organization, characterization, and even
plot. Reacting to his extremes, they called him a romantic.

A consensus is finally emerging that Faulkner must be placed
where he belongs, among the modernists. But what does this
mean? Of course, critics will never agree about terms such as *modern* or *romantic*, but M. H. Abrams has usefully suggested that
such classifications should be linked to the perception of the world
the artist shared with his own time. In *The Mirror and the Lamp*,
Abrams distinguishes between the neo-classical, eighteenth-
century artist as a "perceiving" mind, reflecting the external world
like a mirror, and the romantic, nineteenth-century artist as a
"projective" mind, casting a self-image out onto the world like a
lamp. T. S. Eliot suggested that the modernist movement was
a return to the hard, spare world of classicism, the exact observation of the external object. Although the desire to be faithful to
external reality would be appropriate to the age of photography, the
modernists had an accompanying desire for a new temporal and
spatial reordering and even disordering of the external world, primarily in response to psychology. Gertrude Stein, seeing the impli-
cations of William James's "flow" or "stream" of consciousness for
revealing repressed instinct, suggested that artists return to repetitions and primitive rhythms. Proust decided that his own invol-
untary memories could serve as a guide to help him uncover the
basic laws of human behavior. Given this emphasis on the unconscious, we could say that the modernist movement (and Faulkner)
represents, neither the perceiving nor the projecting mind, but the
promiscuous mind. And the appropriate image is neither the enlightened mirror nor the enlightening lamp, but the darkened bed.

The choice of term would rest on more than a greater frankness
regarding sexuality. The word *promiscuous* means "having diverse
parts," an apt description of the Freudian awareness of the mind's
divisions, the many levels of unawareness below the conscious.
Modernists like Eugene O'Neill even sounded Jungian levels of ra-

cial unconscious. While the romantic had seen the primitive as a purifying spring, the modernist saw it as a muddy river bottom, full of blind creatures that bump in the mire. Romantic nature, wild, was still an English garden, not a wasteland. Promiscuous also means "indiscriminate," "lacking standards of selection." Indeed, modernists did set out to remove personal judgment or censure from the material chosen. Joyce wanted to represent "the thousand complexities" of the mind and as many activities of the body, with the instincts central to both. As Hemingway's Frederic Henry says in *A Farewell to Arms*, "I was not made to think. I was made to eat. My God, yes. Eat and drink and sleep with Catherine." Promiscuous is also apt in its "casual" sense. The modernist writer, knowing that the unconscious leads our "free associations" by the nose, felt free to mix casually with the night crawlers, our dreams, where words refuse to lie still, undoing the pious by calling a funeral a funforall or toppling the innocent with "the cock struck mine." Thus, the promiscuous-minded modern artist played with his material, having his own hidden designs.

In this profusion of free associations and primordial rhythms, the modern artist turned to the bed for primary relationships and ancient rites of passage. Sister Carrie could say goodbye to her family in chapter one and never glance back, but the modernist carried that first bed on his back like Kafka's bug. Moreover, the modernist recognized the universality of the big bed moments, the unwholly Joycean trinity of "Bridebed, childbed, bed of death." In the nineteenth century, the butler simply helped you off with your coat. In the twentieth century, he might snicker at your bald spot. And that mattered. The agony of Nathanael West's Miss Lonelyhearts is knowing that even the most odious human beings suffer an agony as great as his own. Above all, the bed is an apt metaphor because, unlike previous artists, who believed they controlled the illumination of their work (whether reflecting or projecting), the modern artist knew he was one of the featured partners in the performance, the other being the work of art itself. In other words, besides the driving forces of character, plot, or genre, the artist knew that one engine was his own, usually unconscious, obsessions. Therefore, the greater his nakedness, the more prodigious his cover.

Three types of covers may be observed in the modernist movement. Most obviously, writers organized their work by external patterns. Of course, towering geniuses have traditionally turned to organizing frameworks. Chaucer used Boccaccio and Boethius; Shakespeare used Plutarch and Holinshed; Milton used the Bible and the Talmud. With the rise of romanticism, which glorified the individual imagination, the practice of telling tales based on the classics came into disfavor. Although Coleridge evidently used ships' logs for his descriptions in *The Rime of the Ancient Mariner*, he kept it quiet. Modernists such as Eliot and Joyce returned to the practice, sometimes with a vengeance. In *Ulysses*, which defines the modern novel much as *Oedipus Rex* defines Greek tragedy, Joyce patterned his three main characters—Stephen, Bloom, and Molly—on Telemachus, Odysseus, and Penelope in their three primary modes: quest, return, and stasis. Moreover, using what he called "mosaics" of synonyms, homonyms, and images, Joyce paralleled episodes in the *Odyssey*, making his eighteen chapters also relate to parts of the body, disciplines of the mind, times of the day, techniques of discourse, colors, symbols, and other wonders too numerous to mention. Beckett reported Joyce's saying, "I may have oversystematized *Ulysses*." But ironically, Joyce and the modernists set up these elaborate frameworks as they also set out to represent reality (the highest goal of a literature in competition with photography), rearranging the reality of the external world to reflect the reality of the internal world.

A second cover of modernist writers involved fragmentation and distortion. For example, Joyce's Cyclops chapter begins with "I," repeats expressions such as "says I," uses phrases such as "cod's eye" (to rhyme with God's eye), discusses the *I*rish and the Emerald *I*sle, and Joe and John and Jesus (whose names, in Greek, begin with an *I*), and it refers to a local watchtower or a one-eyed merchant, all glancing off references to "blinding." Joyce once said, "I can justify every word and every *syllable* in everything that I write!"

Actually, recent psychological experiments suggest that when we encounter a word, all the meanings we know, no matter how disparate, are available to us on some level. Thus, if I say, "This room has bugs in it," you might promptly produce several meanings for "bugs." But tests demonstrating the human ability to quick-shift show that on the unconscious level you can have all five meanings ready: cockroaches, germs, problems, enthusiasts, or hidden microphones.

It was Freud's studies of dreams, jokes, and slips of the tongue that brought this phenomenon into the modern awareness. In these mundane circumstances are found four types of wordplay: displacement (shifting emphases), condensation (compressing meanings), representation (making symbols) and misrepresentation (garbling and gainsaying with puns and adversatives). Of course, the reason for these routine distortions is that they protect us from those thoughts that lie too deep for tears (or titterings). Given the significance of the unconscious, the artist's task is to pluck the words and set them vibrating in the mind to register additional harmonics. Sherwood Anderson, a profound influence on Faulkner, had himself been influenced by Gertrude Stein's use of repetitions, which drew attention to the words, along with minute variations, which drew attention to the syntax. Anderson encouraged young writers to join the "great revolution in the art of words."[1] Imagine the delight of these modern word bugs to be able to jam words together to make "dimmansions" or spread them out to make "wavyavyeavyheavyeavyevyevy hair"; to slip letters out, making "word" out of "world"; or garble them, making "calvary" out of "cavalry"; or reverse them, making "dog" out of "god." Again, the justification for this wordplay was the creation of realism, to catch what Joyce called that "great part of every human existence . . . which cannot be rendered sensible by the use of wideawake language, cutanddry grammar and goahead plot."

The third cover of the modernist writer—that he chose the ironic mode—follows logically from the first two. For if the writer was both hiding and distorting, he was a dissembler, the meaning

1. Carvel Collins writes: "Examination of *The Double Dealer* quickly makes clear that the people who ran it—with whom William Faulkner associated in . . . 1925 and . . . 1926—were fully aware of the intellectual and aesthetic currents which were making the twenties so important in American literature ("Introduction" 16).

of the Greek root *eiron*. And this, again, despite our shared sense that his fictive world was somehow more real. Of course, as J. H. Robinson, the modern historian, suggested, the complexities of human thought and experience could only be treated in a mood of tolerant irony. But for the racked artist, the tolerance or detachment was as feigned as the fantasy of the modern parent, imagining he or she could avoid conflict with a child by "using" psychology. In fact, sometimes the ironic mode leaves us, like the child, aware of the parent's intensity of feeling but puzzled about its specifics. Critics are still quarreling over the fourth book of *Gulliver's Travels*. Were the Houyhnhnms Swift's ideal or an overnice contrast to the Yahoos? Although earlier writers can usually be centered within the beliefs of their own time, for the modernists, the center would not hold. And as for asking them what they meant, if they were willing to speak, we might learn their conscious desires. But what parent is fully aware of his or her own unconscious desires?

Faulkner was a notoriously untrustworthy commentator on his own writing, and he worked beneath all the covers. It is not surprising that both he and Joyce thought of themselves first as poets, for they both loved to write under the constraints of form and with the freedom of wordplay. Moreover, Faulkner's reading in the modernists is suggested by the book list, ordered for him by his mentor, Phil Stone, who subscribed to the *Dial*.[2] His use of Eliot goes back to his poetry: "Love Song" all but paraphrases "Prufrock." His awareness of Joyce is documented through biography[3] and text, where allusions to and devices from *Ulysses* early appeared in *Sol-*

2. See Blotner, *Library* 123–27, for a list that included F. Scott Fitzgerald, H. D., James Joyce, D. H. Lawrence, Archibald MacLeish, H. L. Mencken, Eugene O'Neill, John Crowe Ransom, William Carlos Williams, and Conrad Aiken's *Modern American Poetry*.

3. Blotner (*Biography*) indicates that Faulkner received and dated a copy of *Ulysses* in 1924 (1.352); that Joyce was common currency in Sherwood Anderson's New Orleans circle (1.329); that Faulkner discussed Joyce with Hamilton Basso in 1925 (1.418); that Faulkner gave his wife *Ulysses* in 1931 to help her understand *Sanctuary* (1.746); and that that same year, Faulkner admitted to Paul Green and Milton Abernathy that he had lied about not knowing Joyce (1.716); in fact, he recited Joyce to them and read aloud from his *Light in August* manuscript (1.721).

diers' Pay and *Mosquitoes*.[4] The title *Mosquitoes* is itself a parody of *Ulysses*, in which Joyce never mentions the *Odyssey*. In Faulkner's book, mosquitoes are called only "it" or "they," with much slapping of wrists or rubbing of legs or fighting of battles: "Its thin whine rose keening to an ecstatic point and in the glass she saw it mar her throat with a small gray speck. She slapped savagely. It eluded her with a wary, practiced skill, hanging fuzzily between her and the unshaded light" (112).

In a 1958 interview with Richard Ellmann, Faulkner said that he "considered himself the heir of Joyce in his methods in *The Sound and the Fury*" (308n). Certainly critics have found evidence of his Joycean use of the lumber room of his library: McHaney's study of *The Wild Palms* suggests that Faulkner evokes, by paraphrase, parody, and allusion, themes from Dante, Hemingway, Schopenhauer, Nietzsche, and Anderson, all in that one book!

Moreover, right from the beginning, some critics did recognize parallels between Faulkner's characters and religious and mythic figures, particularly those described in James Frazer's encyclopedic study of comparative religions, *The Golden Bough*. In *Light in August*, besides the obvious connection between Joe Christmas and Jesus Christ, Joe relates to the golden bough itself. In his description of Turner's painting *Golden Bough*, Frazer says that the pictured Lake of Nemi had been called "Diana's Mirror" because it bordered her sacred grove, anciently patrolled by a priest with a drawn sword: "Within the sanctuary at Nemi grew a certain tree of which no branch might be broken. Only a runaway slave was allowed to break off, if he could, one of its boughs. Success in the attempt entitled him to fight the priest in single combat, and if he slew him he reigned . . . with the title of King of the Wood" (1.11).[5] The tree to be guarded was the sacred oak, and the golden bough, probably the parasitic mistletoe, venerated for its intermediary po-

4. See Slabey ("Faulkner's *Mosquitoes*"), Blotner (*Biography* 1.429), Adams, and Kenner. Gwynn early complained of the Eliotic echoes in *Mosquitoes*.

5. Critics such as Millgate and Moseley have made this connection between the Priesthood at Nemi and *Light in August*. Other discussions of religious and mythic parallels include: Cottrell, Holman, Slabey ("Myth"), Langston, Rubel, Kunkel, Asals, Don Noel Smith, and Pitavy.

sition between heaven and earth, like Christ. In fact, it was thought to be god-empowered, to have been "planted" by lightning. Since it stayed alive in winter, it appeared to hold the soul of the "dead" oak, and it alone could kill the apparently "deathless" god (11.279–303).

The language to support both Joe and Joanna in these multiple roles is pervasive. Joe is constantly linked with words relating to lightning, such as *flash, glint, gold, yellow* or *bolt*, reaching a climax just before his death when "his raised and armed and manacled hands [are] full of glare and glitter like lightning bolts, so that he resembled a vengeful and furious god pronouncing a doom." Joanna, called "priest" and "tree," has a "clump of oaks" in the "exact center" of her property. When Joe battles her, it is "as if he struggled physically with another man for an object of no actual value to either, and for which they struggled on principle alone";[6] to him she is "a dual personality: the one the woman at first sight of whom in the lifted candle . . . there had opened before him, instantaneous as a landscape in a lightningflash, a horizon of physical security and adultery if not pleasure; the other the mantrained muscles and the mantrained habit of thinking born of heritage and environment with which he had to fight up to the final instant" (221–22 / 258).

However, my own studies of *Absalom, Absalom!* and *Light in August* indicate that, in addition to these bookwide themes and correspondences, discovering the themes of Faulkner's chapters or divisions is critical to understanding his works. The two halves of *Absalom, Absalom!* correspond to two stages of a trial in equity, a branch of civil as opposed to criminal law concerned with providing remedies for wrongs that cannot be compensated for in money. And when we examine Faulkner's repetitions in each of the nine chapters, we discover that they represent nine types of evidence in giving testimony. For example, chapter 2 represents hearsay testimony by repeated phrases such as "Miss Coldfield told Quentin,"

6. *Light in August*, pages 222 / 258. Page references, hereafter cited parenthetically in text, are to both the original 1932 edition and the new, 1987, paperback edition of the Corrected Text, in that order, separated by a virgule. (The 1987 cloth-bound edition has different pagination.) Corrections of substance are given in text, in brackets, with the notation *CT*.

"the town learned," "Sutpen told Quentin's grandfather," "it was believed (or said)," or elaborate constructions such as "there were probably others besides Quentin's grandfather who remarked," "Sutpen's future and then unborn sister-in-law was to tell Quentin," or even "General Compson was the first man in the county to tell himself." The bare outline of this novel-trial is as follows:

I. Preliminary hearing
   Chapter 1: Opinions and convictions
   Chapter 2: The hearsay history of Thomas Sutpen
   Chapter 3: The vanishing, immaterial Coldfields
   Chapter 4: Waiting for the best, the very best evidence
II. Removal of proceedings
   Chapter 5: A certain sworn statement
III. Trial in equity
   Chapter 6: Viewing the scene from a northern perspective
   Chapter 7: Admissions and confessions
   Chapter 8: Presumptions that compound the guilt
   Chapter 9: Real evidence[7]

At the same time, these legal maneuverings are highly ironic. The testimony in the first four chapters by actual witnesses to Sutpen's (still to be determined) "crime" consists of "evidence" that violates the four exclusionary rules of opinion, hearsay, immateriality, and best evidence withheld. While such testimony would be allowed in preliminary hearings, still, our sense of fair play is disturbed by the way this confusing, incomplete, and possibly untrustworthy material is thrust at us.

Conversely, in the last four chapters, which constitute the "trial," the evidence seems more acceptable because the forms in which it is presented are legally correct. They include viewing the scene (a practice widespread before photography), admissions and confessions, presumptions, and real evidence. Even though our sense of reality is troubled by the knowledge that all of the information comes from Quentin and Shreve, several generations re-

---

7. Hlavsa, "Vision." This study has since been revised and expanded with the help of Russell Nobels, a lawyer from Mississippi. The idea that *Absalom, Absalom!* reflects a trial in equity was first proposed by Singleton.

moved from the events themselves, we are more likely to believe this kind of testimony. Thus, the legal structure itself, when it is known, adds weight to our intuitive desire to believe that Quentin and Shreve are closer to the truth than Rosa or Mr. Compson.

Light in August also uses chapter divisions to develop underlying structures. As examined in Part Two of this study, Faulkner paralleled the 21 chapters of *Light in August* with the 21 chapters of the St. John gospel. For example, the changing of water to wine occurs in John's chapter 2 where, in Faulkner, Christmas and Brown are introduced as bootleggers. The teaching in the temple occurs in chapter 7, the chapter in which McEachern is trying to teach Joe his catechism. The story of the woman taken in adultery is paralleled by the story of Bobbie, the prostitute, in chapter 8. Most prominently, the crucifixion scene occurs in both 19th chapters. And both chapters 20 involve musings on the living dead—in Faulkner, the "phantoms" of Hightower's past; in John, the risen Christ.

But there is more. Faulkner further expanded each gospel story with related mythic belief and folk practices from *The Golden Bough*. For example, in chapter 9 of John, Jesus heals the blind man, who comes to see both spiritually and physically, while his adversaries become increasingly blind. Although many people in Faulkner's chapter 9 are similarly shown suddenly free from their former blindness, they are also repeatedly shown beating on each other: McEachern at Joe, Joe at McEachern, Bobbie at Joe, Joe at the horse, Joe at the stranger in Bobbie's house, and finally, the stranger and Max at Joe, lying on the floor. But commentary on John 9 notes that even in Jesus' time, blindness was still regarded as an embodied sin to be cast out.[8] Thus, when we examine Frazer's chapters in *The Golden Bough* on the expulsion of scapegoats, we discover that such ceremonies include not only beatings but sliding down ropes, donning costumes or masks, dancing, screaming, cursing, and even spitting, all of which are elements in Faulkner's chapter 9.

---

8. Anchor (371). This modern study discusses the whole range of Johannine studies going back to patristic writings.

When critics complained to Joyce that the puns he used to establish themes were trivial, he retorted, "Yes, some of my means are trivial, and some are quadrivial." As a similarly deliberate craftsman, Faulkner makes every word count, every metaphor, every phrase. He once said that Flaubert was "a man who wasted nothing . . . whose approach toward his language was almost the lapidary's" (Blotner, *Biography* 1.459). Faulkner's use of names is the most obvious example. Anse is for the ants of this world; Snopes for what?—the low, snotty stoops? Narcissa is the mirror; Popeye, the voyeur. What critics had not realized is that the chapter in which we learn a character's name is often significant. For example, in *Absalom, Absalom!* we only learn the names of Clytemnestra and Charles Bon in chapter 3, and this amidst a barrage of historical or fictional references and personae: Sutpen is an "ogre-face" or behind a "Greek mask" in an "edifice like Bluebeard's" (60); Rosa is called "Cassandralike"; Ellen is metamorphosed out of a "shadowy miasmic region something like the bitter purlieus of Styx" (69). These references have led critics to try for analogies with Oedipus or the Orestia, but such theories quickly spin out of control. For example, there is no evidence that Bluebeard only wanted a son, and while Rosa may make Cassandra-like pronouncements, it is *she* who does not understand them. Such individual poses match only if you do not set them in motion. That they nonetheless work as "stills," as possible prototypes for the Sutpen tragedy, is true. But then they occur as part of the chapter's theme of immateriality, so the fact that they cannot move, are weightless and finally immaterial, is part of the message.

Even less observed than the naming game is Faulkner's use of dialect to reinforce theme. For example in *Light in August,* the dialect word *sho* for *sure* occurs prominently in chapters 1, 18, and 21. In these chapters of John, the central theme is Christ's identification at his first appearance to the disciples, at the public trial, and at his final appearance, which begins, "After these things Jesus shewed himself to the disciples at the sea of Tiberias; and in this wise shewed he himself." Thus, *sho* can be both *sure* and the homonym *show*.

How do we know these structural and dictional patterns were

Faulkner's designs? For example, in examining *Light in August*'s individual chapters, I have entitled chapter 2 "External Changes." Now while *change* is a high-frequency word in Faulkner's chapter, the word never occurs in John 2 (the marriage at Cana and the scourge of the temple) although *changers* does. Can the use of this key term be justified?

Only because it works. Following Faulkner's lead, reading John through Faulkner's themes, can reveal patterns unnoticed in John. But first we must determine the direction of Faulkner's lead, and since Faulkner himself is a playful or perplexing guide, each chapter demands close scrutiny. In other words, to solve John, you must first solve Faulkner's chapters as you would a riddle.

Take an anonymous medieval verse:

> All night by the rose, rose,
> All night by the rose I lay,
> Dared I not the rose steal,
> Yet I bore that flower away.

Five types of observation help us to discover the meaning of this riddle: the repetition, the positioning, the accent, the associations, and the anomalies. Thus, we notice "All night," repeated once and placed at line's beginning and "rose," repeated three times and placed at line's end. Regarding "rose," we think of the flower and its tradition of youth, passion, purity, and, in the middle ages, secrecy. We also think of the past tense of "rise," sexually suggestive, especially linked with "All night," the rhymed word "lay," and that striking word "bore." Beyond all, we notice that the manifest content, the riddle, makes no sense: how can one both lie by a rose and bear it away? One can, but only when the action is in the past tense.

Now, were I to title this riddle "The Maid's Deflowering," critics might complain that I don't know that this is the meaning. Nowhere does the word *maid* appear; "deflower" is not "flower"; and even if the poem is about sex, it could be about adultery rather than the loss of virginity. All this is true. However this title does fit the parts—it works. Furthermore, the young man's "roguishness" is increased by imagining his lay involves a young girl. It is not wrong to make assumptions, to use our imagination. If we, as informed readers, can establish a pattern on the strength of the most verifiable evidence, then we may take the next step and extrapolate, bringing to light less obvious (though perhaps equally important) evidence.

In fact, when we use the five types of observation in Faulkner's chapter 2 and discover the theme of change, we find, returning to John 2, that it does apply to all three episodes, a unity previously unnoticed. The first story in John can be called "the changing of water to wine"; the second involves the changes Jesus would effect by driving from the temple those "changers of money"; and the third has Christ foretelling his own resurrection, a change in the "temple of his body." But then John is also making metaphoric patterns in his use of "temple." In fact, wordplay is a distinguishing feature of John.

Faulkner gives us many opportunities for this pleasurable puzzle-solving. Although John is the most literary gospel, the only one with a real sense of plan (Cambridge 36), the unity of his chapters is by no means always apparent, and there are many textual problems. Especially at the beginning of this century, controversies over the single or multiple authorship, the early or late dating, and the many dualisms of light-dark or spirit-flesh, all had led scholars to read John allegorically, for literary clarity or philosophical statement or spiritual vision, depending on the mind-set of the commentator.

Faulkner evidently sensed the textual compatibilities, perhaps because as a modernist writer he was willing to pull the word out of context, make it concrete or invert it. As Freud noted, in dreams any element may be taken negatively or positively, and all time is present time. Or perhaps these compatibilities came to Faulkner from seeking the primitive or archetypal designs behind John's stories. In other words, *The Golden Bough* may have suggested some matches between concrete behavior and abstract thought. For if we turn to Frazer for the folk or mythic traditions surrounding the changing of water to wine, we read of certain people who mark Easter by holding their tongues in buckets of water mixed with fodder, waiting to gulp it at the "miraculous change" (10.124).

Thus, along with chapter 2's external changes—of clothing, of name, of the underworld bootlegger, Joe Christmas, as the Underworld god, Dionysus (whose rites involved changing water to wine)—Faulkner suggests changes of attitude or expectations, but even these are signaled by the concrete—the loosened tongues of Christmas and Brown, separately referring to food in a lunch pail as "muck," or even "Cold muck out of a dirty lard bucket" (39 / 47).

To be sure, if we had to rely on any one chapter for the basic pattern, our analysis would seem altogether too convenient. On the other hand, if every cream sauce has a fishy taste, it is time to look for the trout in the milk. If we, reading Faulkner, are able to discover unifying themes in John and compatible discussions in Frazer, twenty-one times over, certainly Faulkner could have made the same discoveries.

The question is how much of this unifying work was conscious on Faulkner's part? Theories on creativity tend to go in two directions: artists may be more aware than the rest of us, or less. Either they bring the unconscious up to the light, or they descend into the darkness, intuitively guided. Going to either extreme starts throats clearing. If Faulkner attended to details, he might be thought of as obsessive. If the unconscious took over, he might be thought of as lacking art.

There are good reasons to lean toward the obsessiveness. To begin with, this inclination goes with the trade. The writer is obsessed (the word means "to sit on"), playing by the hour with pieces of his own creation (while the critic plays with another's creation!). One can still see the complex notes for *A Fable*, in large and minuscule lettering, all over the walls of Faulkner's working study at Rowan Oak. Moreover, Faulkner was obsessed, with the South, with racism, with religion, with women. His bathroom obsessions are painfully obvious in *Mosquitoes*. Obsessions are useful; they keep us at the task. But just as Faulkner's obsessions led him to do the work, so they led to some overreaching for parallels. In *A Fable* Christ's crown of thorns is signified by a coil of barbed wire (Blotner, *Biography* 1.1501). In *Absalom, Absalom!* David's slingshot is signified by the French architect's suspenders tied to a pole (Rose 33). In *Light in August*'s chapter 4, the "living water" of Christ, testified to by Jacob's well, becomes Hightower's sweat, rolling down his face as he hears Byron's testimony. In chapter 6, Christ's discourse on bread and the eating of his flesh, becomes Joe Christmas, symbolically descended of Ham, eating "bread, with ham between" on the way out of the orphanage, and "bread, with ham between" on the way back.[9] In chapter 20, the raising of Christ from the dead becomes the rising—the erection—of Hightower, masturbating.[10]

Of course, such saucy topics extended the Edwardian revolt against Victorianism. But side by side with this adolescent snickering is a passionate cry of rage. Each outlandish parallel is just one instance of a serious chapter theme. In the above examples, Brown's testimony in chapter 4 brings many people to life, but especially Joe Christmas as "nigger" (91 / 107). Chapter 6 describes the process of making Joe into the dough-man, to be broken and shared by each new communicant. Chapter 20 reveals that Hightower does hold the image of life—in all its tragic absurdity—within his Golgothian bandaged skull.

Faulkner's world is, above all, one of paradox, of extremes. In such a world, it is the women who are harder on Lena than the men. It is the kind mother who is more of a danger to Joe than the cruel father. It is the rational Milquetoast who nightly relives the foolhardy violence of the cavalry charge. And it is the low, brutal scapegoat who finally soars into the sanctity of victimization.

Operating by extremes permitted Faulkner to suggest the whole range of human experience—the realism modernists sought—while he worked with some fairly stock characters: the Earth Mother, the hot spinster, the prostitute with the heart of gold, the weak-kneed intellectual, the mean half-breed. They are not stereo-

---

9. Recall in the Lestrygonian chapter of *Ulysses*: "Sandwich? Ham and his descendants mustered and bred there."

10. Don Noel Smith believes that Hightower's "daily vision represents a form of autoeroticism or masturbation" (173). Our last view of Harry Wilbourne, in *The Wild Palms*, may be similar. McHaney relates the book's title and the passage's palms and hands to jokes about masturbation (*William Faulkner's* The Wild Palms 172–73). And Minter (65) sees masturbatory activity in *Mosquitoes*.

types: they present too many surprises for that. Like many modernist characters, conceived out of their underlying form, they are archetypal, with reinforcing quirks and oddities. But the fact that Faulkner animated these lumps of rage and jest under secret wraps suggests that they were shaped by a fierce sentimentality, an expression of unfulfilled longings.[11] Apparently one of Faulkner's engines was a treacherous tenderness toward his characters, glaringly evident in *The Reivers*. To protect himself from his own pathos, he permitted his characters brutal or ludicrous behavior— behavior which he alone (like the Creator) could explain.

In *Light in August* Faulkner made all of his characters operate by forces they cannot begin to understand, let alone resist.[12] Strap Joe to the analyst's couch, he might dredge up the dietitian, but he would never imagine he was playing the role of Dionysus. Joanna knows only that she is a carpetbagger's granddaughter, not that she is Diana of the Woods. In chapter 6, Faulkner protected himself from the heartbreaking knowledge of Joe, the victimized child, by filling his chapter (in John, the feeding of the multitude) with food jokes: the matron has "jellied" eyes; the dietitian looks to Joe like "something sweet and sticky to eat"; while she thinks of him

11. Notice that Joe's fear of Mrs. McEachern is a fear of sentimentality. Folding back on itself is Jacob's suggestion that only the "sentimentalist would insist upon the parallel between Joe Christmas and Christ" (147). Fiedler early recognized the sentimentality in Faulkner, likening him to Dickens. Two psychological studies of Faulkner are especially important. Analyzing Faulkner's rhetoric, Mortimer finds obsessions with boundaries, the dissolution of time and space, and the undermining of our ability to know, suggesting that they arose from his fear of the "otherness" of women. Focusing on *Absalom, Absalom!* and *The Sound and the Fury*, Irwin finds narcissistic themes in the overlapping Compson and Sutpen stories, especially evident in the recurring motif of the double (found in images of the shadow and the mirror). Freud suggested that the double represents "all the unfulfilled but possible futures to which we still like to cling in phantasy."

12. Abel says, "Most of the principal characters in the novel . . . act as if their wills were determined by some overruling necessity" (39). This is also true of John's characters. Critics are divided on the question of Joe's free will. Benson (546) says, "This Christmas story is of a man who has no choice in any meaningful sense of the word"; Kazin (525) says, "Joe Christmas is nothing but the man things are done to, the man who has no free will of his own." On the other hand, Longley (23) says Joe is "free to choose what he will be." The two views are compatible: as with Christ, the role of the scapegoat is assigned to him, and he accepts it.

among blacks as "a pea in a pan full of coffee beans." Similarly, in chapter 12, Faulkner protected himself from the heartbreaking knowledge of Joanna, the lonely spinster, by filling this chapter (in which Jesus announces, "Except a corn of wheat fall into the ground and die, it abideth alone") with parallels to the harvesting of the Corn Maiden and other slightly ludicrous rainmaking behavior, described in Frazer.

The secrecy has also had the effect of keeping Faulkner's characters more firmly under his own control, less vulnerable to critical scrutiny.

When Milton wrote *Paradise Lost*, he knew, had within, all that his reading and studying had told him; his edifice was the transformation of all those bits of glass and stone and mortar into cathedral. So it is with Faulkner's art. Having studied the principles of giving evidence in a trial in equity, he worked out his ironic nine-part structure for *Absalom, Absalom!*. Having fully stocked the lumber room of his brain-attic with John and Frazer, he demonstrated that he could fashion every element—word, metaphor, description, and incident—to fit the grand design of *Light in August.*

CHAPTER II

The Mythical Method

In using the myth, in manipulating a continuous parallel between contemporaneity and antiquity, Mr Joyce is pursuing a method . . . of ordering, of giving a shape and a significance to the immense panorama of futility and anarchy which is contemporary history. . . . Psychology . . . ethnology and The Golden Bough have concurred to make possible what was impossible even a few years ago. Instead of narrative methods, we may now use the mythical method.

Eliot, "Ulysses"

HEN, IN 1963, Lawrance Thompson suggested that Faulkner had read Eliot's 1923 essay on Joyce (21–22), he was reflecting the growing critical awareness of Faulkner's interest in what Eliot had called "the mythical method." This method included shaping characters and their stories according to parallels from Faulkner's own religious heritage, the Bible, along with one of the primary bibles of the modernist movement, *The Golden Bough*. It was evidently a work that fascinated him. The name he gave to his

Oxford home, Rowan Oak, is one type of the sacred golden bough (11.281), and Blotner observes that Faulkner was reading Frazer at the time he was writing *Light in August*.[1] As for his other works, to name just a few studies, McHaney's "*Sanctuary*" shows Faulkner's use of the priesthood at Nemi; Yonce's study of the relationship between *Soldier's Pay* and *The Golden Bough* shows how early Faulkner had turned to Frazer; and Cross found that the unabridged Frazer was used in *The Sound and the Fury*, a connection first made by Carvel Collins ("Pairing").

As Blotner says, Faulkner was always "setting new technical challenges for himself in successive novels" (*Biography* 1.607). Simply listing the variety of Faulkner's organizations (see Appendix A), we find that no two are alike. Moreover, by now scholarship has uncovered some of those challenges.[2] But since he was more secretive than Joyce, who could not wait for his cafe set to uncover his schemes, Faulkner never disclosed his game plans. Indeed, he once said, "No one but me knew what I was writing about or writing from" (*Lion* 220).

To uncover the challenges of *Light in August*, we should consider the book's anomalies. To begin with, one of the book's puzzles is that the many religious and mythical motifs appear to operate simultaneously. With names like Joanna Burden, Lena Grove, or Joe Christmas, we are almost in the world of Everyman, yet these characters do not stay in their assigned roles. Joanna resembles Diana, while Lena is an Earth Mother. But both have biblical associations, as well. Joanna, the feminine form of John, has

1. Blotner, *Biography* 1.660. Watkins writes, "A little Shegog girl is buried in his yard [at Rowan Oak]. A little girl who had heard that people return to life on Halloween once wrote a letter to the buried child and sent it to Faulkner. He and his family dressed in white, dug a hole in the grave, and buried the letter; and he wrote the little girl that he had delivered her letter to the Shegog child." See also the All Souls' ceremonies in chapter 11.

2. *As I Lay Dying* parallels the Bulfinch version of the Phaëthon-Apollo myth (Solomon), with plot and character references to *The Scarlet Letter* (Douglas & Daniel); *The Sound and the Fury* has patterns of the Christ story, structural ties to Dante's *Inferno* (Murphy), and allusions to Frazer, Freud, and Shakespeare (Carvel Collins, "Faulkner's *The Sound*") and (Naples); *A Fable* uses the synoptic accounts of the Passion (Ficken, "Christ Story"), with parallels to Humphrey Cobb's *Paths of Glory* (Julian Smith).

the Baptist's initials, she appears before J.C., and her head is cut off. And despite the associations of "Lena" with Helena or Magdalena, this "lady" arrives wearing her madonna blue, bearing her "luck" (which might be her "election") and carrying her palm-leaf fan, along with her rather determined innocence. She is, in other words, a Mary. Well, the facts make clear that she is not.[3] Is this a sly dig at the doctrine of the virgin birth or testimony to the possibility of genuine innocence despite actual guilt?

Joe Christmas is a similar puzzle. Like Christ, he has mysterious parentage, his feet are votively bathed, he appears to reject his mother (from John's "Woman, what have I to do with thee?"), he lives fifteen years in obscurity, he experiences an agony in the "ruined garden" (264 / 307), and at 33 (or is it 36? Jesus' age is also only approximated [Luke 3:23]),[4] he experiences a kind of crucifixion, complete with the five wounds, and a prompt apotheosis: "The man seemed to rise soaring into their memories forever and ever." But surely Joe cannot be Christ; no matter how we sympathize with his grim childhood (and who would suggest that Christ was the result of a poor upbringing), Joe is a murderer and, perhaps worse, a man of no message, at least none that *he* can articulate. Try as one might, despite one's intuition of a Christian connection, it is hard to give that connection shape and substance.

And of course, there are other puzzles. Recall the confusion, on first reading the novel, in the two contrasting depictions of Bobbie, from the wayward girl in chapter 8 to the screaming whore in chapter 9. Or recall, in chapter 4, that Hightower suddenly begins to sweat on hearing, not of the murder, but that Joe is "part nigger." Or recall Joe's odd behavior in chapter 5, slapping his drunken partner, "Joe Brown" (Lucas), or stripping himself before Joanna's window, or tramping off to the stable to "smell horses."

Real problems such as these have led critics to some odd conclusions. Ignoring the omniscient author's description of Joe's life,

3. Questioning the Holy Family parallel, Kerr (134) makes the seemingly absurd suggestion that if Lena is Mary and Byron is Joseph, then Lucas must represent the Holy Ghost.

4. See Lamont for a discussion of Joe's age.

which "for all its anonymous promiscuity, had been conventional enough, as a life of healthy and normal sin usually is" (246 / 285), one critic suggests that Hightower and Joe had been homosexual partners. Another calls Christmas a "pervert" or a "sadomasochist." Another gives him an "inferiority complex." Strained as these suggestions are, they arise from our struggles to explain some bizarre behavior.

Then, too, Faulkner's infamous repetitions produce some odd chapter themes. For example, inexplicably, chapter 4 keeps going on about hair: not only is the barbershop a frequent setting or the untidy-haired Mrs. *Beard* a frequent character, even the information that Joanna's head was "cut pretty near off" promptly notes that she was "a lady with the beginning of gray hair," or Christmas will say, "You ought to be careful about drinking so much of this Jefferson hair tonic. It's gone to your head. First thing you know you'll have a hairlip." Or chapter 5—where Joe wants to smell horses—is infused with many smells, breathing, and even the nose, called to our attention by repetition, synesthesia, or by Faulkner's "not" metaphors.

We have similar problems with the book's organization, complained of by earlier critics.[5] Chapter 5, covering the day before the murder, seems to come at an odd moment, *after* the discovery of the body and *before* the flashback to the murderer's childhood. Or there are constant shifts of time and place in chapter 14, the hunt for Christmas, even looping back over events in chapter 13. And why the sudden introduction of a new narrator in the last chapter? Although odd behavior and unusual structure can be found in every Faulkner novel, it is important to ask why, since these questions may very well have answers.

In *Light of August,* most of these difficulties and anomalies can be explained by Faulkner's use of John and Frazer. Consider first the question of structure. Biblical scholars often divide John as follows:

5. Cowley (xxiv-xxv) complains about the structure of *Light in August.* Leavis (92) suggests that Faulkner's "technique" may be a disguise for his "uncertainty about what he is trying to do"; and Reed (115) says that "disjunction here goes far beyond just a confused chronology or overturned conventional expectation."

Prologue: the beginning of chapter 1

Chapters 1–12: the Book of Signs

Chapters 13–20: the Book of Glory—the final days

Epilogue, chapter 21: not by John

So, too, the rather confusing time sequence of *Light in August* may be given as follows:

Chapter 1: the coming and history of Lena

Chapters 1–12: the crime signaled and explained

Chapters 13–20: the final days in Jefferson

Chapter 21: Lena and Byron, described by a new narrator[6]

Furthermore, that many biblical commentators will omit the story of the adulteress in John 8 suggests one explanation for the two views of Bobbie. Many believe that the adulteress story is an interpolation, because the language, grammar, and especially the tone are more like Luke than John, more gentle and compassionate (Cambridge 175–76). Thus, in Faulkner's 8, not just Bobbie, but all the characters—Max, Mame, McEachern, and even Joe himself—are presented in a much kinder light than elsewhere. Scholarly considerations could have also determined the odd placement of Faulkner's chapter 5, reflecting the questionable placement of the same chapter in John, since Jesus' movements at the beginning of chapter 6 seem geographically to follow his location at the end of chapter 4.

Furthermore, Faulkner's text and John's gospel contain parallel stylistic anomalies. In the gospel's last chapter, not by John, notice the repeated *thats* and *whiches*: "And there are also many other

---

6. Although subdivisions of John vary, even these differences may be found in Faulkner. For example, Westcott groups the latter part of John 1 with the chapters up to the end of 4, an organization that might be reflected by Lena's echoing words at the end of chapters 1 and 4.

But the Cambridge Bible groups John's chapters 1 through 5, an organization that might be reflected in Faulkner's Jefferson setting, before the shift to the orphanage, in chapter 6. Coindreau (36) and others see a three-part structure in *Light in August*, with 5–12 in the middle. Pitavy (16) would also separate 1–4 because the reiteration of Lena's words is put in the mouth of Byron, who did not witness her Jefferson arrival. "The author's artistic intention is therefore obvious: he wishes the first four chapters to form a perfect circle in themselves." Ficken ("Critical" 2–8) divides the novel into nine time periods.

things which Jesus did, the which, if they should be written every one, I suppose that even the world itself could not contain the books that should be written." Likewise, in his last chapter, Faulkner not only presents a completely new narrator, he even makes sure that the introduction to this narrator is amusingly slowed by its *thats* and *whiches*: "On his return home he told his wife of an experience which he had had on the road, which interested him at the time and which he considered amusing enough to repeat. Perhaps the reason why he found it interesting and that he felt that he could make it interesting in the retelling is that he and his wife are not old either, besides his having been away from home (due to the very moderate speed which he felt it wise to restrict himself to) for more than a week" (468 / 545).

FIGURE 1. The rustic corn goddess, Isis, was often worshipped as the Madonna by early Christians. (*Courtesy Kelsey Museum of Archaeology, University of Michigan*)

As for the Frazer connection, the evidence supports Cross's contention that Faulkner used, not the abridged, but the complete Frazer. For example, regarding chapter 5's references to smells, breathing, and even the nose, smells were used medicinally in primitive societies. Actually, biblical scholars conjecture that the pool at Bethesda was a healing spa or hot springs and that the periodic "troubling" of the waters was the boiling up of noxious vapors (Cambridge 123). Frazer cites several ancient volcanic regions, known for their curative powers. This discussion is not in the abridged Frazer. Nor is the description of the shepherds' festivals of St. George and the Parilia (3.324–48), which Faulkner features in 10 to develop John's discourse on the Good Shepherd.

Thus, Faulkner's "mythical method" of creating *Light in August* worked in the following way. Evidently he began with the lumber room of his childhood Christianity (to be discussed in my chapter 3). Drawing on a solid familiarity with the Bible and with Frazer, he assigned each of his major characters at least one corresponding pair of religio-mythic counterparts. The basic list is as follows:

Joanna	John the Baptist	Diana
Joe	Jesus	Dionysus
Lena	Mary	Isis
Lucas	Judas	Osiris
Byron	Joseph	Adonis
Hightower	Pilate	Hippolytus
Bobby	the woman sinner	Persephone / Demeter

Even this was no casual selection. Faulkner assigned his mythic figures from Frazer in accordance with their compatibility with the biblical figures. For example, Isis (Lena), out looking for Osiris (Lucas), was early confused with the Virgin Mary (6.118; see fig. 1). And the choice of Adonis for Byron probably reflects both his association with Bethlehem (1.257) and Frazer's comment that Adonis (Byron) was often confused with Osiris (Lucas), the figure Isis (Lena) is seeking. Of course, as in myth, the figures are not fixed. In the parallel to the sacred golden bough, Joe can represent the runaway slave, the parasitic mistletoe, the lightning which plants it on the tree, the new priest, who is King of the Wood, and even the originating god. Inevitably, those things touching or housing the sacred become sacred themselves. Or several characters can be different aspects of one archetype: Joe Christmas is the crucified Christ, while Lena's child is the newborn babe. Or one character can play several compatible roles: Hightower, a Pilate figure, can also play Nicodemus or the doubting Thomas. Or a character can take up several roles in one chapter: in chapter 5, Joe Christmas is the halt man, waiting to be cured; then he is the angel, troubling the waters; and finally, like one of Proteus' avatars, he becomes the troubled waters themselves.

However, while Faulkner's characters have their Christian counterparts, they do not equal the characters in John. Having established his religio-mythic pantheon, Faulkner arranged that in each chapter both major and minor characters reflect John's themes by engaging in practices described in Frazer. But again *which* mythical figure and *what* folk practice is chosen from Frazer is determined by themes from John's chapter. For example, appropriately, the Underworld wine god, Dionysus, is represented by the underworld bootlegger, Joe Christmas, who was "just down on his luck for a time, and . . . didn't give a damn much how he rose up." Also appropriate is Joe's introduction in chapter 2, where the theme is change, from John's story of the changing of water to wine. One of the chief miracles of the Dionysian Mysteries was the changing of water to wine (Moffatt 49), and Dionysus himself was said to have evaded his enemies, the Titans, "their faces whitened with chalk," by changing into various shapes before he was killed and mutilated, in one story, in the form of a blackskinned goat.

Still, when the covers are off the modernist writer, the truth can be both better and worse than we had supposed. For example, fortunately there is reason for Faulkner's having introduced a new narrator in his 21st chapter to parallel the new narrator in John 21, for he demonstrates the power of faith (despite some fishy appearances) to guide and sustain the good and simple people of this earth. Unfortunately, his version of the drawing-in of nets is that Byron, as the typical male, is not just the poor fish that didn't get away; he is the one that jumped into the net.

But the good and bad of the modernist techniques must be faced.

In the novel, especially, the central problem is that interferences with the narrative line place at high risk one of our most important pleasures in reading, namely, our love of story. What happens when modernists such as Joyce and Faulkner interfere with the story line?

And what about the puns? Many people don't like puns, especially bad puns, which simply interrupt their train of thought. In fact, someone has said that encountering puns in a modernist novel can be like coming on metallic prizes in a cake—more disturbing than pleasant. Then too, many people actively resent Faulkner's obscurities and the vague hints of goings-on. Often, his writing makes one feel like a child in a roomful of adults who are speaking of something fascinating (like sex) in riddles and grimaces. Moreover, the explanations for the anomalies do not make them disappear; indeed, they seem to send us off to other, unrelated, worlds. Worst of all, with no explanations, we can lose our way completely. There is an elitist, rejecting side to the ironic mode, which even the cognoscenti may dislike.

Just as the modern painter used bright colors, thick outlines and abstract shapes, so Faulkner used his materials, the words themselves, the odd structures and the ironic, dissembling mode to disturb and distract us. Indeed, they suggest that the train of thought may have more than one destination. Reality does encompass strange and distant lands, all within our personal or collective past. Freud's main thesis is that our sense of what is real must be expanded to include some rather peculiar impulses and behavior. While Forster was saying "Only connect," Faulkner was demonstrating that the connections are there, willy-nilly.

The fragmentation works in a similar way. As one critic noted, "Faulkner's characters are fragments of men needing each other to compose the full image."[7] In *A Fable*, Christ is crucified as Corporal Brzewsky, the English Boggan, the American Brzewski, and the Negro, Rev. Tobe Sutterfield, alias Tooleyman (Tout le Monde). Where each character enacts a chapter theme, there are no he-

---

7. Kaplan (111). Rovere also uses the word *fragmented* to describe Faulkner's characters (ix).

roes or villains, only better or worse people at better or worse moments. "Hero" becomes a momentary "heroism," and "betrayals" must be considered individually and in context.[8] When Lucas rebels from his master, Christmas, we say, "He would!" yet when Byron rebels from his master, Hightower, we say, "He should!"[9] McEachern's stubborn indoctrination has a disastrous effect on Joe, yet the same behavior by Grandfather Calvin, who would "beat the loving God" into his children, produces a returning son who engages his father in "deadly play and smiling seriousness." When the sheriff harks to Brown's assertion that Christmas is black with the crescendoing, "Nigger? . . . Nigger?" we see a good man disappearing into the haze of his racist background. When Grimm castrates Joe and shouts, "Now you'll let white women alone, even in hell," we see a bad man using racism as a blind for his own paranoia.

This thematic engagement of all the elements, working like poetry, is what makes the minor episodes so strong in Faulkner. At any point in his novels, the main action up on center stage is reflected and reechoed from every corner of the theater. Thus, Faulkner strengthens the realism of his fiction; life does consist of more than center stage. And while the ironic use of external structure seems to undercut that realism, it turns out that the script reflects age-old patterns of human behavior.

Undoubtedly, Faulkner's distortions in favor of John's chapters or Frazer's discussions make for some odd "believing before knowing." Take Joe's desire to "smell horses" "because they are not women" (101 / 119). To introduce the theme of smells as curative agents (appropriate to the healing theme in John 5), Faulkner calls on our irrational identification of horses with potency. And it is precisely this bypassing of the rational which may be the source of surprise—and pleasure—for each fresh reading of the novel.

The point is, if we do not read Faulkner in the light of these modern techniques, we misread Faulkner. Not recognizing the

---

8. Reed (144) makes a similar point when he says "apparently no conventional guide to virtue" exists for any character.

9. McCamy (9) also noted the "disciple" relationship of Byron and Hightower.

connections between the two stories of *The Wild Palms*, editors disengaged the alternating sections of "The Old Man," and as McHaney notes, the convict's "No to life" must be balanced by Harry's "No to death" (*William Faulkner's* The Wild Palms 194). Not recognizing the significance of the manner and order by which the story is told in *Absalom, Absalom!*—where information may be withheld not by Faulkner but by those giving testimony—commentators set about "unscrambling" the book with genealogical charts and chronological checks. Not recognizing the humorous parallel to the fourth gospel's 21st chapter, critics found fault with Faulkner's introduction of a completely new narrator at the ending of *Light in August*.

Ana-lysis means literally *up-loosening*, as in unyoking the team, opening the mouth, or releasing captives. By unlayering the layers of *Light in August*, we learn that the story is more than the story. Because we know behavior has many causes, only a work that has many levels of explanation will satisfy our sense of ourselves as complex, and above all, willful human beings. So our experience of reading and analyzing a work of literature opens us to new connections. Of course, no matter how we explain the odd or awful behavior of Faulkner's characters, we will never solve the mystery of them as they are imagined. But the process of seeking will have sent us around the world and back in time, revealing new connections with other lives and suggesting why we are so repelled by and drawn to Faulkner's mythic vision.

CHAPTER III

The Christian Legend

Q. *Sir, . . . the basic crucifixion image in* A Fable *occurs over and over again in your books. It occurs in* Light in August. *It happens in a kind of way even in* Sanctuary. *It happens in* Requiem for a Nun. . . .

A. *Remember, the writer must write out of . . . what he knows and the Christian legend is part of any Christian's background, especially the background of . . . a Southern country boy. . . . It has nothing to do with how much of it I might believe or disbelieve—it's just there.*

Faulkner in the University

LTHOUGH HE never wrote religious tract, Faulkner's work is powerfully infused with Christian icons. As a modernist writer, what did he think of them? Certainly we can agree that he is frequently denouncing the dead forms of religion. But then so was Jesus. Since so much of his work focuses our attention on biblical material, it may be helpful to explore Faulkner's knowledge of the Bible and his attitudes toward Christianity.

The knowing came early, but the learning continued throughout his life. Affectionately, Faulkner reported that his great-grandfather, who must have combined the sternness of a McEachern with the kindness of a Grandfather Calvin, required all the members of the family to have a Bible verse memorized before breakfast (Blotner, *Biography* 1.124). Several books in his library suggest that his interest in the Bible as narrative survived those early rigors. One, autographed in 1932, was the Merrymount Press multivolumed edition of the King James Bible, printed with paragraphing and without numbered verses or commentary, which, as Meeter notes, "prints verse as verse," so interpolations are more readily apparent. The other, *The Son of Man: The Story of Jesus*, by Emil Ludwig, combines the synoptics in story form, with the complexities removed. As for biblical commentary, we learn that Faulkner was reading the college-level, annotated Cambridge Bible from Laurence Stallings's 1932 observation of him in Hollywood: "Unlike practically everyone else, he has remained cold sober. He bought one book to read over his lonely nights. It is a second-hand twelve-volume . . . Cambridge edition of the Holy Bible."[1] But Faulkner didn't need to own biblical commentary in order to know it. The university library in Oxford, Mississippi, had a good exegetical collection. Moreover, during much of the writing of *Light in August*, Faulkner—like the typical New Yorker—was meeting friends on the steps of the New York Public Library (Blotner, *Biography* 1.744), where the Reading Room shelves the standard biblical commentaries (along with the complete Frazer).

Just as Faulkner the writer was carried by the artistic currents of his day, so was Faulkner the thinker. Along with other modernists,

---

1. Blotner, *Biography* 1.777, his ellipses. Blotner may have confused this with the Merrymount Press edition (*Biography* 1.790). Since the Cambridge Bible was not found in Faulkner's library at the time of his death and since no Cambridge edition is twelve volumed, Meeter believes Stallings's story is insufficient evidence that Faulkner read this commentary. Although I have no reason to assert that Faulkner did use the Cambridge over any other commentary, it could be that Stallings simply got the number of volumes wrong and that Faulkner got rid of the Cambridge edition before he left Hollywood.

Faulkner was writing against a background of Victorian religiosity. The Christ story—itself filled with ironies—was owned and operated by the Sincere who were trying to keep the Store going by capitalizing more and more of Its Goods. When the modernists seized it for their ironic mode, they seemed impious. Consider the shocked response to *A Man Who Died*, D. H. Lawrence's Passion according to Frazer's Osiris. But often the modernists believed themselves to be more, not less, religious. Having experienced the first world war, they believed they struggled with a scale of evil unknown to their elders. The suggestions of what Jung called the "living primordial images" lying behind the domesticated church only challenged these young writers. If religion was to have personal validity, one would have to work on it. Many set out to solve the problem of God and evil, going from scholarship to séance. Yeats made his religion out of Irish history and the occult; Pound, out of American history and Confucius. Others, keeping within Christianity, made their separate peace with God. Perhaps Joyce meant it ironically, but the lapsed Catholic said, "I have found no man yet with a faith like mine."

When Faulkner was questioned about supplanting a faith in God with a faith in Man, he said, "Probably you are wrong in doing away with God in that fashion. God is. It is He who created man. If you don't reckon with God, you won't wind up anywhere. You question God, and then you begin to doubt, and you begin to ask 'Why? Why? Why?' and God fades away by the very act of your doubting Him" (*Lion* 70). He also said, "Within my own rights I feel that I'm a good Christian" (*Faulkner in the Univ.* 203), and at Nagano, although he said that at times "Christianity gets pretty debased," he affirmed his belief, even espousing personal immortality: "I do believe in God, yes. I believe that man has a soul that aspires towards what we call God, what we mean by God" (*Faulkner at Nagano* 23–24). On the other hand, during one of his frequent depressions, Faulkner reportedly said that although he used "Christian lore and imagery," he felt "there was no such thing as personal immortality" (Blotner, *Biography* 2.1046). As usual, Faulkner's words about himself may be less trustworthy than the writings themselves.

Faced with the new gospel of comparative religions, many writers of Faulkner's day considered the Christian story mere primitive superstition, while others gave it naturalistic explanations. Frazer himself asserted that "to dissolve the founder of Christianity into a myth" is "absurd" (9.412n). Rather, he suggested that Jesus' role in the annual Passover ceremony was an "accident" that his enemies forced upon him because of his "outspoken strictures" (9.422).

If we examine *Light in August*, we may move closer to an understanding of Faulkner's position. Unlike those who sought to explain Christ in naturalistic terms, without the mystery and miracle, Faulkner singles out John, the fiercest version of the Christ story. John's Jesus says, "Woman, what have I to do with thee?" He says, "For judgment I am come into this world, that they which see not might see; and that they which see might be made blind." He says, "If a man abide not in me, he is cast forth as a branch, and is withered; and men gather them, and cast them into the fire, and they are burned." Of course, biblical commentators have explanations for these pronouncements, citing John's dualisms or his determinism, but for most readers, for the child, which is the stage when most of us come to the Bible, those explanations are needed.

But equally unlike those who were reducing Christ to "mere" primitive superstition, Faulkner reasserts the power of that violent natural world, which could make a community of decent, hard-working men so angered by the dark "contemptuously still" face of Joe Christmas that they want to run him through the planer (28 / 34).

Thus, for some modernists, neither the Christian nor the primitive world was less powerful when the family ties between them were revealed. From his constant use of biblical structures and figures, it should be obvious that Faulkner was obsessed with religion, or more precisely, he was obsessed with a need to place his own religion into a universal context, into cultures that exist across such vast tracts of time and space, they might indeed have been universal because they represent completely different worlds. His purpose in doing so was moral. He loved the people of his religion, but he wanted them to be aware that the savage roots of

Christianity go down not only into history but also into their own hearts. Because ultimately Faulkner believed we are one. Like Eliot, who maintained that myth opened modernist writers to the "vanished mind" of our own past, Faulkner believed he could hold his Mississippi folk in the light of the biblical tale as it is illuminated by mythic or folk behavior. In fact, the one could be electrified by the other.

Thus considered, the connections between *Light in August* characters and the various Christian figures assume an even greater importance. To begin hierarchically, that Old Doc Hines, whom blacks "perhaps . . . took . . . to be God Himself" (325 / 379), that Hines is God the avenging Father of Joe Christmas is most evident in chapter 15, which opens in John, "I am the true vine and my Father is the husbandman." Since for John's Jesus, "I and my Father are one," Hines shows that he is both the true source of the murderer and his destroyer. Well. God? Creator of evil and destroyer? Is this the (Manichean) God that Faulkner believed in?[2] Hines is simply insane, a fanatic, obsessed with—the chosen race. As soon as we say the words, the parallel emerges of Hines with the parochial God of the Old Testament (not a stranger to John), the vengeful Yahweh of the Israelites, the chosen people.

This suggests that Faulkner was using the specifics of the Hebraic-Christian tradition as leverage to roll away the stone from the deeper principles. It also appears that he had some fun at the task. Again, consider Lena. As the Virgin Mary, she suffers some lowering of status, for the parallel reminds us that she is a fallen woman. Indeed, so might the Virgin have been. On the other hand, Lena is a good and kind person, especially worthy in her innocent belief in the word of Lucas, and in her ability to carry her burden lightly. So might the Virgin have been—even without the virginity. Evidently Faulkner wanted to restore the human ambiguities to the Christian story.

Faulkner's parallels to the enemies of Christ also place Faulkner within a context sympathetic to the essentials of Christianity. If

---

2. Doyle (10) sees *A Fable* as Manichean, noting that frequently Faulkner "simply juxtaposed good and evil as if to say, 'This is the whole of life.'"

all were Black Mass, all reversed, we might expect Faulkner to have given the betrayer, Lucas-Judas, some redeeming features. Lucas has none. And we cannot even assume, along with Lawrance Thompson, that Faulkner was "contrasting certain pagan attitudes with certain Christian attitudes for the purposes of honoring the pagan" (80).[3] The pagan rite behind Percy Grimm comes from the self-castrating Priests of Attis. Faulkner's design is much more potent than simple inversion.

Notice also that the do-nothing, Hightower, as Pilate or doubting Thomas, comes in for some of Faulkner's greatest scorn. Although he does finally realize that he is as guilty of castrating the church as the "professionals" who have "removed the bells from its steeples," even this does him no good, returning as he does to his nightly "charge." Unlike Lena and Byron and the people of the town, who receive him with "hunger and eagerness," wanting to believe, Hightower never had any faith to begin with. That's his problem; religion is irrelevant. Real religion, the kind that depends on faith and charity, is not possible for the impotent rationalist.[4]

Actually, Faulkner's attitude toward Hightower is best understood by reading Frazer on "The Burden of Royalty." Among many folk, the sacred ruler is responsible for the whole course of nature, so "the least irregularity on his part may set up a tremor which shall shake the earth to its foundations." From the moment he ascends the throne, "he is lost in the ocean of rites and taboos." Because of the heavy strictures, "few kings are natives of the countries they govern," and if the office is accepted, "they sank under its weight into spiritless creatures, cloistered recluses, from whose nerveless fingers the reins of government slipped." Most of this suggests Hightower, but Jefferson has another cloistered ruler

3. The element of Faulkner's believing in belief is also absent in Kohler's suggestion that Faulkner's treatment of Hebraic-Christian myth is like Joyce's use of Homer and Mann's adaptation of Faustian legend (475). Slabey ("Myth" 329) may be closer to the mark when he suggests that *Light in August* is a "Kierkegaardian attack upon the '*un*Christian elements' in a presumably 'Christian' society." Similarly, O'Dea (54) asserts that Faulkner's Christianity rests not on dogmatic stances but on "the ethical preambles necessary for the advent of the divine."

4. As Hardy says, one of Faulkner's favorite themes is the inevitable defeat of "purely rational purpose" (140).

in Joanna Burden, and even her role has precedence in the practice of a priesthood shared by a war chief and a taboo chief, the latter office being, like Joanna's, hereditary (3.1–25).

Undoubtedly, the most problematic casting in the play is Joe Christmas as Jesus Christ. Obviously, Joe is not always Jesus in Faulkner's narrative parallel to John, even though he does, along with others, often act out Jesus' words and actions. But his name and the bookwide affinities, especially in the crucifixion chapter, force us to make the connection with Christ,[5] and it is this characterization especially that has led many to believe that Faulkner was engaged in Black Mass. But this position assumes Joe's guilt, regarding what he does (or may have done, or may have been forced to do) without acknowledging the ambiguities. Does Joe kill McEachern? If all we know is the swing of the chair, we are still within our own dreams. Does Joe murder Joanna? If we believe he kills her in self-defense, we are still within our rights. He might even be justified as what Faulkner called in *Absalom, Absalom!* "the murderer who kills not out of lust but pity" (121). As we are essentially innocent when we have good and sufficient reasons for our guilt, so Joe is essentially innocent, forced as he is by both McEachern and Joanna into representing what each of them most despises.[6]

But any explanation of Joe must take into account the parallel with John and the use of Frazer, two perspectives that would seem to be irreconcilable. John, especially, would scorn the notion that Christ was a "typical scapegoat," while the effect of Frazer's work was to shatter the Christian sense of uniqueness. Moreover, to present a Christ figure as a "typical scapegoat" means that *Light in*

---

5. Brumm asserts that the sufferings of the innocent heroes of American literature, like Joe, "who often leave an entire world in ruins behind them, would be meaningless if Christ did not lend them the significance of innocence suffering magnificently" (219). It might be argued that Joe's sufferings should not be meaningless: that precisely as we fail the innocent sufferer, so we fail all humanity.

6. Brumm says, "At bottom even the cruel Joe Christmas is a basically innocent person who is prevented from being innocent all his life" (219). Walter Taylor maintains that "Faulkner was trying to show that this 'criminal' was no more guilty or innocent than society itself. [He was] caught up in processes that produced first the 'criminal,' then his crime, then his inevitable martyrdom"(79).

August cannot be a tract for the literal truth of Christianity. However, these disparities can be reconciled in the modern perspective of moral thinkers such as Unamuno or Santayana, who held that Christ was "constructed by the imagination in response to moral demands." This takes the burden of belief out of the hands of science and returns it to the individual will, testing it by its ability to generate understanding of and sympathy for the human condition. Such believers would not refuse to look through the Galilean telescope; rather they would recognize that the telescope can be extended by what religions have imagined beyond and within. Belief in God creates God within. Belief in the "Christian myth" renews its efficacy in human affairs.[7]

When we recall the tenderness with which Faulkner treats the faith of Byron and Lena, it suggests that he believed in belief. He once called God "the most complete expression of mankind" (*Lion* 70). Such a perspective places the burden for God's very existence on man and suggests that even as Faulkner appears to have doubted the uniqueness of Christ's role as savior, he recognized the importance of salvation. This is why, although he was part of the twentieth century's religious skepticism, he could still create characters who express Christianity's deepest paradoxes, perhaps made more profound when they are known to lie behind a thousand masks.

It also suggests that he believed individuals must discover their relationship to God in terms of the imperatives of the human community. During Joe's agony in the garden, he thinks "*God loves me too*" (98 / 115). This dawning realization suggests he is discovering his unique role in the eyes of God, which will lead to his becoming a person in the eyes of men. The paradox may be understood by examining his twofold creation, as flesh and spirit. His flesh is the creation of Hines and the dietitian, who pronounce him "nigger bastard," thrusting him into an intermediary, nonplace, between white and black.[8] His spirit is the creation of the McEacherns, who produce an impotent Satan, thrusting him into an intermediary,

---

7. Vickery (236) says Faulkner believed that "the communal and anonymous brotherhood of man can be re-established if each man . . . accepts responsibility for all time as well as for the particular time in which he was born.

8. Jenkins noted this first parentage of Joe (73).

nonplace, between the rocklike damnation of the father and the drowning forbearance of the mother.[9]

Understanding the pattern of Joe's beginnings helps us to understand his ending, for it is there that he loses both intermediary positions of nonbeing, like Jesus, binding himself to the human community, allowing events in time to grind inexorably over him.[10] In killing Joanna, Joe finally becomes flesh in the form of nigger-murderer, the only possible explanation the community could have for his relationship with Joanna. Now he will enter the world of blacks, violently impress his being upon them by challenging their leaders, seizing their pulpit and putting himself—literally—in their shoes. In killing himself, provoking the community's involvement in and then revulsion over Grimm's excesses, he finally becomes spirit in the form of suffering man, rising into their memories, forever "serene" and even "triumphant." [11]

Still this explanation of Joe as Jesus remains incomplete unless we return to the modernist techniques of fragmentation, external structuring, and irony. Remember that our concept of Jesus comes from four quite different perspectives, the most singular being that of St. John. For the synoptics, good acts made one like God; for John, God made one like God. Christ was begotten by the Father. Joe Christmas makes us squirm because, although he does repre-

9. Faulkner said that Joe tried "to live outside the human race" (*Faulkner in the Univ.* 118). Walter Taylor argues that it is Joe's childhood isolation from blacks that makes him "the incarnation of a myth" (84): because he is raised as a Puritan white with the secret belief that he had black origins (63), Joe's original sin of "nigger" takes on the shape of "nigger-devil," the shadow or guilty projection of a Puritanical white society. He also notes that on Joe's final night with the McEacherns, he repeatedly "vanishes," becoming nothing (70).

10. Krieger comments that in his death "Joe seems closest to Christ" (324). But in keeping with the irony of the Christ story, Greer (166) is also correct in his assertion that "it is the social definition of the Negro, the unclean, rejected, and despised aspect of man," that kills Joe Christmas.

11. Vickery (72–74) suggests that Joe takes on the mythic role of Negro, but that in his death he becomes "the man"—the term is repeated. Indeed, "the man" echoes Pilate's ironic words (only in John) "Behold the Man." Sundquist argues that Joe's death is "sacrificial in that it depends on the 'mechanism of reciprocal violence,'" the origin of ritual sacrifice, which grows "from a vicious circle which a community is unable to break without selecting a surrogate victim who can contain the violence by taking it upon himself" (93).

sent a Christ which is, like John's, highly mysterious and eschato-
logical, he does not reflect Luke's "gentle Jesus," Matthew's "great
Rabbi," or Mark's less articulate "man of action."[12] It may be that
these perspectives are reflected by the other three main characters,
Lena, Hightower, and Byron, as if Faulkner reasoned that the synoptics themselves would have been part of John's story.[13] The four
narrators of *Absalom, Absalom!*—Rosa, Mr. Compson, Quentin,
and Shreve—represent a similar fragmentation, and notice that the
nonsynoptic fourth, Shreve, like John, is the most removed from
the original vision, yet he intuits the most.

This may be only one reason for Faulkner's having chosen John.
Another might be aesthetic: John's narrative is both more unified
and more literary than any of the synoptics. There is also the fact
that, unlike the synoptics, who primarily addressed the Jews,
John's message was universal. There is even the possibility that
Faulkner may have been saving the synoptics for another work,
namely, *A Fable*.[14]

But the International Bible (20) has noted that despite his mysterious origins and his confident divinity, John's Jesus may be the
most suffering *man*: only in John do we find Jesus weary (4:6); do
we hear "Jesus wept" (11:35); does he say, at the Passion, "I thirst"
(19:38). In using John, Faulkner may be suggesting that Joe Christmas is not the abstract Christ but one whose physical suffering
might give us pause. But then equally, in using Frazer to expand on
John, Faulkner may be suggesting that Joe's slayers are not John's
abstract "authorities" but humanity itself, each fumbling one of
us, whose counterclaim might give us pause.[15]

12. He is given John's symbol of the eagle (150–51 / 176–77).

13. Holman suggests that each of the main characters "is a representation of
certain limited aspects of Christ" (166).

14. See Ficken ("Christ Story"). On the other hand, Culley believes that Faulkner's vision is closest to John's because for both, final judgment has been shifted to
the present. Discussing *Go Down Moses* and *Requiem for a Nun*, she argues that
Faulkner reflects John's view that the choices man makes now will determine his
judgment at the Apocalypse: "Faulkner's insight is that we become our choices"
(67).

15. Waggoner remarks that the novel "asks pity for Christmas by making us see
that the terrible things we do and become are all finally in self defense" (103).

Typical of primitive scapegoats, Joe hardly knows why he has been chosen.[16] But we know. Because we have heaped our worst impulses on him—the hate, the filth, the fear—we now want to be rid of him. And his death will be a repudiation of those impulses. As in our dreams, we entertain these dreadful desires that we may be washed clean, renewed. So the animus to heap our sins on the weakest among us and then be rid of him is both despicable and somehow laudable, if either of these terms can be applied to such wishful thinking.

Thus, in modernist writing, the fragmented parts must be reassembled and viewed ironically through the external structure. In *Absalom, Absalom!* this means that Quentin's final forswearing of the South ("I don't hate it!"), matching Miss Rosa's opening indictment of the demon she loves, is not Faulkner's central message, any more than Genesis or Revelation is the central message of Christianity: rather it is a chosen act of sacrifice (such as Bon's) or of suffering (such as Bon's son) and, so that others might be saved, the reporting of that act. Similarly, in *Light in August*, Joe Christmas is not the new Christ, although his death does serve, like Christ's, to break into the circle of time, spilling blood to rid us of our guilt.[17] But after our wrong has been entombed in Hightower's "place of skulls," a renewed spirit arises again in the form of Byron and Lena's new life and child, part of the older, more encompassing circle—beyond guilt—which embraces all time and blood. Using modernist techniques, Faulkner demonstrates that the traditional beliefs can be broken apart, distorted, and reassembled in the unlikeliest of forms and folk—a maid, a stable, a man—of the Mississippi clay.

16. Calling Joe a "monstrous mockery" of Christ, "not willing Savior but tormented and compulsive victim of history's perversions of Christianity," Hardy (148) says this figure "is the only kind that properly can appear to a society that has already completely rejected Christ."

17. As R. G. Collins says, Joe's sacrifice "sanctifies life. Because of the common identity of mankind, that man who dies as the victim of society throws into symbolic relief the life and death relationship of mankind. It is, indeed, death which gives life its meaning and value" ("*Light*" 148).

CHAPTER IV

The Basic Assumptions, Beginning with the Word

Language [is] that meager and fragile thread ... by which the little surface corners and edges of men's secret and solitary lives may be joined for an instant now and then before sinking back into the darkness where the spirit cried for the first time and was not heard and will cry for the last time and will not be heard then either.

Absalom, Absalom!

 FAILED POET, Faulkner loved words above all else. At the level of the word, meaning becomes poetry because all possibilities are packed in upon one another, ready to explode. This temporary fusion of meaning creates the potential for all the poetic devices such as irony and paradox, but it also creates the potential for humor, which arises from an unexpected breaking off of a connection, unexpected often because it reminds us of latent aggressions or hostilities.

From the previous chapter, one might have thought that Faulkner's work was all solemnity, but much of it is closer to being comedy.[1] When Faulkner was asked about naming characters like Gail Hightower: "It seems to me that those people named themselves, but I can see . . . [they] came from . . . my memory of the old miracle plays, the morality plays in early English literature" (*Faulkner in the Univ.* 97). Those works also taught, using a combination of high jinks and high seriousness.

But what's so funny about *Light in August* and how can it be likened to the sometimes romping hilarity of morality plays? To illustrate the connection, suppose I tell you about a great big fellow named King who finds and adopts a valuable little animal and is killed trying to protect it. That's not very funny on the surface. But now I add that this fellow was shot holding onto the ledge of a Manhattan skyscraper. If you are not a movie buff, you still might miss the humor. In fact, the story can now be a private joke for those who guess that the "fellow" is King Kong and the "valuable little animal" is Faye Wray. This is not to say that the story of King Kong is inherently funny; the humor arises both because my story turns out to be based on a campy movie and because *fellow* and *animal*, used ambiguously, turn out to mean "gorilla" and "woman." To maintain the humor within a serious dimension, we may occasionally have to forget the grim underlying message.[2] But then one job of humor is to release us from our disapproving superego in acceptably short bursts of hilarity. Just so, the morality plays could treat raucously the direful themes of betrayal and death.

Thus, one of the basic assumptions we might make about much of Faulkner's work is that, in wanting to out-Joyce Joyce, he was often having fun, creating his own games, perhaps at the reader's expense, but more probably out of the ripeness of his own creativ-

1. Brooks (72) believes *Light in August* is in the comic mode even if it is "a grotesque and savage comedy." Comparing it to Joyce's *Ulysses*, which, "though it has much pathos and horror in it, is also finally a comic work," Brooks suggests that "Faulkner's comedy is frequently a makeweight to the terrible." "Its function is to maintain sanity and human perspective in a scene of brutality and horror" (71).

2. Campbell and Foster (111) hold that "the atmospheric function of Faulkner's humor" is to increase the horror "by the very casualness of the humorous contrast offered."

ity. And like the poet, like Dante, he must have delighted in making the game multidimensional. To give a small, but telling example from *Light in August*: in John 4 the woman at the well gives testimony to the "living water" of Jesus (as opposed to the dead well of Jacob). In Frazer, we find that offerings to sacred wells could both make water flow (like the "living water") and make one confess (like the giving of testimony). So, in Faulkner's chapter 4, there is much giving of testimony and a hint of the "living water," but the two themes are marvelously compressed at chapter's end in Lena's innocent country expression, "Here I have come clean from Alabama." To be sure, this glance off "O Susanna" ("I've come from Alabama, my true love for to see") reflects Lena's thoughts of Lucas. It may even poignantly reflect Faulkner's thoughts of his recently buried first child, named "Alabama." But both of these thoughts could have been reflected with expressions like "come clear from Alabama" or "come a-ways from Alabama." In fact, elsewhere he did put significantly different words in Lena's mouth. In chapter 1, her final words suggest the theme of "the coming": " 'My, my, . . . here I aint been on the road but four weeks, and now I am in Jefferson already. My, my. A body does get around' " (26 / 32). And in chapter 21, her final words suggest a second coming: " 'My, my. A body does get around. Here we aint been coming from Alabama but two months, and now it's already Tennessee' " (480 / 559).[3] But in chapter 4, the expression he

---

3. On the principle that we should never underestimate Faulkner's learning, this chiasmus (a reversing parallel form) was probably deliberate. He used it at the climax of *Absalom, Absalom!*:

> *And you are———?*
> *Henry Sutpen.*
> *And you have been here———?*
> *Four years.*
> *And you came home———?*
> *To die. Yes.*
> *To die?*
> *Yes. To die.*
> *And you have been here———?*
> *Four years.*
> *And you are———?*
> *Henry Sutpen.* (464–65)

chose—come clean—also fortuitously unites the themes of cleansing and confession.

Thus, even in Faulkner's most serious works, the element of humor cannot be discounted. For example, in *Absalom, Absalom!* the legal pattern is evident primarily through Faulkner's peculiar stylistic devices, especially his repetitions, which include synonyms and even homonyms—puns—supported by image and episode. So in the chapter giving immaterial evidence, the episodes include people seeing or not seeing (giving material witness to) other people, before they themselves vanish (become immaterial, which they are in a legal sense anyway). The narration includes accusations of what is "evident" and "apparent" amid discussions of "ogre-faced" or "masked" characters, false fronts, as if what is apparent is merely fiction or immaterial. And the diction even includes immateriality in the form of cloth, the long-gone uniforms and flags of the Confederacy.

Indeed, the parallels we find in even the most solemn moments suggest that Faulkner found the potential for humor irresistible. In *Light in August*'s crucifixion chapter, while Joe Christmas is poignantly being linked to many particulars of the Passion, we also find an amusing parallel to Pilate's sign over the cross, which John alone universalizes into Greek, Latin, and the local Hebrew: Stevens is a "Phi Beta Kappa"; Grimm commands a platoon "vide his active commission"; while the soldiers use the local language: "There was something about it too assured and serenely confident to the [be (*CT*)] braggadocio; tonight when they heard the marshal's feet on the stairs, one said, 'Ware M.P.'s' and for an instant they glanced at one another with hard, bright, daredevil eyes; then one said, quite loud: 'Throw the son of a bitch out,' and another through pursed lips made the immemorial sound" (432 / 504–5).

Besides the humor, what other basic assumptions have been uncovered here that could be applied to other Faulkner works?

First, we should assume that all we have to go on is the text since

---

Its use in *Light in August* is appropriate to the theme of the Second Coming, especially since the technique was a favorite of John's. Pitavy (149) finds chiasmus and other rhetorical devices in chapter 3, where, in John, Nicodemus the scribe exemplifies dead learning.

Faulkner's own comments on his writing will be useless and even misleading. For example, having established a complex legal framework for *Absalom, Absalom!*, having used the central figures of two Compson lawyers, with Henry and Bon reading for the law, Faulkner responded to a question about the conjectured New Orleans lawyer as follows: "There probably was a lawyer. I don't remember that book, but yes, yes, there was a lawyer. That sounds too logical in Mississippi terms. Yes, he was—there was a little lawyer there" (*Faulkner in the Univ.* 77). And regarding the title, *Light in August*, with all the potential classical and biblical allusions (particularly to John), Faulkner refers vaguely to "fauns" in his "country":

> [In] August in Mississippi there's a few days somewhere about the middle of the month when suddenly there's a foretaste of fall, it's cool, there's a lambence, a luminous quality to the light, as though it came not from just today but from back in the old classic times [with] . . . fauns and satyrs and the gods and—from Greece, from Olympus. . . . It lasts just for a day or two, then it's gone, but every year in August that occurs in my country, and that's all that title meant, it was . . . a pleasant evocative title because it reminded me of that time, of a luminosity older than our Christian civilization.[4]

We should also assume that we have only the published text to go on. The handwritten manuscript of *Light in August* does occasionally have more thematic supports, but it can also have fewer.[5] For example, reinforcing chapter 5's theme of curing by immersion, the manuscript has Joe recall his "manhate" for McEachern, using imagery of dense air, which, said to "flow away," suggests a kind of metaphoric immersion: "until at last it would seem to him that he could feel the ~~bed, the vv~~ floor, swelling and bulging upward around him, lifting him toward the low ceiling, compressing the dark air between him and the ceiling until it was too dense for breathing. And he would lie there, rigid, breathing like a man bur-

---

4. *Faulkner in the Univ.* 199. Many critics have discussed the "light" motif: Hirshleifer (237–38), Cottrell (213), Krieger (330), Ficken ("Critical" 24–28) and Don Noel Smith (196n), who says "the light with which Christ is identified in the book of John might well have had some influence."

5. There is a complete manuscript at the University of Virginia and two fragments elsewhere. Fadiman's study of this material is useful.

ied in cotton, until at last dawn would begin. Then the hate, the ceiling, the darkness would begin to flow away."[6] The manuscript also includes references to Bethesda's function as a healing place: "the invisible, dimlighted city hospital" distantly blew upon Joe's "sweaty face . . . the smell, carbolical, aseptical of the hospital" (Mms. 47–48).

On the other hand, in chapter 3 of the manuscript, Hightower hides his face from the reporters with his hat, while, in the published version, he uses an open hymnbook, books being central to the discussion in John 3 of the letter versus the spirit of the law. But most of the changes are slight, the manuscript being almost a fair copy.[7] As Meriwether says, Faulkner "evidently took pains to save only the finished word" (60).

A third assumption regarding Faulkner's work is that the chapters or divisions might well be considered as separate thematic units—like separate poems. We must also notice what characters are introduced within those poems. For example, in *Light in August*, Hines is given five different names, marking five different chapter themes. In chapter 6, he is called "janitor" (meaning "door") to mark the entrance (or intaking) of the sacramental meal. In chapter 15, he is little Uncle Doc, to mark the puppets of ancestor worship. In chapter 16, he is Old Doc Hines, to mark the effigies of Old Man Death. In chapter 17, he is "the man" or "he," to mark the taboo of speaking ancestor names. And in chapter 19, he is called "grandfather," to mark the hereditary role of the scapegoat.

This focus on chapter units also means that each character must

---

6. Mms., 45. That chapter themes were on Faulkner's mind right up through the transcription of this (almost) fair copy is indicated by occasional changes, which often add to or remove thematic references.

7. See my chapter 6, n. 8, for a discussion of a page from an earlier manuscript that strongly reinforces chapter themes. It is interesting that in a letter referring to the lost page, Faulkner wrote, "For God's sake see if I left it in the office. It is a complicated chapter and I cant reconstruct it" (Blotner 1.109n). That this fragment is not reflected in the Virginia manuscript suggests that the manuscript is not an early draft. Indeed, because problems with or changes in the Faulkner manuscript often reflect problems in John, my own suspicion is that Faulkner deliberately and humorously left a manuscript that would set his scholars along paths similar to those of John's.

be judged in the context of each chapter. For example, Bobbie's tenderness in chapter 8 reflects the fact that all the characters suspend and have been suspended from the judgments of this world, whereas in chapter 9 all the characters are driving away evil and are themselves driven away. It also suggests that Bobbie's sluttishness, Joe's brutality, or McEachern's blind lunacy in 9 is as temporary as the earlier, kinder, passing judgment. Thus, Faulkner may have found a way to overturn the ordinary sequential force of the novel which suggests that what we later learn about a character is more "true" than what we learn first. And it further allows us to keep contradictory views of Faulkner's women characters.

Similarly, events must be judged as part of chapter themes. For instance, in chapter 7, Joe Christmas savagely attacks the black girl in the shed, teaching her (in the temple) that her behavior is wrong. But it is in the next chapter (the judgment of the adulterous woman), that he now judges his and her behavior with compassion: *"I know now why I struck refraining that negro girl three years ago and that she must know it too and be proud too, with waiting and pride."* She is waiting for another who will judge her worthy of correction for sexual degradation.

Of course, we must also assume that themes can overlap from chapter to chapter. But without knowing the underlying structure, critics who are accustomed to tracing the binding threads of a Shakespeare play can go astray in a Faulkner novel. Take *Light in August*'s references to urns. The Keatsian timelessness of Lena's movement "like something moving forever and without progress across an urn" in chapter 1 has been compared with the "deathcolored and foul" urns of Bobbie's menstruation in chapter 8 or with Hightower's wish for a life like a "classic and serene vase" in chapter 20. This is to compare apples and oranges along with horse chestnuts because they all have peelable skins. Actually, in chapter 1 the urn emphasizes the unbroken continuity, in chapter 8 it is the container, and in chapter 20 it resurrects earlier (dead) motifs.[8]

8. Fadiman shows that the urn image of chapter 1 was added late to the manuscript, which suggests to her that Faulkner wanted to contrast the "life-styles" of Joe and Lena (153). I believe that the addition is another instance of Faulkner's concern for the thematic unity of his chapters.

On the other hand, motifs can run through the whole book, especially when they are justified by the structural framework. Legal terminology may be found throughout *Absalom, Absalom!* To list only some of the more remarkable examples, Rosa repeats that she holds "no brief" or that she does not "plead," since "there were plenty to aid and abet" Sutpen (24), plenty of "witnesses" (28), for the "indictment" (14), as she "saw the notes of hand on pride and contentment and peace . . . fall due" (18). She also says that she owned her home *"in fee simple"* (153), while Grandfather describes Sutpen's *shoulders* as "forensic" (275). Or the theme of "light," pervasive in John, is also evident in *Light in August*: indeed, both "Lucas" (for the Latin, Lucifer) and "Lena" (for the Greek, Helena, or torch) mean "light." From John's standpoint, there is no question about his use of "light." But Faulkner must be playing with many meanings, from bright to transparent, from igniting to luminous, from elucidating to facile, from alighting to eased. Lucas will "light out," one country term, when Lena is "light," another, suggested by Faulkner, for having given birth.[9]

Or consider the amusing parallel for John's repetition of the word *bearing*. In John 15 we read about the branch's bearing fruit; in 16, we read about the disciples' bearing the truth and a woman's bearing a child; while in 18, we read about bearing witness. A similar repetition occurs in Faulkner. In 15, we read of offerings "borne intact" to the Hineses, while Hines and Christmas are repeatedly borne about. In 16, Hightower says that people cannot bear pleasure, while Mrs. Hines bears Milly, Milly bears Joe, both having "bore and suffered" the devil within Hines, who, along with his wife, is called a bear. In 18, Brown's note requests money be given *"toe barer,"* while Byron's thoughts include this extraordinary repetition: "Well, I can bear a hill . . . I can bear a hill." "It seems like a man can just about bear anything. He can even bear what he never done. He can even bear the thinking how some things is just more than he can bear. He can even bear it that if he could just give

---

9. See Blotner, *Biography* 1.702. R. G. Collins ("Game" 82) discusses the names Lucas and Lena as representatives of "light." In Spanish, giving birth is referred to as *dar luz a*, which means giving the baby to the light.

down and cry, he wouldn't do it. He can even bear it to not look back, even when he knows that looking back or not looking back wont do him any good" (401 / 467).

In general, however, it may be a useful working hypothesis to treat each chapter as separate and to assume that Faulkner has created a pattern that will emerge by studying all levels, including the puzzling anachronisms, the striking images, and the odd conjunction of episode. The opening and closing paragraphs should be noticed, and above all, any repetitions of words, including synonyms and homonyms. This is where a concordance can be invaluable.

Unfortunately, none of the published Faulkner concordances divide the words by chapter, nor do they list separately words that are repeated on one line. So one must actually divide out the chapters and count the multiple entries.[10] My handmade concordance of *Light in August,* made up before the published version appeared, listed the words by page and chapter. When a word had a high rate of occurrence in one chapter, that word could be listed for possible thematic connections with others in the same chapter. Then as themes emerged, it became possible to return to the text to find related words whose occurrence rate was not so obviously significant. In fact, the procedure was no mere tabulation: some words could be buried in others. In chapter 1, while the concordance spots the "word" of Lucas, the father (echoing "In the beginning was the Word"), only the careful reader can add "mouthword" and perhaps even the meaningful "inwardlighted" with its homonyn for *word.*

In fact, some apparently insignificant words are not listed in the published concordance. The word *all,* for example, used in chapters 11 and 12 along with other evidence, signals All Saints' and

---

10. In *Absalom, Absalom!*'s chapter 1, which illustrates the theme of opinion evidence, the word *knew* is doubled on one line and quadrupled on another: "because our father knew who his father was in Tennessee and who his grandfather had been in Virginia and our neighbors and the people we lived among *knew* that we *knew* and we *knew* they *knew* we *knew* and we *knew* that they would have believed us about whom and where he came from even if we had lied" (15, my italics). Notice the irony of "knowing" in a chapter filled with opinion evidence, especially since, as the passage suggests, even a lie would have been believed.

All Souls' Day celebrations in honor of the dead (Joanna and her past).

But the concordance did help to filter out less useful observations. The word *know* first came to my attention in reading chapter 4, but the concordance shows it is important throughout the book, as the biblical concordance shows it is in John.[11] On the other hand, the high occurrence of *change* in chapter 2, or *cut* in chapter 12, hardly noticeable in context, turned out to be significant.

An instructive example is in chapter 8, where, in John, the setting for the woman taken in adultery is the "treasury" (the only use of that word in John), actually a place where boxes were kept to receive charitable gifts (Cambridge 183). In Faulkner, the word list for that chapter includes a theme appropriate to the restaurant setting, namely, money and changemaking:

Word	Occurrences in chapter 8	All other occurrences
acquire	2	—
cents	5	3
cheap	4	4
counter	20	11
dime/-s	9	4
money	15	38
nickel/-s	11	10
owe/-s	4	2
parsimony	2	—

But another group is less obvious:

box/-es	9	12
bureau	8	4
case/-s	5	1
cup/-s	7	5
urn	2	1

11. Schlepper (185), calls it "extraordinary" that some form of *know* occurs so often (over 850 times) throughout *Light in August*. It was a word Faulkner loved (see the previous note), but so did John, where the cognates of *know* occur 114 times, more than the combined synoptics.

Although we might recognize the role of money in the chapter, it is not until we notice these possible containers of money that, returning to the chapter, we find many "hiding places," from bundles, to baskets, to pockets, to caves, to the hidden valley where Joe kills the sheep, to the guarded portal of the restaurant, to the cache for Joe's rope and Mrs. McEachern's change, itself in a tin can. So the theme, widened to include the judgment of the woman in the treasury, becomes woman-as-treasure, a secret sexual store to be guarded or weighed, that is, judged, in this chapter, charitably. So Bobbie is, in this chapter, Joe's secret treasure, even if one that can be had for small change. But had our attention not been drawn to this grouping by the concordance, we might not have been alert to these wider speculations based on the connection with John.

Or consider this thematic cluster, found in chapter 5, which, in John, presents the lame man waiting to immerse himself and be cured in the waters of the pool at Bethesda.

Word	Occurrences in chapter 5	All other occurrences
dew/-ed	5	3 (all in ch. 14)
gurgle/-ing	2	—
spring (stream)	5	10 (6 in ch. 14)
water/-'s/-s	4	13 (4 in ch. 14)
wet	4	4 (scattered)

Notice here that the liquid theme is not exclusive to chapter 5; it is also significant in chapter 14.

To demonstrate the whole procedure, we might examine the wordlist turned up by the concordance for chapter 11 (the number of occurrences outside the chapter is in parentheses):

beans 3 (1)	father/-'s 36 (51)	mother/-'s 19 (32)
beets 2	fireflies 4 (2)	play/-ed/-ing 5 (22)
bolt 3 (2)	foreign 2	priest/-s 6 (2)
born 10 (34)	frail [beat] 2	race/-'s/-es 7 (8)
buckboard 5	French/-men 5 (1)	rape/-ed 2
bury/-ied/-ing 6 (5)	frockcoat 3	resist/-ance/-ed 6 (2)
calico 2	gown 3 (1)	retrospect/-ive 2

California 3	grave/-s 6 (2)	Saint Louis 2
Catholic/-s 4 (2)	grizzled 3	saloon/-s 3
cedar/-s 4 (1)	grove 4 (8)	Sante Fe 2
crashed/-ed-ing 5 (12)	hurl/-ed 3 (2)	sister/-'s/-s 6 (4)
crude 3 (3)	keg 2	slaveholders 3
despoil/-ed 3	kin 2	Spanish 6
dig/-dug 3 (3)	land 5 (4)	tar 2
dish/-es 8 (23)	lilac 2	veil 3 (1)
drifted/-ed/-ing 6 (6)	locked 5 (19)	waist 2
east 2 (2)	messenger 9 (1)	wedding 8 (2)
		west/-ward 4 (1)

Chapter 11 is John's story of Lazarus, brother of Mary and Martha, raised from the dead by Jesus, who commands that he be loosed of his graveclothes. As echoes of this story, three groups of words are obviously justifiable, namely, those related to death and burial (including *bury, dig, grave, land, despoil,* and possibly the pun *waist*); those related to clothes (including *frockcoat, calico, gown,* and *veil*), and those related to kinship (including *race, born, kin, father, mother, sister,* and *wedding*). Moreover, these words lead to others in the chapter. For instance, in the category of kinship, *forebears* appears once here and nowhere else; *dam* appears once here and once elsewhere; and although *blood* appears almost twice as often in 19, the crucifixion chapter, it does appear eight times here, where it means family.

But three other groups also occur: some kind of battle or struggle (including *bolt, locked, crashed, hurl, resistance, rape,* the repeated "I'll be bound," and possibly the puns *beets* or *buckboard*); some victual words (including *beans, beets, dishes,* or *keg*); and some kind of "foreignness," the opposite of kinship (including *foreign, French, Spanish, Catholic, slaveholders, priest,* and such "foreign" places as *California, Santa Fe* and—spelled out—*Saint Louis*).

The justification for these themes will be found in Frazer, not scattered widely, but clustered in a particular chapter or division (see Appendix B). On the other hand, where to look will often be far from obvious. Sometimes it is. If John's chapter on the teaching in the temple includes the word *circumcision*, we should turn to discussions of initiation rites in Frazer. But in chapter 11, even if the main theme is "the dead" (it could be "magicians"), Frazer's index has more than a page of references to death and the dead. However, following the weddings and battles and the odd comparison of Joanna to a tree, we are led to discussions of the homeopathic belief that control over the land and its fecundity comes about by raising the dead. Thus, in chapter 11, Faulkner presents Joanna in language that links her not only to the dead but also to those forms—interchangeable in myth—of tree, priest, and god. The primitive will often revitalize such figures by marriage ceremonies, complete with wedding finery and feasting, between man and goddess or maid and tree, and the honor will be won by battles or contests.

Naturally, in reading Frazer or John, one must be alert to the kinds of ideas and attitudes that would have fired Faulkner. For example, commentary on John 11 notes that revivification of the dead is usually accomplished by the voice (International clxxxiv). Fascinated with the power of words, with language's "meager and fragile thread" that binds us so briefly, Faulkner may have had this in mind for Joanna's revivification, with Joe thinking: "She is like all the rest of them." "When they finally come to surrender completely, it's going to be in words" (227 / 265).

But we should ask, how important is it to know Faulkner's game plans? To begin with, knowing about Faulkner's knowing cannot help but make his achievement even more impressive. Take his use of John as a parallel for *Light in August*. After all, the gospel is often disjointed or repetitious, with many textual problems. Of course, many of John's chapters do have obvious unities: the story of the loaves and fishes is followed by Jesus' discourse on the bread of life. Perhaps these instances emboldened Faulkner to look further, for as we will see in Part Two, apparently Faulkner himself discovered some surprising unities in John's chapters, and Faulkner himself discovered their connections with primitive and mythic traditions in Frazer. After centuries of biblical exegesis, it may be hard to believe that Faulkner could have been charting new territory, but then he was looking at John with a creative rather than a scholarly eye.

Then too, knowing Faulkner's game plans can settle some crucial questions. For example, what happens to Hightower at the close of chapter 20 has been a source of great confusion, with Faulkner even having to set the record straight. Hightower, he had to tell us, does not die (*Faulkner in the Univ.* 75). That might have been obvious had we known that Hightower is playing there the doubting Thomas, who must be shown everything before he believes. Such a figure would be allotted nothing more dramatic than one dim moment of insight before he returns to his nightly "charge."

Then, the various pronouncements on character might be reexamined. Take Joe's "sadism." To begin with, sadism is a dismissive term, as reductive as calling Molly or Caddy a nymphomaniac. It separates the bad boys and girls from the rest of us. But more importantly, we will find that each instance of what might be thought of as sadistic behavior is not only part of a particular chapter theme from John, but can be justified by specific societal demands described in Frazer. Therefore, Joe's actions should be read less in terms of individual psychology—as important as that is— and more in terms of the larger design, which is yet consistent with Joe's psychology.

Still another reason for knowing what Faulkner is about involves his humor, his enjoyment in creating many levels of understanding. Like Joyce, burying flower references in his *Ulysses* chapter on the Lotus Eaters, Faulkner must have enjoyed burying animal references in chapter 10 (John's discourse of the Good Shepherd) in honor of shepherds' festivals: "here bobbie," "here kid," "chicken feed," "keep," "leave it lay," and "hey kid."[12] It might even include "*install*ment" (207–8 / 242–43); certainly the poet in Faulkner would have wanted us to pause over every word.

Of course some of the humor may have a darker side. Often it seems regrettably compatible with Frazer's barely disguised contempt for the "primitive"—the word itself can be offensive. *The Golden Bough* has many instances of reaching for humorous effect

---

12. Joe's semiconscious awareness of Bobbie's departure is like Molly Bloom's drifting off to sleep, and both passages are rendered without punctuation.

by apparently ludicrous comparisons. For example, discussing the Todas, a pastoral people who live on milk, although Frazer's source calls their priest a "dairyman," he insistently makes this "milkman": "Heavy restraints are laid in their entirety only on milkmen of the very highest class. Among the Todas there are milkmen and milkmen; and some of them get off more lightly in consideration of their humbler station in life" (3.16).

Elsewhere, Frazer suggests that a woman of the Gallas who acts possessed of the holy spirit Gallo is only tired of housework (1.395–96). Or, quoting an African king—"God made me after his own image; I am the same as God"—Frazer footnotes: "A slight mental confusion may perhaps be detected in this utterance of the dark-skinned deity. But such confusion, or rather obscurity, is almost inseparable from any attempt to define with philosophic precision the profound mystery of incarnation" (1.396n). This kind of nonsense must have been all too compelling for that Old Boy Faulkner, expressing as it does, the fantasy that we can distinguish between "them" and "us."

But in the context of Faulkner's abiding compassion, most of the humor is fairly benign and even fun. For example, in chapter 6, Faulkner creates a parallel between the dietitian and the janitor—with their "mad eyes looking into mad eyes" (119 / 140)—and the "seers," the sacred men and women of the temple. According to Frazer, the "sacredness' of these ancient divines was used to explain both their madness and their begats, even their dirtiness. The Syrian "holy men" often wore "filthy garments," yet none would shrink from them because they were thought to be acting in God's name and speaking with his voice. Among the Semites, sanctuaries were "the seats of profligate rites," and the offspring of the divines were believed to be the emanations of "uncouth but worshipful idols" (5.57–109). Now Faulkner would have found these ideas just as funny as Frazer did. And he must have enjoyed creating his bitterly humorous parallel of the janitor, a "small, dirty man," who says, "Don't lie to me, to the Lord God," who, with the temple prostitute, herself exemplifying "womanfilth" "before the face of God" (124 / 145), creates "out of the mouths," their offspring: the "little nigger bastard."

Of course, exploring the puzzles of Faulkner's structural designs does not mean that we have "explained" Faulkner's genius. After all, his genius does not lie in riddles to be unriddled but in our sense that he is touching on the greatest enigma of all—the human condition. When Picasso looked at African masks, he saw his own people. When Joyce turned to the tales of the tribe—whether of ancient Greece or modern Ireland—he saw the universality of human impulses. Similarly, when Faulkner read of folk customs, even if he was amused at their oddities, he nevertheless believed that they made all too much sense. Ghoulishly, in *As I Lay Dying*, when Vardaman bores a hole in Addie's coffin (and her head) after twice opening the window, he is following a practice, described in Frazer, of releasing the soul from the body (4.198–99).

We should allow ourselves to be guided by the echoes of Faulkner's laughter—raunchy, sexist, cute, or grim. Let me give one last example. Although I knew that Hightower represented Hippolytus (with his many associations to horses), I must have read Frazer's extended description of this figure many times before I noticed this singular formulation: "Diana, for the love she bore Hippolytus, persuaded the leech Aesculapius to bring her fair hunter back to life by his simples" (1.20). Simples? Taken aback for a moment, I finally decided this referred not to Hippolytus' elementary parts but to Aesculapius' herbs. But the word had made me laugh. Had it made Faulkner laugh? Sure enough, when I looked up the word *simple* in the concordance, it led me to a passage in chapter 16, where Hightower is responding to the lowly Byron—who is trying to bring him back to life: " 'Ah yes,' he says. 'That's all. That's simple. Simple. Simple.' Apparently he cannot stop saying it. 'Simple. Simple' " (368 / 429).

So the work should be fun. And exhilarating. Because we can assume what we have known all along: that Faulkner was writing on the highest levels of literary expression, where it may be that the brain so teems with ideas and images that the writer needs only the container to hold and shape the ripeness of it all. Still, the fact that Faulkner's Mississippi folk have immortal forms beneath their not-so-simple adventures, that's what's so funny about *Light in August*.

PART TWO

Faulkner's Modernism in Chapter and Verse

CHAPTER V

The Prologue and Book of Signs

Light in August, Chapters 1–12

Chapter 1: The Light Witness to the Word

REFLECTING GOD's first words in Genesis, "Let there be light," John begins with the well-known prologue: "In the beginning was the Word, and the Word was with God, and the Word was God. The same was in the beginning with God. All things were made by him; and without him was not any thing made that was made. In him was life; and the life was the light of men. And the light shineth in darkness; and the darkness comprehended it not." With several asides, the next section presents John the Baptist's witness ("I am the voice of one crying in the wilderness, Make straight the way of the Lord") and his testimony of initial disbelief, even as he "saw the Spirit descending from heaven like a dove." The final section presents the first gathering of Jesus' disciples, suggesting a widening sphere of believers, as one tells another of having found the "Lamb of God," or an Israelite "in whom is no guile," while Jesus himself predicts that "hereafter, ye shall see heaven open, and the angels of God ascending and descending upon the Son of Man."

Faulkner's opening chapter reflects this same sequence. We are first presented with Lena, carrying the word of Lucas, who is, after all, the father (although, like God, "he ain't any hand for letters"): "I reckon me and him didn't need to make word promises" (15 / 19). She had told him "to just send me word" (16 / 20). "Like as not, he already sent the word and it got lost." She had told him, "You just send me your mouthword" (17 / 21). "But me and Lucas don't need no word promises between us. It was something unexpected come up, or he even sent the word and it got lost" (17 / 22). It is this "word" which makes the Armstids witnesses to the truth, while the final section presents Lena being passed along to more and more witnesses.[1]

Regarding John's themes, we begin with the coming of the holy (and wholly) innocent Lena, the descent of the angel (into time, into carnal knowledge), as a witness to the father's word. Nor is she alone in witnessing. As in the gospel itself, where believers and nonbelievers fulfill prophecy, here too all reflect the central witness, for when Lena appears with the Word, the word she carries is the reverse of her own belief. Even as the life within is the light of men (or men make light of her life within), the darkness (she in her innocence or they in their knowingness) comprehends it not. Of course, the kind folks, the Armstids, the men at the store, they all believe they have the true knowledge of Lucas, borne to them by Lena's very innocence. Without ever having seen him, they know exactly what sort of fellow he is. Yet it is their practical kindness to her that belies their own cynicism. Through them, the Lord does provide. Thus, all take the function of John the Baptist, who "came for a witness, to bear witness of the Light, that all men through him might believe." All witness the appearance of the word made flesh, express their (right) knowledge of the unseen father ("No man hath seen God") and, by helping the innocent bearer of the word, themselves become witnesses.

Here also is our first view of Lena as the Virgin Mary.[2] Called a

---

1. Pitavy (57–58) notices the repetitions of "savage," "gray," and "brusque," in connection with Mrs. Armstid. Such words have been associated with John the Baptist, the "voice crying in the wilderness."

2. For a discussion of Lena as Mary, see Langston (50).

"lady travelling," she appears in August, the time of Caesar Augustus and the Assumption of the Virgin; she wears Mary's color, blue; and she carries the palm-leaf fan.[3] Faulkner's description of her lean-to room is like a Renaissance painting of the simple maid's election, her "luck," receiving the Holy Ghost through the window: "She slept in a leanto room at the back of the house. It had a window which she learned to open and close again in the dark without making a sound." "She had lived there eight years before she opened the window for the first time. She had not opened it a dozen times hardly before she discovered that she should not have opened it at all. She said to herself, 'That's just my luck'" (3 / 5–6). Yet we know it is not the Holy Ghost which comes in through the window but Lena who climbs out.

The mythical figure closest to this paradoxical combination of sanctity and comedy is Isis. As Frazer says, "In art the figure of Isis suckling the infant Horus is so like that of the Madonna and child that it has sometimes received the adoration of ignorant Christians" (6.119, see fig. 1). But originally Isis was a fertility goddess, "a rustic Corn-Mother" with homely, clownish features, "adored with uncouth rites by Egyptian swains" (6.117). That her rites and processions became "distinguished by a dignity and composure, a solemnity and decorum" (6.118) is suitable to Lena, whose movements are described as "serene" and "deliberate," and who eats with a "tranquil and hearty decorum."

Isis was also a wanderer, out searching for her brother-husband, Osiris, whose parts were "scattered" (6.10), the word Faulkner uses repeatedly to describe Lucas.

Symbolizing the wanderings of Isis (or the coming of the Baptist, or the descent of the dove, or the ascending and descending of the angels), many movements in the chapter are up and down. In the first sentence, Lena is "watching the wagon mount the hill toward her." Then we hear of her getting down from the wagon as a child, or of her (unnecessary) climb out the window to leave home, or of

---

3. In his book on *The Wild Palms*, McHaney (165) observes that in Frazer's *Golden Bough*, the palm tree is a fertility symbol especially associated with childbirth.

her movements into and out of the wagons on the way to Jefferson. Dialect expressions also reflect this theme: Lena says "the foreman was down on Lucas," or "a young fellow needs timé to get settled down" (16 / 20–21), or "I just got too busy getting this chap up to his time," or "something unexpected come up," or "I just decided to up and not wait any longer" (17 / 22).

But the most interesting symbol of the coming is the shoe. One of the Baptist's singular lines is "He it is, who coming after me is preferred before me, whose shoe's latchet I am not worthy to unloose." Important to biblical studies, some form of this expression appears in all four gospels; so scholars have used the variants to compare them.

Frazer also discusses the shoe and its latchet in connection with heralding. To loosen or impede good or bad spirits, they will be used along with other homeopathic charms such as knotting or unknotting strings; braiding or unbraiding hair; clasping or unclasping hands; opening or closing doors, drawers, boxes, and locks; wearing or not wearing rings. For example, "knots may be used by an enchantress to win a lover and attach him firmly to herself." They may be used as protection, or "to stop a runaway. In Swazieland you may often see grass tied in knots at the side of the footpaths. Every one of these knots tells of a domestic tragedy. A wife has run away from her husband, and he and his friends have gone in pursuit, binding up the paths, as they call it, in this fashion to prevent the fugitive from doubling back" (3.305).

The loosening of knots may also be efficacious. "Moslem pilgrims to Mecca are in a state of sanctity or taboo and may wear on their persons neither knots nor rings." Especially at childbirth, various peoples will "untie all knots in a house" (3.293–94) or open all locks and doors, "the lids of all chests, boxes, pans" (3.296), or the husband "loosens the plaits of his hair and the laces of his shoes" (3.297–98). So also "at certain magical and religious ceremonies the hair should hang loose and the feet should be bare" (3.310–11). God commands Moses at the burning bush to remove his shoes. Dido, performing rites to bring back Aeneas, "stands by the altar with her dress loosened and with one foot bare" (3.312). To account for this practice, Frazer suggests "the magical virtue attributed to knots; for down to recent times . . . shoes have been universally tied to the feet by latchets" (3.313).

The imagery and diction of Faulkner's chapter reflect these actions. As a child, Lena would come to town with her father, carrying her shoes, witnessing even in those early days:

> Six or eight times a year she went to town on Saturday, in the wagon, in a mail-order dress and her bare feet flat in the wagon bed and her shoes wrapped in a piece of paper beside her on the seat. She would put on the shoes just before the wagon reached town. After she got to be a big girl she would ask her father to stop the wagon at the edge of town and she would get down and walk. She would not tell her father why she wanted to walk in instead of riding. He thought that it was because of the smooth streets, the sidewalks. But it was because she believed that the people who saw her and whom she passed on foot would believe that she lived in the town too. (1–2 / 3)[4]

Described in the present as coming "afoot," Lena lifts down, or carries, or places beside herself, or walks in, her brother's dusty shoes. Moreover, while Armstid watches "across the footboard," Martha breaks the china effigy with her shoe, or when Lena asks for "sour deens," she is told that all she can buy for a nickel is "shoeblacking."[5]

The chapter also has a number of string images,[6] as in this description of the wagon, which "seems to hang suspended in the middle distance forever and forever, so infinitesimal is its progress, like a shabby bead upon the mild red string of road. So much is this so [so is this (*CT*)] that in the watching of it the eye loses it as sight

4. That the theme of shoes, also unlaced, will come up again in the early kidnaping of Joe Christmas and his final capture only reinforces its recognition of a spiritual power unloosed.

5. Ficken ("Critical" 128) points out the repetition of the unlaced shoes, as does Baldanza (69), who ascribes it to the novelistic technique of "theme clusters."

6. Critics such as Porter (112) have suggested that the beads on the string form an image echoing Bergson's metaphor for static moments along the flux of time. But we have two reasons to look to Frazer to account for the repetition of this theme. Besides their use in following a runaway, strings were also important to Osiris (Lucas): "At his festival women used to go about the villages singing songs in his praise and carrying obscene images of him which they set in motion by means of strings" (6.112).

and sense drowsily merge and blend, like the road itself, with all the peaceful and monotonous changes between darkness and day, like already measured thread being rewound onto a spool" (5–6 / 7–8). Then Lena is found with "no wedding ring" (9 / 12) or "plaiting with rapt bemusement a fold of her skirt" (17 / 22), while Martha bangs the stove lids or opens the dresser drawer, unlocks a metal box, and pulls the china rooster from a cloth sack. That she knots and reknots the coins which Lena later unknots, has a spellbinding or unbinding function, just like all the spitting at Lena's passing, for spit can be used to bind a knot (3.302) or break a spell (3.279).[7]

Overall, one of the noteworthy features of John 1 is the strange triad of thundering timelessness, the history of the Baptist, and a series of scenes on successive days. This same mixture is evident in Faulkner's chapter.[8] For example, after the book opens in the present tense, with Lena watching the wagon, the description of her own beginning is capped with this Keatsian timelessness: "backrolling now behind her a long monotonous succession of peaceful and undeviating changes from day to dark and dark to day again, through which she advanced in identical and anonymous and deliberate wagons as though through a succession of creakwheeled and limpeared avatars, like something moving forever and without progress across an urn" (5 / 7).

And these timeless "avatars" are thematically linked. Three times John the Baptist says words such as "After me cometh a man which is preferred before me: for he was before me." The theme of one coming after who was before and of one finally seen who had been only heard, is developed in several of Lena's reveries, but most fully here:

> As though out of some trivial and important region beyond even distance, the sound of [the wagon] seems to come slow and terrific and without meaning, as though it were a ghost travelling a half mile ahead of its own shape. "That far within my hearing before my

7. In an unpublished master's dissertation, Frazier (70) also observes the connection between Faulkner's knots and Frazer.

8. Kreiswirth notes "Faulkner's curious shifting of verb tenses" in this opening chapter (61).

seeing," Lena thinks. She thinks of herself as already moving, riding again, thinking *then it will be as if I were riding for a half mile before I even got into the wagon, before the wagon even got to where I was waiting, and that when the wagon is empty of me again it will go on for a half mile with me still in it. . . .* Thinking, "And if he is going all the way to Jefferson, I will be riding within the hearing of Lucas Burch before his seeing. He will hear the wagon, but he wont know. So there will be one within his hearing before his seeing. And then he will see me and he will be excited. And so there will be two within his seeing before his remembering." (6 / 8–9)

Of all the gospels, John alone carries the sense of timeless continuity from the beginning, with the expectation that at this moment in time, the continuity will be broken, the expectation fulfilled. In chapter 1, Faulkner similarly suggests this "steady and unflagging" continuity that contains the expectation of a break, like the smashing of the china rooster or the "series of dry sluggish reports" in the "hot still pinewiney silence of the August afternoon" (5 / 8).

The final effect of both opening chapters must be described as exalted. Both herald a joyous event, joyous because, like a myth, it is as familiar as the seasons; eventful because, like Christianity, it happens in our own time and space in ways we could not have imagined. In his portrait of the decorous, pregnant Lena, ascending and descending the wagons in and out of her heavy men's shoes, Faulkner has managed to capture both this joy and surprise. The appearance in history, all-knowing as it believes itself to be, of the timeless innocent, carrying lightly her belief in the word, is the restorative good news to which we will return throughout the novel, with unreasonable relief.

Chapter 2: External Changes, like Water to Wine

Chapter 2 of John contains three main episodes: the changing of water to wine, the scourge of the temple, and the foretelling of the resurrection, in Jesus' metaphoric "destroy this temple, and in three days I will raise it up." After the first, the disciples "believed in him"; after the second, they remember prophetic scripture; and after Jesus is risen, John here reports, they remember his words and believe.

In Faulkner's chapter 2, the many introductions to people are similarly told from a later, enlightened perspective, as if each first impression had to be reconsidered. Recalling the first time he heard Christmas's name, Byron thinks:

> And that was the first time Byron remembered that he had ever thought how a man's name, which is supposed to be just the sound for who he is, can be somehow an augur of what he will do, if other men can only read the meaning in time. It seemed to him that none of them had looked especially at the stranger until they heard his name. But as soon as they heard it, it was as though there was something in the sound of it that was trying to tell them what to expect; that he carried with him his own inescapable warning, like a flower its scent or a rattlesnake its rattle. Only none of them had sense enough to recognise it. (29 / 35)

The chapter begins "Byron Bunch knows this," and goes on with what people knew and did not know about Christmas and Brown and Joanna and Hightower, and even Byron himself. All of the speculations are based on external changes, of name, or particularly, of clothing. Christmas is first described: "He looked like a tramp, yet not like a tramp either. His shoes were dusty and his trousers were soiled too. But they were of decent serge, sharply creased, and his shirt was soiled but it was a white shirt, and he wore a tie and a stiffbrim straw hat that was quite new, cocked at an angle arrogant and baleful above his still face. He did not look like a professional hobo in his professional rags, but there was something definitely rootless about him" (27 / 33). When the foreman asks if Christmas is going to work "in them clothes," the superintendent says, "That's his business." "I'm not hiring his clothes," so the foreman says, "Well, whatever he wears suits me if it suits you and him" (28–29 / 34–35). Further, "as they watched him . . . working in that tie and the straw hat and the creased trousers, they said among themselves that that was the way men in his country worked; though there were others who said, 'He'll change clothes tonight. He wont have on them Sunday clothes when he comes to work in the morning'" (29 / 35–36).

When Brown arrives, his clothing is also discussed; he is described as a man who cannot wear pants. And the men theorize about his change of name, referring again to clothing:

> There was no reason why his name should not have been Brown. It was that, looking at him, a man would know that at some time in his life he would reach some crisis in his own foolishness when he would change his name, and that he would think of Brown to change it to with a kind of gleeful exultation, as though the name had never been invented. The thing was, there was no reason why he should have had or have needed any name at all. Nobody cared, just as Byron believed that no one (wearing pants, anyway) cared where he came from nor where he went nor how long he stayed. (33 / 40)

Likewise, regarding Byron, Mrs. Beard "knows only that shortly after six o'clock each Saturday Bunch enters, bathes and changes to a suit of cheap serge which is not new, eats his supper and saddles the mule which he stables in a shed behind the house which Bunch himself patched up and roofed [note the change in the shed], and departs on the mule. She does not know where he goes" (43 / 52).

This reading of character by external changes is the dominant motif in Faulkner's second chapter. All of the characters are introduced as strangers, foreigners, or outcasts,[9] and as Frazer notes, "A passing stranger may be a god" (7.236), a tradition found in the Bible (Hebrews 13:2). With Joanna, the Yankee, "something dark and outlandish and threatful" still surrounds her; Byron is "a man of mystery among his fellow workers"; Hightower is "the fifty-year-old outcast." But particularly Christmas, the foreigner, is twice symbolized by the snake; his frequent "vanishing" and "reappearing," coupled with his bootlegging and its ties to the underworld, suggest that the "other country" he comes from is actually the Underworld: "There was something definitely rootless about him, as though no town nor city was his, no street, no walls, no square of earth his home. And that he carried his [this (CT)] knowledge with him always as though it were a banner, with a

---

9. Burroughs (191) remarks on the significance of the stranger-god motif. Vickery (75) cites Joe, Joanna, and Hightower, "the Negro, the Yankee, the Apostate" as key figures "in a society which defines itself by exclusion." Indeed, one could add Lena, the Fallen Woman, and even Byron, the Overconscientious Worker.

quality ruthless, lonely, and almost proud. 'As if,' as the men said later, 'he was just down on his luck for a time, and that he didn't intend to stay down on it and didn't give a damn much how he rose up'" (27 / 33).

As mentioned, the language Frazer uses the describe the Underworld wine god, Dionysus, is particularly applicable to Joe, but also to the theme of change. Associated with the "winnowing-fan" (Christmas works on the sawdust pile), the infant Dionysus, whose father was Zeus in the form of a serpent, is said to have brandished his father's lightning and evaded his white-faced enemies by changing into various shapes before he is finally killed and mutilated as a bull (7.12–13). As a blackskinned goat, Dionysus is called "kid" (7.17), as is Christmas, with his insistently "parchment" skin, by Max and company. As a tree spirit, Dionysus is found "in a plane-tree" (7.3), while Joe ignores Byron (himself a yeargod) "as if he were another post" (30 / 37). And the Dionysian Mysteries apparently involved the changing of water into wine.

On a more comic level, the avatars apply to that other wine god, also an underworld figure, Joe Brown as Osiris, here transformed into Christmas's disciple: "He wore now the new suit and the straw hat, and he stopped at the shed and stood there looking at the working men as Christmas had done on that day three years ago, as if somehow the very attitudes of the master's dead life motivated, unawares to him, the willing muscles of the disciple who had learned too quick and too well. But Brown merely contrived to look scattered and emptily swaggering where the master had looked sullen and quiet and fatal as a snake" (40–41 / 48–49).[10]

Like Dionysus, Osiris was beset by conspirators, who threw him into the Nile. When his body was found, it was rent into fourteen pieces and "scattered" (6.10). Recall that Brown is repeatedly described as "scattered," so much so that "now there was nothing left but the transparent and weightless shell blown oblivious and without destination upon whatever wind" (34 / 41).

The theme of change may also be found in Faulkner's humorous

---

10. Many critics have noticed the master-disciple relationship. See Kunkel (148), Moseley (142), and Kerr (129).

inversion of the planing mill into a temple-sanctuary, primarily again on the basis of proper clothing and decorum. Byron and Lena "might be sitting in their Sunday clothes, in splint chairs on the patinasmooth earth before a country cabin on a sabbath afternoon" (49 / 58). Similarly:

> Some of the other workers were family men and some were bachelors and they were of different ages and they led a catholic variety of lives, yet on Monday morning they all came to work with a kind of gravity, almost decorum. Some of them were young, and they drank and gambled on Saturday night, and even went to Memphis now and then. Yet on Monday morning they came quietly and soberly to work, in clean overalls and clean shirts, waiting quietly until the whistle blew and then going quietly to work, as though there were still something of Sabbath in the overlingering air which established a tenet that, no matter what a man had done with his Sabbath, to come quiet and clean to work on Monday morning was no more than seemly and right to do. (36–37 / 44)

Faulkner further develops the theme of change by using Frazer's descriptions of the folk belief in water-to-wine transformations. On Easter night, when bonfires were lit and smoke used to read omens (10.121), certain villagers would "draw water in buckets" which they would mix "with the fodder and drink of the cattle," and because they believed that at a mystic hour "the water turned to wine as far as the crowing of a cock could be heard, . . . they laid themselves flat on their stomachs and kept their tongues in the water till the miraculous change occurred, when they took a great gulp of the transformed water" (10.124).

The tongue testing and the pail with the fodder appear at key moments in Faulkner's chapter 2. At the very instant Byron has his altering insight (realizing that Christmas has not changed his clothes because he is broke), he is offering his food, which Christmas proudly rejects as "muck" from a "pail." And soon after, Byron notes they had not hired "the stranger's tongue" anymore than his clothes (31 / 37).

They may also be found in the echoes of John's literal and figurative assault on the temple.

In John's version of the scourge on the temple, Jesus takes a whip of "small cords" and drives out "those that sold oxen and sheep and doves," and the (twice mentioned) "changers of money." Faulkner expands these motifs by echoing Frazer's Festival of Fools, when mock priests or bishops, dressed impiously, would transform the church altar into a tavern, eating sausages, chanting obscenities, and running riot through the whole church. One noteworthy prank was to bring an ass into the church, glorify it with a regular Latin liturgy and imitate its braying (9.335).

Brown is repeatedly associated with the term *fool* (his laughter echoing like "a meaningless sound in a church" [36 / 43]), and he is also called a mule and "a horse . . . a worthless horse. Looks fine in the pasture, but it's always down in the spring bottom when anybody comes to the gate with a bridle" (33 / 39–40) (again, suggesting the theme of change). More important, in Brown's last days at the mill, he is spoken of as a "public servant," selling hooch for a password of "six bits"; although he is not "chained to that scoop" and he "aint quite sold yet," he clutches the shovel "as though it were a riding whip," he, whose name is Burch. But after he, too, rejects "cold muck out of a dirty lard bucket," the final expulsion comes when he blabs, "lay into it, you slaving bastards" in a "loud voice cropped with teeth." Mooney lets him have it. "You aint calling me that . . . are you?" Whereupon, "Brown's mobile face performed one of those instantaneous changes which they knew. Like it was so scattered and so lightly built that it wasn't any trouble for even him to change it" (41 / 49). In association with the animal imagery, the tethering, the selling, and the whip, this "scattered" suggests that Brown is the defiler, the turncoat, the ass, who must be thrown out of the temple.

The figurative assault is on a temple which Jesus says he will raise up again in three days, meaning "the temple of his body." The Faulkner parallel again involves the mill, namely, Byron's use of it as a sanctuary, "where the chance to do hurt or harm could not have found him" (50 / 60). Echoing the Festival of the Innocents (similar to the Festival of Fools) when a Boy Bishop took possession of a church during an intercalary period to perform its offices (9.336–38), each Saturday, Byron takes over the mill, bearing the "stacked burdens of staves" (the staff signals the bishop's authority), living by the whistle, counting his worth on a huge watch made of silver. The destruction of the temple occurs when he falls in love, for it is with a temple which, according to his *raising,* should have been physically sacred: "Then Byron fell in love. He fell in love contrary to all the tradition of his austere and jealous country raising which demands in the object physical inviolability" (44 / 53).[11] Even Lena's odd suspicion of Byron—she who expected nothing but kindness all the way from Alabama—suggests that she shares his "foreknowledge of something now irrevocable, not to be recalled" (50 / 60).[12] So they come together with their notions of themselves intact, only to have those notions destroyed. And although the reader knows, can interpret as John does, that the very act of destruction—only an external change—will be one of rebuilding, this is little help to Byron, who, "already in love, though he does not yet know it" (50 / 59), signals the change in his miserable sense that "he could have bitten his tongue in two" (51 / 60).

Chapter 3: *Rulers Inscribed by the Rules*

The third chapter in John contains the discourse between Jesus and Nicodemus, the Pharisee, one of the ruler-scribes who taught adherence to the letter at the expense of the spirit. A second scene, between John the Baptist and his followers, may be a variant of the first, since both instruct by the technique of misunderstanding and both teach the need to distinguish between flesh and spirit in order to be born again. And the lesson is exemplified: Jesus receives the ruler; he teaches the rabbi; he quotes text to the scribe. The irony is patent. The ruler, master, scribe, the old order, will be supplanted by the new.

The central character in Faulkner's chapter 3 is Hightower, dead learning personified, who also confuses spirit and flesh, and who

---

11. The "temple of the body" is suggested ironically in another Faulkner character, Temple Drake.

12. Ficken ("Critical" 74) calls her suspicion of Byron a "new element in Lena."

may need to be born again, since he was "born about thirty years after the only day he seemed to have ever lived in" (57 / 66). In developing the theme of the ruler-scribe, Faulkner draws on Frazer's chapter "The Burden of Royalty." Evidently so much of a people's well-being rests with the ruler that he "exists only for his subjects; his life is only valuable so long as he discharges the duties of his position by ordering the course of nature for his people's benefit. So soon as he fails to do so, the care, the devotion, the religious homage which they had hitherto lavished on him cease and are changed into hatred and contempt; he is dismissed ignominiously and may be thankful if he escapes with his life" (3.7–8). From the moment the ruler "ascends the throne he is lost in the ocean of rites and taboos" (3.8). For one tribe, the priestly king was "unapproachable by his subjects. Only by night was he allowed to quit his dwelling in order to bathe" (3.9). For another, he "must be celibate; if he is married he must leave his wife" (3.15). Another ruler may come down from the hills only once a year "to make purchases in the market." Still another "may not touch a woman nor leave his house; indeed he may not even quit his chair, in which he is obliged to sleep sitting, for if he lay down no wind would arise and navigation would be stopped" (3.5). Because of these strictures, "few kings are natives of the countries they govern" (3.18), and the burdens of royalty are such that "either men refused to accept the office, which hence tended to fall into abeyance; or accepting it, they sank under its weight into spiritless creatures, cloistered recluses, from whose nerveless fingers the reins of government slipped into the firmer grasp of men who were often content to wield the reality of sovereignty without its name. [Sometimes] this rift . . . could deepen into a total and permanent separation of the spiritual and temporal powers" (3.17).

Jefferson has two such cloistered rulers, Hightower and Joanna Burden, both names relevant.[13] But then a shared priesthood is not unusual: on Fiji there is a Sacred King and a War King; in western Africa, a fetish king and a civil king; in British New Guinea, a

13. Brooks (59–60) notes many parallels between Joanna and Hightower, as does Baldanza (70).

taboo chief and a war chief. Usually, the office of taboo chief is hereditary; on one island in Polynesia "religious and civil authority were lodged in separate hands, spiritual functions being discharged by a line of hereditary kings, while the temporal government was entrusted from time to time to a victorious warchief" (3.20–24).

Joanna's connection with the taboo of race is inherited: "It still lingers about her and about the place: something dark and outlandish and threatful, even though she is but a woman and but the descendant of them who the ancestors of the town had reason (or thought that they had) to hate and dread. But it is there: the descendants of both in their relationship to one another [another's (CT)] ghosts, with between them the phantom of the old spilled blood and the old horror and anger and fear" (42 / 50–51).

Hightower's obsession with his grandfather's charge makes him the war chief, but this is what creates the conflict with the town. Brought in to be, as he says, "both master and servant of their believing" (69 / 81), and supposed to teach spiritual power, Hightower can only talk of temporal power. In fact, he becomes, like Nicodemus, an object lesson; so that when Byron arrives, it is the town which teaches him: "and they told him," "they told Byron," "but the town said," "the old people said," "the women, the neighbors . . . telling one another."

Their text is Hightower, who lives behind his "monument," bearing a "legend" which he "lettered" himself, "with bits of broken glass contrived cunningly into the paint, so that at night, when the corner street lamp shone upon it, the letters glittered with an effect as of Christmas" (53 / 62). The "effect" of Christmas is the emphasis, for the "legend," offering "Art Lessons / Handpainted Xmas & Anniversary Cards / Photographs Developed" (no birthday cards), bears no relation to reality, since "he had had no art pupils and few enough Christmas cards and photograph plates, and the paint and the shattered glass had weathered out of the fading letters." The sign is read only by strangers, for whom the words are as devoid of meaning as for the occasional negro nursemaid who "with her white charges would loiter there and spell them aloud with that vacuous idiocy of her idle and illiterate kind" (53 / 62–

63). As for Hightower, "the sign which he carpentered and lettered is even less to him than it is to the town; he is no longer conscious of it as a sign, a message" (54 / 64).

The scribal theme pervades his story.[14] Hightower writes letters to get to Jefferson, and he continues writing them to Memphis, after his wife's death. While he is preaching, the townspeople feel he is "using religion as though it were a dream. Not a nightmare, but something which went faster than the words in the Book" (56 / 66). When his wife explodes in church, Hightower is "frozen in the shape of the thundering and allegorical period which he had not completed" (59 / 69). When he hides his face from the reporters with an "open hymn book,"[15] his expression is "like the face of Satan in the old prints" (63 / 74). And Byron notes "with a kind of musing and respectful consternation" (67 / 79) the books in Hightower's study, books that do him no good when it comes to delivering the black child. If all these books, letters, and signs sound useless, they only reflect the message of Nicodemus, who confuses the letter of the law with the spirit of the law, and who must learn to distinguish between flesh and spirit.

Hightower also confuses flesh and spirit. Although he contributes to a home for delinquent girls, he seems not to understand why they are delinquent, for when the neighbors hear his wife weeping in the parsonage, they know that "the husband would not know what to do about it because he did not know what was wrong" (57 / 67). Like the Public Magician, he must stay hidden and protected from ordinary intercourse—which Faulkner has amusingly reflected in his lack of intercourse with his own wife.

And his lack of intercourse with the people of the town. He comes to Jefferson to be at the scene of his dead grandfather's adventure, "as if he did not care about the people, the living people"

14. Examining the stylistic peculiarities of this chapter, Pitavy (149) finds studied inversions, chiasmus, preciosity in the use of words, and sonorities.

15. The manuscript reads, "[A]nd next day when the picture came out in the Memphis paper it was taken from the side, with him in the middle of a step, holding ~~his hat~~ the hymn book in front of his face. And behind the ~~hat~~ book his lips were drawn back ~~like~~ as though he was sailing. Only his teeth ~~was~~ were tight together and his face looked like ~~how~~ they draw the face of Satan" (Mms. 28).

of the town (56 / 65). He persistently confuses "cavalry" with "calvary," the fleshly heroism of boys with the spiritual leadership his parishioners yearn for, looking at him "up there in the pulpit with his hands flying around him and the dogma he was supposed to preach all full of galloping cavalry and defeat and glory just as when he tried to tell them on the street about the galloping horses, it in turn would get all mixed up with absolution and choirs of martial seraphim, until it was natural that the old men and women should believe that what he preached in God's own house on God's own day verged on actual sacrilege" (57 / 67).

Notice the parallel does not suggest that Hightower, receiving Byron by night, is Jesus, receiving Nicodemus; rather, the theme of one who lives in darkness, who "loved darkness rather than the light" and who "must be born again," can be applied to Hightower, who lives behind "bushing crape myrtle and syringa and Althea," [16] who only lived the night his grandfather was killed: "as though the seed which his grandfather had transmitted to him had been on the horse too that night and had been killed too and time had stopped there and then for the seed and nothing had happened in time since, not even him" (59 / 69). And now Byron says, "I dont reckon there is anybody in Jefferson that knows that he sits in that window from sundown to full dark every day that comes, except me. Or what the inside of that house looks like. And they dont even know that I know" (67 / 79).

But this can be turned around. If Hightower is caught in his obsession, so is the town caught in its fixed responses. In language which echoes "the wind bloweth where it listeth, and thou hearest the sound thereof, but canst not tell whence it cometh, and whither it goeth," Faulkner signals a similar confusion of flesh and spirit over Hightower's "high brown" cook, in the minds of the townspeople: "Because that was all it required: that idea, that single idle word blown from mind to mind" (66 / 77), a confusion whose end is signaled by "then all of a sudden the whole thing

---

16. The association of death with crape myrtle is obvious, but "syringa" means "hollowness," while Althea caused her son's death and committed suicide. Pitavy remarks that Hightower's garden symbolizes his "cramped and useless life" (91).

seemed to blow away, like an evil wind" (67 / 78). Thus, Faulkner is suggesting that the townspeople's obsession with the dead issue of race will inevitably lead them away from their naturally good hold on the truth, just as will the aristocrat's obsession with the dead past, particularly the glorious martial past.[17]

Instructed by the two, Byron, at least appears to be free of confusion, believing "that the town had had the habit of saying things about the disgraced minister which they did not believe themselves for too long a time to break themselves of it. 'Because always,' he thinks, 'when anything gets to be a habit, it also manages to get a right good distance away from truth and fact'" (69 / 80).

On the other hand, these observations can apply to Byron himself.[18] Regarding Hightower, Byron knows why he stays "almost within sight of, and within hearing of, the church which had disowned and expelled him": "It is because a fellow is more afraid of the trouble he might have than he ever is of the trouble he's already got. He'll cling to trouble he's used to before he'll risk a change. Yes. A man will talk about how he'd like to escape from living folks. But it's the dead folks that do him the damage. It's the dead ones that lay quiet in one place and dont try to hold him, that he cant escape from" (69 / 81). But Byron, too, is a prisoner of habit, fearful of "doing harm," of risking change, and he too must escape the dead, in the form of Hightower himself. Thus, when Byron instructs us, we should be alert to his own need to be "born again."

Chapter 4: Reflective Testimony by the Waters of the Well

Now we must widen our speculations on Hightower as we have with other characters. Chapter 1 focused on Lena enacting the

17. Kerr (132) says Hightower's vision, "symbolizes the Southern chivalric ideal," Vickery says Hightower mirrors the South's "legends of its own past" (76), while R. G. Collins ("*Light*" 100) says Hightower "represents the historical American South in its most tenuous mythic form: the South of tradition in which the Civil War stands as cultural, historical, and emotional climax."

18. Ficken observes ("Critical" 90) that Byron has also been guilty of withdrawing from life.

theme of witnessing while she also suggests the figures of the Virgin Mary and Isis. Chapter 2 focused on Christmas enacting the theme of change while he also suggests Christ and Dionysus. In chapter 3 Hightower embodies the dead learning of a Nicodemus. But besides this thematic role, he also suggests the mythic figure of Hippolytus, whose name means "horseloosed," appropriately, because horses were sacred to Poseidon, his grandfather (1.27). Most important, horses were excluded from his sacred grove because of the manner of his death: preferring to spend his days hunting with the chaste Artemis, he spurned Aphrodite, so she had him dragged to death by horses. Here we recall Hightower's spurning of his wife's sexuality; his chaste contributions to unwed mothers, a special concern of Artemis (1.37); above all, his obsession with horses, particularly his grandfather's. Note that entering Hightower's "sanctuary" (293 / 341 & 424 / 494), Byron is described as a "puny, unhorsed figure" (70 / 82).

This suggests the difference between the two chapters: in 3, we found echoes of the original myth. Hightower is ensnared by the past, by the horses of his wild obsession, which is yet "chaste": even the original hunt was for chickens. In chapter 4, he takes the role of Hippolytus' priest, a life-service (1.24), who was expected to stay in his sanctuary and ensure the fruitfulness of the land by receiving offerings of grain and particularly locks of hair, felt to be the source of power (witness Samson), especially sexual power (1.31).

As discussed, the theme of hair recurs often in Faulkner's fourth chapter (see my chapter 1). But the hair appears not simply because of Hippolytus-Hightower. The reason it was offered "to the shadowy dead" was that it could make water flow and, in a similar way, make someone talk, give testimony (11.158). Both of these themes are central to this chapter in John.

In John 4, the two main episodes involve "tricks" which, like any magician's tricks, depend on the belief of the audience. In the first, Jesus tells the Samaritan woman that he represents the "living" water, as opposed to the nearby well of Jacob, and reveals information about her (that she has had five husbands) which no stranger could have known; yet her subsequent testimony depends on her prior belief in the Messiah. So also in the second episode, the healing of the nobleman's son, as soon as Jesus says, "thy son liveth," the nobleman "believed."

To understand Faulkner's parallel for these episodes, we must examine the chapter's unique structure.

Although Faulkner's chapter 4 has two parts, the break occurs with no apparent time lapse, in the middle of a conversation between Hightower and Byron. Moreover, the second part, with its fairly sustained narrative, comes as a relief after the constant switching from the present to the past and back again, with Byron and Hightower talking about Lena, or the fire, or Brown, or Christmas, or Joanna.[19] This deliberate disjointing of elements makes one wonder what the characters are reacting to, the strangest sequence being the last, when after Byron repeats Lena's question— "Is he still enough of a preacher to marry folks?"—Hightower responds,

> "Byron . . . Byron. What is this you are telling me?"
> Byron ceases. He looks quietly at the other, with an expression of commiseration and pity. "I knowed you had not heard yet. . . .
> They look at one another. "What is it I haven't heard yet?"
> "About Christmas. About yesterday and Christmas. Christmas is part nigger. About him and Brown and yesterday." (82–83 / 97)

This constant shifting has a stylistic counterpart in the opening dialogue of John 4, between Jesus and the woman at the well, where elaborate introductions punctuate each utterance:

> Jesus saith unto her, Give me to drink. . . .
> Then saith the woman of Samaria unto him, How it is that thou, being a Jew, askest drink of me, . . . a woman of Samaria? . . .
> Jesus answered and said unto her, If thou knewest [who was speaking] to thee . . . thou wouldest have asked of him, and he would have given thee living water.
> The woman saith unto him, Sir, thou hast nothing to draw with, and the well is deep: from whence then hast thou that living water?
> . . .

---

19. While Kreiswirth notes that Byron's narrative "moves back and forth in time" (72), Parker calls it "a coyly staggered succession of withholdings and revelations" (90).

Jesus answered and said unto her, Whosoever drinketh of this water shall thirst again: But whosoever drinketh of the water that I shall give him shall never thirst. . . .

The woman saith unto him, Sir, give me this water, that I thirst not. . . .

Jesus saith unto her, Go, call thy husband. . . .

The woman answered and said, I have no husband.

Jesus said unto her, Thou hast well said, I have no husband: For thou hast had five husbands; and he whom thou now hast is not thy husband. . . .

The woman saith unto him, Sir, I perceive that thou art a prophet. . . .

Jesus saith unto her, Woman, believe me, the hour cometh, . . . and now is, when the true worshippers shall worship the Father in spirit and in truth. . . .

The woman saith unto him, I know that Messias cometh, which is called Christ. . . .

Jesus saith unto her, I that speak unto thee am he.

Although there may be ingenious parallels within the particular sections (such as the woman saying "I have no husband" just as Byron is trying to explain Lena's lack of a husband to Mrs. Beard), the individual points of reference are less important than the parallel witnessing and staccato style.

Diction, too, relates this strange episode in Faulkner to the well of Jacob. References to wells and water frame the conversation. Byron and Hightower "sit facing one another. . . . Both their faces are just without the direct downward pool of light" (71 / 84). Overleaf a grimace crosses Byron's face like a water-surface ripple: "His upper lip just lifts momentarily, the movement, even the surface wrinkling, travelling no further and vanishing almost at once" (72 / 85). Punning words such as *licks, drinks, reflection,* and *well, well, well* lace the conversation. Most important, the first sequence is climaxed, as if all this back and forth has operated like a pump, in the sudden mobility of Hightower's "parts" and the gush of water: "He does not move. For a moment longer he does not move. Then there seems to come over his whole body, as if its parts were mobile like face features, that shrinking and denial, and Byron sees that the still, flaccid, big face is suddenly slick with sweat" (83 / 98). From that point on, the water continues to flow until "the sweat [is] running down his face like tears" (93 / 109). Like the lifeless well of Jacob (once a source of belief) or like the sanctuary of Hippolytus which received locks of hair to make the rivers flow, or like sacred wells which have rainmaking powers (2.159), Hightower represents a dead tradition from which, despite his "shrinking and denial," life may yet be forced.[20]

Regarding the next forward movement of the story, we should review Joanna Burden's association with John the Baptist.[21] Joanna is the feminine form of John, her initials are J. B., and "Burden" suggests prophetic weight. Moreover, she comes to Jefferson before J. C. with her alien message of brotherhood, and like the Baptist, whom Jesus calls "a burning and shining light," she and her burning house are focal points of the story. Most important is the severed head, its position suggesting a Janus pose of the past and the future.[22]

However, to the countryman who finds her, Joanna is simply a body to be saved from the fire, especially difficult because she— it—is coming apart: when he rolls her in a bed cover, he "swung it onto his back like a sack of meal and carried it out of the house and laid it down under a tree" (85 / 100–101). This body is "like a sack of meal" which appears on the scene like an offering just when, in John 4, Jesus is speaking of the harvest of souls: "Say not ye, There are yet four months, and then cometh harvest? . . . Lift up your eyes, and look on the fields; for they are white already to harvest. And he that reapeth receiveth wages, and gathereth fruit unto life eternal: that both he that soweth and he that reapeth may rejoice together. And herein is that saying true, One soweth, and another reapeth." And when Joe Brown seeks the wages, the reward money, for Christmas's labors, Byron comments, "It beats all how some folks think that making or getting money is a kind of game where there are not any rules at all" (90 / 106).

---

20. Remarking on the repetition of Hightower's "shrinking and denial," Ficken suggests it is because "the outside world is once again forcing itself into his quiet and secluded life" ("Critical" 97).

21. On Joanna as John the Baptist, see Cottrell (208–9).

22. As an avatar of Dianus, Janus is also a link to Joanna as Diana.

But then this remark is made before the transformation of Joe Christmas from mere "foreigner" to "nigger," after which we find a whole new group of believers. Faulkner relates his story to John by using tricks of time, as in the original: "A certain nobleman, whose son was sick at Capernaum . . . heard that Jesus was come . . . and besought him that he would come down, and heal his son: for he was at the point of death. Then said Jesus unto him, Except ye see signs and wonders, ye will not believe. The nobleman saith unto him, Sir, come down ere my child die. Jesus saith unto him, Go thy way; thy son liveth. And the man believed the word that Jesus had spoken." When his servants met him, saying, "Thy son liveth," he asked the hour when the boy began to heal, and they said, "Yesterday at the seventh hour the fever left him. So the father knew that it was at the same hour, in the which Jesus said . . . Thy son liveth: and himself believed, and his whole house."

That "seventh hour" has prompted much comment. Why did it take so long for the father to return to Capernaum, only fifteen miles from Cana? Many excuses have been invented for the father's "dilatoriness" (Moffatt 122).

In Faulkner, we have two instances of the "seventh hour." The first is clear: Brown testifies that the murder was done at 7 o'clock in the morning. The second is obscured: Brown testifies that he first saw the fire "about eight o'clock," whereupon the sheriff says, "And that fire wasn't reported until nigh eleven o'clock." "And that house was still burning at three P.M. You mean to say a old wooden house, even a big one, would need six hours to burn down in?" (89 / 105). But those hours add up to seven, not six, and representing the time it took for the fire to end, are a fitting symbol for the seven hours it took for the fever to end.

Why has the parallel been obscured? The answer may lie in the chapter's peculiar style. Throughout, we find what could be called "doubling-up constructions," such as "he knew before he knew what had happened" (76 / 90), or "not knowing that I knew" (82 / 96), or "folks dont know if she ever knew or not" (73 / 86); or even doubling doubles, as in: "That would be for me to do too. To tell on two days to two folks something they aint going to want to hear and that they hadn't ought to have to hear at all" (72 / 86).

This doubling-up, the stylistic expression of the chapter's theme of shared or reflective expectations, extends to images and incidents. Recall Hightower and Byron sitting across from each other; a number of such pairs repeat and reflect one another. Byron and Lena echo:

> "What is it them men were trying to tell you? What is it about that burned house?"
> "It wasn't anything," he said, his voice sounding dry and light to him. "Just something about Miss Burden got hurt in the fire."
> "How got hurt? How bad hurt?"
> "I reckon not bad. Maybe not hurt at all. Just folks talking, like as not. Like they will." (77–78 / 91)

There are the descriptions of Hightower's "parallel" forearms or palms or "twin" spectacles. He has "two faces, one imposed upon the other" (82 / 97). And so, remarkably, has Joanna, "laying on her side, facing one way, and her head was turned clean around like she was looking behind her" (85 / 101). And there is a proliferation of expressions such as "looking this way and that," "louder and louder," "faster and faster," "going and going," with the climactic " 'Nigger?' the sheriff said. 'Nigger'?" (91 / 107).

Returning to the central testimony of Joe Brown, the prophet who "hath no honour in his own country," the reader hardly needs to know the time discrepancies to recognize that Brown is lying. And we see that belief in his testimony depends on a single, shared prejudice: that Joanna Burden, "nigger-lover," was murdered by Joe Christmas, "nigger." But all of the eyewitness testimony given in chapter 4 similarly rests on this kind of reflective relationship between the teller and the told: "Byron can see in the other's face something latent, about to wake, of which Hightower himself is unaware, as if something inside the man were trying to warn or prepare him. But Byron thinks that this is just the reflection of what he himself already knows and is about to tell" (74 / 88). Yet the doubling-up is not exact, not mirrorlike, except as mirrors distort. The appropriate image is the pool in the well, which both reflects and echoes from its own depths. Thus, lines are repeated, but not exactly. Stories are retold, but with changes. The times are given, but with some distortion.

Expressing this theme, Byron says, "Like not only finds like; it cant even escape from being found by its like. Even when it's just like in one thing" (80 / 95). This could be a thoughtful comment on the message in John. Although two wonders occur, Jesus wishes that truth, not tricks, should teach, and in fact, the witness of the Samaritan woman and the nobleman rests on prior belief. In Faulkner, Joe Brown makes patent lying believable to the townspeople by telling them the only "truth" they can hear, that Joe Christmas, nonentity, is really Joe Christmas, "nigger." Now he lives. That the "truth" is irrelevant to the murder makes no difference. The same principle can be applied to Hightower's reception of Byron's story. Hightower keeps saying, "But I don't see, but I don't see." The one piece of information which makes him see is that Christmas has come to life to the people of Jefferson in the form of "nigger." Now he himself is needed, and with this knowledge, the "living water" wells up in him and begins to flow until it is "running down his face like tears."

Thus, when Lena's words at the end of chapter 4, "My, my. Here I have come clean from Alabama, and now I am in Jefferson at last," echo her words at the end of chapter 1: "My, my . . . here I aint been on the road but four weeks, and now I am in Jefferson already," we sense that the movement from witness to belief can be directed by stubborn faith or stony prejudice.

Chapter 5: The Suspension of the Halt Man

The setting of John 5 is the pool of Bethesda surrounded by the impotent, the blind, and the halt, waiting to be immersed after an angel has "troubled" the water. When the halt man complains that no one will put him in the pool, Jesus says, "Rise, take up thy bed, and walk," and he does so. When the Jews then berate Jesus for healing on the Sabbath, he counters that God works on the Sabbath, whereupon they criticize him the more for equating himself with God.

In Faulkner's chapter 5 the central theme of "suspension,"[23] implicit in John's story, ranges from being immersed to being dismissed, from being undecided to being stopped, with images such as the town lights looking like "low bright birds in stillwinged and tremulous suspension" (107 / 126). Central is Joe, here suspended in life as he will be in death, and in preparation for that role, he is being baptized.

The elements Faulkner uses from John include the pool, the immersions, the cures, the rising and taking up of the bedding (the Greek *krabbatos* is the vulgate for a poor man's pallet), a kind of Sabbath, and a final suggestion of the "troubled" waters. But this chapter is unusual in that one character will take three roles. First Joe is the curative agent, striking the waters. Then he is the halt man, repeatedly immersing himself. Then he becomes the waters themselves, as if his "troubled" state will cure his "halt" condition. Needless to say, the acting out of these roles makes for some mysterious behavior.

To begin with, Joe strikes the drunken Brown with "hard, slow, measured blows, as if he were meting them out by count" (96 / 113). His deliberateness is usually cited as "sadistic." But such "strokes" occur often in the chapter, usually in the same measured manner, from the trivial striking of matches to the significant striking of the clock, at chapter's end. Moreover, Joe is shown encountering a racism that has debilitated an entire society, from Brown's open "Take your black hands off of me, you damn nigger-blooded—" (96 / 113), to Joanna's implicit praying over the black savage; from the "abyss" of the ironically named Freedman Town, to the heights of the challenge above town by the black, Jupe.[24]

Thus, Joe is sadistic in the measure necessary to one who must lance a malignancy in order to cure it. Appropriate to the hospital setting of Bethesda, he removes his buttons "with the cold and

23. Millgate (136) refers to this chapter as "one of Faulkner's most extended experiments in suspended time," and Ficken also observes that Joe is here in a kind of "temporary suspension" ("Critical" 114). Joyce used the theme of suspension in the "Wandering Rocks" chapter of *Ulysses.*

24. This character may indeed be Jupiter, for he seems to "stoop, out of the sky" (109 / 129).

bloodless deliberation of a surgeon" (100 / 117).[25] And in striking Brown, he is like the angel curatively "troubling" the waters, for Brown is described as if he were the waters—full of drink, gurgling, drooling, going limp—to whom Joe commands, not "shut up" but "shut it."

Joe's behavior is also appropriate to his coming role as killer.[26] Because hunters or warriors were "in an atmosphere of spiritual danger," they were placed in a "state of seclusion or spiritual quarantine in which, for his own safety, primitive man puts his human gods and other dangerous characters" (3.157). Under such circumstances, Joe deals with Brown's stumbling around and falling over his cot like other warriors:

> No member of the party was permitted to step over the legs, hands, or body of any other member who chanced to be sitting or lying on the ground; and it was equally forbidden to step over his blanket, gun, tomahawk, or anything that belonged to him. If this rule was inadvertently broken, it became the duty of the member whose person or property had been stepped over to knock the other member down, and it was similarly the duty of that other to be knocked down peaceably and without resistance. (3.159–160)

Hands were especially tabooed (3.158); Faulkner uses the word *hand* sixteen times in two pages, and in some singular ways: "He smoked the cigarette down without once touching it with his hand" (98 / 115). "He would waken her with his hard brutal hand" (99 / 116). "He touched himself with his flat hands, hard, drawing his hands hard up his abdomen and chest inside his undergarment" (99 / 117). "His right hand slid fast and smooth as the knife blade had ever done, up the opening in the garment. Edgewise it struck the remaining button a light, swift blow" (100 / 117–18). Joe's remarkable behavior—striking off a button with his hand and stripping himself—suggests the behavior of the dugong net holy man,

25. In the manuscript *Light,* Joe sees "the invisible, dimlighted city hospital," and feels on his sweaty face "the smell, carbolical, asceptical of the hospital" (Mms. 47–48).

26. Millgate (135) notices the "quasi-rituals" of Christmas's behavior in preparing to kill Joanna, as do Ficken ("Critical" 113) and Kerr (126), who includes the striking of the clock as Gothic.

who must perform certain rituals for a successful catch. Living entirely secluded, he must nightly strip himself of all his "ornaments," which he may otherwise never remove, and bathe "near where the dugongs feed" (3.192).

The bathing is crucial. Purification ceremonies usually include immersions. The Nootkas, for instance, went into the water "five or six times a day" (3.160). In fact, the ceremony of baptism, for which John 5 is a justification (the angel representing the Judaic laws that were superseded by belief in the living waters of Christ), suggests that sins are physical presences to be washed from the body.[27]

Depicting Joe's second Johannine role, as the halt man seeking to cure himself, Joe is immersed in many liquids, real and imagined. Beneath Joanna's window, he seems "to be watching his body . . . turning slow and lascivious in a whispering of gutter filth like a drowned corpse in a thick still black pool of more than water" (99 / 117). When he walks naked, "the dark air breathed upon him . . . the cool mouth of darkness, the soft cool tongue. Moving again, he could feel the dark air like water; he could feel the dew under his feet as he had never felt dew before" (100 / 118). Then he is immersed in "thightall" weeds. Then, most aptly, he is immersed in a process of change from dark to light: "He stood with his hands on his hips, naked, thighdeep in the dusty weeds, while the car came over the hill and approached, the lights full upon him. He watched his body grow white out of the darkness like a kodak print emerging from the liquid" (100 / 118).[28]

His next act is most significant. Returning to the cabin, he is about to lie down "when he stopped, halted, halfreclining" (101 / 119). Like the halt man, he takes up his "bedding," and then he goes to that Christian symbol for beginnings, the stable.[29]

---

27. The baptismal motif in Faulkner's chapter 5 is noted by Roberts (171n).

28. Ficken comments ("Critical" 104–5) on the extremes of light and dark in this chapter.

29. The manuscript *Light* depicts still more immersions, with Joe thinking back: "In the home of the people who had adopted him he would lie in bed waiting for dawn to come. His bed was in the ~~attie~~ loft, the attic, there, reached only by a narrow stair leading up from the room where the people who had adopted him slept.

But the immersions continue. The next morning "the dew was heavy in the tall grass. His shoes were wet at once. The leather was cold to his feet; against his bare legs the wet grass blades were like strokes of limber icicles" (102 / 120). When he builds a fire, "he could feel the heat moving up his legs" (103 / 121), and even his reading suggests immersion, suspension:

> He turned the pages in steady progression, though now and then he would seem to linger upon one page, one line, perhaps one word. He would not look up then. He would not move, apparently arrested and held immobile by a single word which had perhaps not yet impacted, his whole being suspended by the single trivial combination of letters in quiet and sunny space, so that hanging motionless and without physical weight he seemed to watch the slow flowing of time beneath him. (104 / 122–23)

The sun acts as Joe's guide. Befitting this day of rest (the meaning of "sabbath"), this Sun-day opens "peacefully on before him." The "yellow day contemplated him drowsily, like a prone and somnolent yellow cat" (104 / 122).[30] Joe's suspension on this "halt" day of rest suggests the importance of the intermediary position in var-

---

And it he would lie there, on his hard, lumpy, shuckfilled mattress, beneath the close slope of the gable roof, feeling the manhate from himself (Mrs McEachern he ignored save when he deliberately and coldly cut off the buttons which she sewed on his washed clothes) seemed to increase in time [?] with each one of the man's snores until at last it would seem to him that he could feel the bed, the v floor, swelling and bulging upward around him, lifting him toward the low ceiling, compressing the dark air between him and the ceiling until it was too dense for breathing. And he would lie there, rigid, breathing like a man buried in cotton, until at last dawn would begin. Then the hate, the ceiling, the darkness would begin to flow away, going faster and faster, as though suddenly [?] the coming of dawn had broken down a flood gate somewhere, so that (he would be at his single window now; it too facing east) despair and impotence seemed to rush unimpeded as sight itself through the dark orifice, and to diffuse itself upon a region, a country without boundary and colored golder than promise or desire. He would stand, leaning there, freed for the moment of the dark throes of ad tragic throes [thoughts?] of adolescence, breathing deep and quiet. 'Now I can sleep a while,' he would think. 'Now I can get through another day'" (Mms. 45).

30. This metaphorical reading of the Sun-day has literary precedent. Recall that Pope wittily separated the meaning of "Sunday" and "Sabbath" in his "Epistle to Dr. Arbuthnot": "No place is sacred, not the Church is free, / Ev'n Sunday shines no Sabbathday to me" (lines 11–12).

ious cures. Just before the dawn of Easter Sunday may be salutary (10.123), or on Midsummer Festival, it is best "to rise at the peep of dawn, to wet the hands in the dewy grass, and then to rub the moisture on the eyelids, the brow, and the temples, because the dew is believed to cure maladies of the head and eye. [For] diseases of the skin, [one should] roll on the dewy grass" (5.247).

Joe's suspension in the sun relates further to a primitive cure for jaundice. As noted, one motif which follows Joe is lightning-related words such as *yellow, gold,* and *glitter.* The association is both simple—in a racist society, Joe would be known as "high yellow"—and elaborate, relating to Frazer's central symbol, the golden bough, probably the parasitic mistletoe, its gold color perhaps from the belief that at certain times it "blazed out into a supernatural golden glory" (11.285); its intermediary position between heaven and earth perhaps from its having been "planted" on the oak by God's lightning (11.279–303). Thus, Joe would be "jaundiced" because of his impotent condition here in chapter 5, and because of his tabooed "high yellow" position between black and white.[31] The primitive cure for the disease was "to banish the yellow colour to yellow creatures and yellow things, such as the sun, to which it properly belongs," so the priest would chant, "up to the sun shall go thy heartache and thy jaundice" (1.79).

Because the "foul friends" of illness were also fumigated away (9.112), the themes of smells, breathing, even the nose, also arise in this healing chapter. In the first paragraph, "breathing heavily," Brown "began to sing in a saccharine and nasal tenor. The very longdrawn pitch of his voice seemed to smell of whiskey" (95 / 112). Then Joe goes to the stable "to smell horses," where he lies "upon the loosely planked floor of the sagging and gloomy cavern acrid with the thin dust of departed hay and faintly ammoniac with the breathless desertion of old stables" (101 / 119–120). Then he pierces the whiskey cans, making the air so "redolent with alcohol" that the brush he uses "hid the stain but it could not hide the scent, the smell" (105 / 124).

31. Hall suggests that the yellow fever that kills Judith and Charles Etienne in *Absalom, Absalom!* "is symbolic of the racial hatred that has infected and destroyed the South" (112).

But the theme also arises because the pool at Bethesda was probably a healing spa, the periodic "troubling of the water," the boiling
up of noxious vapors (Cambridge 123). Several ancient volcanic regions were known for their curative powers, "especially to heal diseases of the skin" (5.209), as dark skin may be considered in a racist
society. In some caves the vapors were deadly enough to kill animals instantly, although the priests of the Great Mother Goddess
would "go up to the very mouth of the cave, stoop, and creep into
it . . . holding their breath" (5.206).

This same action may be observed in Joe's descent into Freedman Town, looking "like a phantom, a spirit, strayed out of its own
world, and lost" (106) before he "found himself"

> surrounded by the summer smell and the summer voices of invisible
> negroes. They seemed to enclose him like bodiless voices murmur-
> ing, talking, laughing, in a language not his. As from the bottom of
> a thick black pit he saw himself enclosed by cabinshapes, . . . as if
> the black life, the black breathing had compounded the substance of
> breath so that not only voices but moving bodies and light itself
> must become fluid and accrete slowly from particle to particle. . . .
> It was as though he and all other manshaped life about him had been
> returned to the lightless hot wet primogenitive Female. (106 / 125–
> 126)

But his immersion into "the original quarry, abyss itself" (108 /
128) produces a unique effect. Here Joe begins to run, and his "running" is like the troubled water itself. Turning into a "narrow and
rutted lane," he "plunged up the sharp ascent," an unusual direction to be associated with the word "plunged." Now the lights glint
and glare on him. On the hill, he slows, becomes "cool" and moves
"unerringly." His way is "sure, despite the trees, the darkness." He
never loses the path, "which he could not even see" (108 / 128).
When he meets a group of blacks, he hears their murmur "above
the noise of his own blood." When he moves toward them, they
react by "giving him a wide berth." Appearing as vague shapes and
sounds, they drift: "they approached, looming, like two shadows
drifting up." Now Jupe is above: "The head of the negro, higher
than his own, seemed to stoop, out of the sky, against the sky"
(109 / 129). After Jupe asks, "Who you looking for, cap'm," the
"two heads, the light and the dark, seemed to hang suspended in

the darkness, breathing upon one another. Then the negro's head seemed to float away," to "dissolve and fade again into the pale road" (110 / 129). Whereupon Joe moistens his lips, lights a cigarette, his hands shaking, and he thinks, "All this trouble." Then he says it aloud, "All this damn trouble." And to bring it full circle, the chapter closes with "slow, measured, clear" strokes, this time of the clock.

Appropriately, the closing discourse of John 5 promises that "the hour is coming, and now is" when the graves shall be opened. In the chapters that follow, we will find a resurrection of Joe's past, revealing the roots of the racial sickness he has experienced repeatedly on this last, halt day.

Chapter 6: The Dough-Man Multiplied, out of the Mouths

The story of the loaves and fishes is reported in all four gospels, twice in Mark and Matthew, and theories abound as to which account depends on which. John's version is unique in its emphasis on the five loaves of bread, probably because of the accompanying discourse on the bread of life.

Now a less brilliant parallel for this story might present a picnic, at which more and more find themselves satisfied, the "miracle" arising from the sharing. But Faulkner knew that when John said the five barley loaves multiplied, he meant there were twelve baskets of leftovers. The same tough insistence arises in the accompanying discourse on the Bread of Life, which John alone calls flesh: "for my flesh is meat indeed." To parallel these themes of food replication and the eucharist, Faulkner gives us the process, the multiplication of that which sustains, by the primitive technique for replication, homeopathic magic.

According to Frazer, the belief that "things act on each other at a distance through a secret sympathy" operates either by the law of contact, which assumes that "things which have once been in contact with each other are always in contact," or by the law of similarity, which assumes that "things which resemble each other

are the same" (1.53–54). Although both principles may work together, the immersions in chapter 5 represent contagious magic,
while the replications in chapter 6 represent homeopathic magic.

After all, the principle behind the multiplication of the loaves is
of like producing like. Presumably, Jesus could have made food out
of thin air, but instead, he makes bread out of bread. So when the
primitive wishes to multiply something, he will make a likeness
of the desired object or act out its behavior. Frazer reports that the
Cora Indians create a wax or clay model of food which they bury in
a mountain cave. The Todas of India make an offering of a silver
buffalo (1.56). The Arunta mimic the appearance of the emu, wearing long-necked headdresses and peering in all directions. Or to
multiply the witchetty grub, they squat in a long narrow structure
and then shuffle out, pantomiming and singing of its emergence
from the chrysalis (1.85). In fact, Frazer notes that animal representations in prehistoric caves and Egyptian hieroglyphics have been
edible prey rather than dangerous carnivores, suggesting a strong
belief in the efficacy of artistic representation. We must take care
what monsters we create.

The ceremony of the eucharist is related to this homeopathic
principle of like producing like. Bread, made of grain, symbolizes
(as does wine) the primitive hopes for next year's crop. Grain is
used to reproduce grain. Moreover, the mouth is anciently a dual
symbol of both destruction and creativity. You take in the power of
what you eat; you give power to what you say. Thus, the primitive,
wishing to ensure next year's crop, will mark this year's with firstfruit ceremonies. Beginning with purgatives, the Creek Indians
drink "a bitter decoction of button-snake root in order to vomit
and purge their sinful bodies" (8.73), or the Seminoles drink a nau-
seous "Black Drink" (8.76). Frazer suggests that these purgatives
have their parallel in the eucharistic fasting, both honoring the sacredness of the new food. But then even confession, given before
communion, can be seen as a cleansing of the soul by the mouth.

Once purified, the people take the first of the harvest, make a
dough-man, and break it into pieces so that all may eat of it. In
France, a man made of dough was hung on a tree and then kept in
the mayor's house until, the vintage over, it was broken in pieces

and handed out for the people to eat (8.48). The Aztecs made images of their god, using a "paste" of seeds or maize which could be kneaded into a dough with the blood of children (8.90). Important (also to discussions of the Hineses in chapter 15) are the loaves shaped like men called *maniae* by the Romans, since *mania*, meaning "ashes of the dead," was also the name of the Grandmother of Ghosts, to whom effigies were dedicated as substitutes for human victims (8.94–95).

Faulkner's chapter 6 describes Joe's beginnings at the orphanage. Of course, Joe is "bred" in this chapter on bread, and, appropriate to Joe Christmas as J. C., Bethlehem means "House of Bread." Also appropriate to the eucharist is that Joe—a descendant of Ham by his possibly "tainted" blood—is fed "bread, with ham between" on the way out of the orphanage, and "bread, with ham between" on the way back. Moreover, Joe goes from the bleak, "cinderstrewn-packed compound" with its fence like "a parade of starved soldiers," to the eating of toothpaste, to what McEachern promises: food and shelter under the care of Christian people, even as he ironically dispatches the "heathenish name" of Christmas under the banner of "He will eat my bread" (136).[32]

However, the real multiplication going on in this chapter is both less physical and more sustaining. Echoing the ceremonies of the Arunta, squatting in and shuffling out of long, narrow structures, singing of the witchetty grub, Faulkner shows the process of Joe's birth as a "grub." Born "out of the mouths" as the "little nigger bastard," Joe is both the disgusting pink worm at the heart of the South's rose, and he is the eucharistic food, the little dough-man, to be broken and fed to more and more communicants.

Central to the process is the dietitian, the one who determines how much and what kind of food will be fed. Joe thinks of her as "a mechanical adjunct to eating, food and diningroom, the ceremony of eating at the wooden forms." He is led to the toothpaste because of her although he "had never heard of toothpaste either, as if he already knew that she would possess something of that

---

32. Critics, such as Peterson, Morrisseu, and Rosenzweig, have observed the importance of food in Joe's development.

nature." In fact, while he thinks of her as "young, a little fullbodied, smooth, pink-and-white . . . making his mouth think of something sweet and sticky to eat, also pinkcolored and surreptitious" (112 / 132), she also thinks of him in terms of food—the *"pea in a pan full of coffee beans"* (122 / 143).

The replicating birth process itself involves many long, narrow structures, including tubes, passageways, and especially corridors.[33] Joe's earliest memory is of "a corridor in a big long garbled cold echoing building." There, "in the quiet and empty corridor . . . he was like . . . a shadow. Another in the corridor could not have said just when and where he vanished, into what door, what room. But there was no one else in the corridor at this hour" (111 / 131). Going directly to the tube of toothpaste in the dietitian's room, he watches "the pink worm" coil onto his finger, until, hearing voices, he slips behind the curtain and "squatted," feeling the "once cylindrical tube," and tasting "the cool invisible worm as it coiled onto his finger and smeared sharp, automatonlike and sweet, into his mouth" (113 / 133–34). It is this worm which produces the first creation, a kind of test-tube concoction:

> Motionless now, utterly contemplative, he seemed to stoop above himself like a chemist in his laboratory, waiting. He didn't have to wait long. At once the paste which he had already swallowed lifted inside him. . . . In the rife, pinkwomansmelling obscurity behind the curtain he squatted, pinkfoamed, listening to his insides, waiting with astonished fatalism for what was about to happen to him. Then it happened. He said to himself with complete and passive surrender: "Well, here I am." (114 / 134)

"Here I am," he says, as if he had not been there before. That I-am, the *ego eimi*, as in "I am the bread of life," has great significance in John. It reflects the solemn I-am of the Old Testament—I AM THAT I AM, or "I am Yahweh" (Ex. 3:14)—a formula found also in pagan religions (International cxix ff.).

Joe's I-am has come from his vomiting, a reaction to his fearful

33. "Corridor" occurs fourteen times here vs. three other occurrences in the book. Ficken ("Critical" 125–26) noted that corridors are the dominant image in this chapter.

ingesting of the dietitian's "pink worm," an apt metaphor for illicit sex. When the dietitian promptly sings out the name of this grub, this transubstantiated pink worm, as "little nigger bastard," she exemplifies and fosters the multiplication process. It is a process which involves taking something in—usually with the eyes—something which, reacting with an inner guilt or fear, multiplies within, and produces a monster through the mouth. In the next few days, because Joe is "always against her eyelids or upon her retinae," the dietitian finally seeks him in the "empty corridor," and offers him money to buy "some to eat every day for a week." What poor Joe envisions is a boundless multiplication of the toothpaste—"the ranked tubes . . . like corded wood, endless and terrifying"—which causes "his whole being" to coil "in a rich and passionate revulsion." And that response produces in the dietitian a "long shuddering breath," with this doubled monster: "You little nigger bastard! You nigger bastard" (117 / 138).

The chapter is rife with such strange engendering, one of the funniest occurring between the janitor and the dietitian, the sacred men and women of the temple, the seers ("mad eyes looking into mad eyes, mad voice talking to mad voice as calm and quiet and terse as two conspirators" [119 / 140]), who are responsible for Joe's conception "out of the mouths." Telling the janitor she knows that Joe is "part nigger," the dietitian leaves, repeatedly yawning, even "terrifically." She yawns "tremendously, her face emptied now of everything save yawning and then emptied even of yawning." Then she thinks, "They'll send him to the nigger orphanage." She yawns again, but this time "with utter relaxation." Going to her room, she gets into bed, and begins "to open her legs and close them slowly." "Her body [is] open to accept sleep as though sleep were a man" (121 / 143).

The conception leads to the birth. Coming up the corridor, the janitor pushes her door. As she puts "her weight against it, holding it to," his weight is "firm and steady against the crawling door, beyond the crawling gap." She speaks as to "an unpredictable child or a maniac," yet she cannot stop the "slow inward crawling." Once inside, his eyes repeatedly "envelop" her. As her "mouth hung open like the mouth of an idiot," his eyes "contract upon her shape and being." When she does produce a mouth monster (Yes, Joe will be sent to a "nigger orphanage"), "the eyes released her and enveloped her again" before the janitor leaves, pronouncing his final "Womanfilth" (123–24 / 144–45).

Two other points remain. John 6 also recounts the episode of Jesus walking on the water. Because the people know he did not leave with his disciples in the only boat, the next day they wonder how he came to the other shore. Joe's being carried off in the middle of the night, "riding high in the invisible arms," is a similarly miraculous departure, like the departure of Alice, another orphanage child, who had simply vanished, "grown heroic at the instant of vanishment beyond the clashedto gates, fading without diminution of size into something nameless and splendid, like a sunset" (128 / 151).

In the chapter's closing pages, Joe is finally spawned out into the world by the "matron."[34] This episode reflects the final paragraph in John 6 which names the betrayer, "Judas Iscariot, the son of Simon." In changing Joe's name from Christmas, heathen, to McEachern, Christian, Simon McEachern has created his own son of Simon.

Yet the primary betrayal is by the matron, who tells McEachern she knows nothing about Joe's history and that McEachern is welcome to change Joe's name since she is "not interested in what they are called, but in how they are treated" (136 / 160). Exactly the opposite is true. Because Joe has been called "nigger," he is placed "at once" in a home of a man whose "cold" eyes examine Joe as "he might have examined a horse or a second hand plow, convinced beforehand that he would see flaws" (133 / 156–57). Just how Joe will be treated in such a home is obvious, especially when McEachern says, "I make no doubt that with us he will grow up to fear God and abhor idleness and vanity despite his origin" (134 / 158). Between the sin of origin and original sin, all will be one for this ruthless Christian.

---

34. Earlier the sacred men and women of the temple call her "madam."

Chapter 7: *Teaching in the Temple; Learning the Will*

Chapters 7 through 10 of *Light in August* all touch on Joe's final night at the McEacherns.[35] This overlap of chapters also occurs in John, for up through mid-10, Jesus is at the Feast of Tabernacles, an annual commemoration of the tent-dwelling in the wilderness. So Joe's period with the McEacherns is a time apart, a time of adversity, of learning to be a man.

That teaching is the main theme of Faulkner's chapter 7, as it is in John 7, where Jesus is teaching in the temple, is apparent in McEachern's grim struggle to teach Joe his catechism.[36] Although this incident seems to represent a failure to teach, Joe remembers: *"On this day I became a man"* (137 / 161). Clearly some kind of teaching is going on, even if it is not the kind the teacher believes. This is true throughout the chapter, where the actual teaching is pervasive and profound, yet beyond the control of the teacher. McEachern drills the eight-year-old in his catechism; the other boys introduce the fourteen-year-old to sex; or Mrs. McEachern woos the seventeen-year-old with secret favors. Each time the lesson is the style, not the substance. Faulkner has a similar ironic inversion in chapter 3, where he shows Byron learning more by perception than by precept, the one often contradicting the other. There the suggestion is that we learn by seeing what others do; here we learn by doing what others do. There it is signs; here it is simulation. We become what we are by imitation.

Since Joe is becoming a man, he most obviously imitates the man he has as model, even if it means choosing his father's cruelty over his mother's kindness. So the chapter depicts Joe's resistance to McEachern's will, in the sense of desires, in direct imitation of his will, in the sense of determination. The two meanings are present in Jesus' words in the temple: "If any man will do his will, he shall know of the doctrine."

In the opening description, the parlor includes its own imitations: a "yellow imitation oak melodeon" and "fruit jar filled with

35. Ficken remarks on the overlapping of these chapters ("Critical" 129n).
36. This parallel is noted by Holman (157).

larkspur." Joe's clothing is "cutdown" or "like the man's," and his shoes are like McEachern's except polished "as a boy of eight would polish them." The previous night, for doing such a clumsy job on McEachern's shoes, Joe was beaten and the shoes were polished again. Today will be different. The physical descriptions of the two reflect the struggle to come:

> The boy did not look up. He did not move. But the face of the man was not more rocklike (138 / 162). McEachern rose, deliberately, without haste. . . . "Come," he said. He did not look back. The boy followed, down the hall, toward the rear; he too walked erect and in silence, his head up. There was a very kinship of stubbornness like a transmitted resemblance in their backs. . . . They went on, in steady single file, the two backs in their rigid abnegation of all compromise more alike than actual blood could have made them. (139 / 163)

Each confrontation extends the theme.[37] When Joe returns late, he receives his beating from the "stolid and rocklike" McEachern as if his own body were "wood or stone; a post or a tower upon which the sentient part of him mused like a hermit, contemplative and remote with ecstasy and selfcrucifixion" (150 / 175–76). When they battle over Joe's selling the heifer, they are "shapes, almost of a height" (153 / 180) or they stand, "the two of them almost toe to toe" (154 / 181).

The theme of imitation extends to others. Mrs. McEachern raises "one half lifted hand in stiff caricature of the softest movement which human hand can make" (140 / 164). She looks "as if whatever she saw or heard, she saw or heard through a more immediate manshape or manvoice, as if she were the medium and the vigorous and ruthless husband the control" (138 / 162–63).

The episodes themselves present Joe's learning by imitation. His refusal to learn the catechism copies McEachern's refusal to forgo the demand. After Joe rejects Mrs. McEachern's secret offering of

---

37. Carole Anne Taylor (53) comments that "Joe takes awful pride in perversely fulfilling McEachern's own statutes of manhood as he triumphs in that implacable, masculine certainty that dominates his memory of how and when he became a man."

food ("carrying the empty tray as though [like (CT)] it were a monstrance and he the bearer, his surplice the cutdown undergarment which had been bought for a man to wear" [145 / 170]), he later eats it in secret. After he lines up to do violence to the black girl, he so empathizes with her that he must take her place as the recipient of violence. Each time he has internalized his teacher, like that moment when, above the girl, "it seemed to him that he could see her—something, prone, abject; her eyes perhaps. Leaning, he seemed to look down into a black well and at the bottom saw two glints like reflection of dead stars" (147 / 172).

As noted, Faulkner often calls attention to some unity of theme in John. Here, in the context of Jesus' teaching in the temple, marveled at because of his youth, Jesus justifies his doing good works on the Sabbath with a reference to Sabbath-day circumcisions. Faulkner may be suggesting the theme of circumcision with this singular metaphor: "The fluting of young frogs ceased like so many strings cut with simultaneous scissors" (149 / 174). Certainly he features primitive traditions described in Frazer on the initiation into manhood.

Entitled "The Ritual of Death and Resurrection," Frazer's chapter describes the boys' receiving blows, falling down as if dead, being carried off to sacred enclosures, lying with arms crossed, eating sacred, untouchable food, all with a mute acceptance of punishment and the shedding of blood. Some initiates receive a "terrible blow with a cane, which is supposed to kill them" (11.247), while others "dropped down like dead in some public place" and were "carried off, sometimes in a real cataleptic state" (11.252). In West Africa, at the certain signal, "all the men and lads whose hour is come fall into a state of lifeless torpidity, from which they generally arise after three days. But if the fetish loves a man he carries him away into the bush and buries him in the fetish house, often for many years. When he comes to life again, he begins to eat and drink as before, but his understanding is gone and the fetish man must teach him and direct him in every motion" (11.256). Symbolizing the grave, the separate sheds or stockades housed the candidates for varying periods of time. Food was brought, often at great sacrifice (11.253), and sometimes as a sacramental meal, "too sacred even for the elders' hands to touch" (11.246n).

Besides being beaten, falling down, lying trancelike, arms crossed, Joe is found in separate enclosures throughout the chapter. Like chapter 2's inversion of the planing mill into temple, here the stable is transformed into sanctum. Although McEachern chides Joe, "You would believe that a stable floor, the stamping place of beasts, is the proper place for the word of God," his son's martyrdom turns his words into prophecy when Joe stands "erect, his face and the pamphlet lifted, his attitude one of exaltation. Save for the surplice he might have been a Catholic choir boy, with for nave the looming and shadowy crib, the rough planked wall beyond which in the ammoniac and dryscented obscurity beasts stirred now and then with snorts and indolent thuds" (140 / 165). And McEachern makes Joe kneel in his room, transforming that enclosure.[38]

Equally important is the shed with the black girl. Among some tribes, initiation sheds provided "orgies of unbridled lust" (11.253), but usually women were so strictly forbidden that they might be killed for trespassing (11.261). Either custom explains Joe's sudden recognition and expulsion of the black girl, especially since the reason such ceremonies are associated with death and rebirth is that, at circumcision, the young man's soul may be extracted and exchanged with his totem (11.225–26).

As suggested, Joe has several "totems," several teachers. McEachern has taught principally like the Pharisees, the lawgivers who misunderstand Jesus' role because they misread his origins: "Search, and look: for out of Galilee ariseth no prophet."[39] With McEachern in mind, however, we realize that it would make no difference if they did know the prophet's origins; they would still see no good in him. For regarding Joe's conviction that he "got some nigger blood" (184 / 216), he muses that were McEachern told, his "immediate and predictable reaction to the knowledge would so obliterate it as a factor in their relations that it would never appear again" (157 / 184). No, for McEachern, "recognition"

---

38. Nemerov (256) observes that Joe is "born into manhood in a stable."
39. Baker calls McEachern a "neo-Pharisee" (158).

can only be of evil, the inescapable unfolding of Joe's original sin. This is the totem Joe exchanges with him.

The mother's lesson may be just as deadly. She seems kindness itself. Washing Joe's feet, she is given a "crown": "She knelt before him while he watched the crown of her head and her hands fumbling a little clumsily about his feet" (156 / 183). Like Nicodemus at the end of John 7, unsuccessfully trying to influence the Pharisees, she fails to influence McEachern, who rebukes her, "You are a clumsier liar than even he" (155 / 181). Yet it is not her kindness which Joe learns, but her lies, her secrecy.

But then the learning of secrecy is part of most initiation rites. Usually the boys are enjoined "under pain of death" never to reveal the secrets of the shed (11.250), or they are given "a secret language only understood by the initiated" (11.259). Moreover, secrecy is a major concern in John 7: when Jesus' brothers urge him to show himself, he refuses, saying his "time is not yet full come." But when they had gone up to the feast, he also went "not openly but as it were in secret."

Despite what Joe thinks of Mrs. McEachern's "woman's affinity and instinct for secrecy, for casting a faint taint of evil about the most trivial and innocent actions" (157 / 185), he masters it by imitation, and it is his learning of this behavior that forces McEachern to acknowledge his manhood: "You have revealed every other sin of which you are capable: sloth, and ingratitude, and irreverence and blasphemy. And now I have taken you in the remaining two: lying and lechery" (154 / 181).

Taken him, he has. By the end of the chapter, we observe Joe's entrapment: " 'She is trying to make me cry,' he thought, lying cold and rigid in his bed, his hands beneath his head and the moonlight falling across his body, hearing the steady murmur of the man's voice as it mounted the stairway on its first heavenward stage; 'She was trying to make me cry. Then she thinks that they would have had me' " (158 / 185–86). Learning to be hard like the man, Joe has become captive to every sin McEachern would wish on him, even the one McEachern is incapable of himself. With his rock-etched commandments which can be levitated instantly to heaven, this righteous Christian cannot imagine the clumsy, human shift of facts necessary both to lying and to forgiveness.

Chapter 8: Passing Judgments; Casting Stones

For a number of reasons, the story of the adulteress in John's chapter 8 could be termed "passing judgment." The term can mean that judgment is passed on someone, like the accusers judging the adulteress, or it can mean that judgment is passed on to someone, like the accusers themselves. It can mean that judgment is passing—changing—or it can mean that judgment is altogether bypassed, so it becomes accepting, and note that the changing and the accepting are also in the gospel story: judging themselves, the accusers are forced to accept the guilt of the woman. The term can mean that judgment is made in passing, so that it is only a surface calculation or misjudgment, as in Jesus' words here, "Ye judge after the flesh." It can even be a physical movement, as in the gospel's closing return to the theme of stonecasting: "Then took they up stones to cast at him; but Jesus hid himself, and went out of the temple, going through the midst of them, and so passed by."

All of these meanings are found in Faulkner's chapter 8, applying not only to characters, but also to time, space, and mass, with much consulting of watches and clocks, much gauging of size and distance, and much reckoning of small change. From the opening paragraph, with Joe's "passing swift as a shadow" across Mc-Eachern's window, we read of the length and handling of the hidden rope after a year's practice. As he takes his wrapped suit from its hiding place in the loft, he "knows" by feeling the folds that McEachern had "found it." When he has "passed" the quiet house, which looks "threatful, deceptive," and even "treacherous," he checks his watch, although "he did not need the watch to tell him that he was already late," although "he had never owned a watch before and so he had forgot to wind it" (160 / 188). But, he complains, "the watch was dead because he had had no chance to wind it. He had been made late by them who had given him no opportunity to wind the watch and so know if he were late or not. Up the dark lane, in the now invisible house, the woman now lay asleep, since she had done all she could to make him late" (161 / 189). "Passing judgment" here means that Joe is blaming his dead watch on the McEacherns, who, if only in this one particular, are blameless. Other faulty judgments are suggested when he thinks he sees movement in the "treacherous shadows" of the lane, which he then thinks might have been "something in his mind projected like a shadow on a wall" (161 / 189).

In the opening episode, judgments are harsh. In the flashback that follows, judgments will be more charitable, like the (for John) uncharacteristically charitable adulteress story, itself an interruption. In the flashback, because the characters make passing judgments, they must pay for their miscalculations, but these payments further lead to their being injudiciously "accepting," a term used as widely as "passing."

When McEachern brings Joe to town, having miscalculated how long his business would take, he looks at his watch, then "at the municipal clock in the courthouse tower and then at the sun, with an expression of exasperation and outrage." Then he looks at Joe "also with that expression, the open watch in his hand, his eyes cold, fretted. He seemed to be examining and weighing for the first time the boy whom he had raised from childhood" (162 / 190–91). It cannot be helped; they must buy lunch. But the restaurant McEachern chooses because it is "cheap" is described by and includes more surface calculations:

> At the cigar counter McEachern paid the brasshaired woman. There was about her a quality impervious to time: a belligerent and diamondsurfaced respectability. She had not so much as looked at them, even when they entered and even when McEachern gave her money. Still without looking at them she made the change, correctly and swiftly, sliding the coins onto the glass counter almost before McEachern had offered the bill; herself somehow definite behind the false glitter of the careful hair, the careful face, like a carved lioness guarding a portal, presenting respectability like a shield behind which the clotted and idle and equivocal men could slant their hats and their thwartfacecurled cigarettes. (163–64 / 192)

McEachern judges it a place "to avoid and shun," and although it "passed from the surface of thinking" (165 / 193), Joe's inevitable return is again in the context of McEachern's miscalculations, along with an uncharacteristic and ill-judged payment:

Again McEachern had to see the lawyer. But he was prepared now. "I'll be there an hour," he said. "You can walk about and see the town." Again he looked at Joe, hard, calculating, again a little fretted, like a just man forced to compromise between justice and judgment. "Here," he said. He opened his purse and took a coin from it. It was a dime. "You might try not to throw it away as soon as you can find someone who will take it. It's a strange thing," he said fretfully, . . . "but it seems impossible for a man to learn the value of money without first having to learn to waste it. You will be here in one hour." (166 / 195)

For Joe, the miscalculations, the payments, and the acceptance begin with his first judgment of Bobbie, made on the basis of size: "Even a casual adult glance could tell that she would never see thirty again. But to Joe she probably did not look more than seventeen too, because of her smallness. . . . It was because of her smallness that he ever attempted her, as if her smallness should have or might have protected her from the roving and predatory eyes of most men, leaving his chances better" (161–62 / 189–90). When he returns, he miscalculates the cost of the pie and coffee and must pay in his desperate humiliation: "He did not believe that he could bear to see her again," although eventually "he could get the nights passed" (170 / 200). So also when he goes back to settle his "debt," he must pay: "He walked in laughter. He had passed through the door upon it, upon the laughing of the men" (172 / 202), before he encounters Bobbie's genial acceptance.

The next episode presents Joe coming to accept menstruation, another time measurement, when Bobbie forgets her due date. Joe pays and accepts twice. First, in still another flashback, when an older boy told him about the "periodical filth," Joe "shot a sheep. He found the flock in a hidden valley and stalked and killed one with the gun. Then he knelt, his hands in the yet warm blood of the dying beast, trembling, drymouthed, backglaring. Then he got over it, recovered. He did not forget what the boy had told him. He just accepted it" (174 / 204). But if with "the slain sheep he had bought immunity" (176 / 206), Bobbie's clumsy retelling sends him fleeing "backward, past the slain sheep, the price paid for immunity" (177 / 208). The "hardknowing" of "something liquid, deathcolored, and foul" (178 / 209), makes him vomit, yet the next week he is back, taking Bobbie, but in language which suggests she is another sheep, another payment: " 'Where are we going?' she said. He didn't answer, drawing her on. She had to trot to keep up. She trotted clumsily: an animal impeded by that which distinguished her from animals: her heels, her clothes, her smallness" (178 / 209).

In the remaining episodes Joe is shown giving Bobbie a "stale and flyspecked box of candy" (179 / 210), happily bewildered that he can spend the night with her, miscalculating her acceptance of him, paying for it, then finally "accepting" (167 / 196) her prostitution.

Meanwhile, McEachern, also misreading surface evidence, judges Joe's daytime performance as a good sign to be paid for with the heifer: "After a while even McEachern accepted a fact. He said: 'I have been watching you lately. And now there is nothing for it but I must misdoubt my own eyes or else believe that at last you are beginning to accept what the Lord has seen fit to allot you'" (170 / 200). Right to chapter's end, McEachern judges Joe with "dour and grudging approval."

This theme of passing judgment is related to Frazer in several ways. One involves the primitive method of transferring evil, appropriate to the adulteress story, the casting of stones. On a journey over high passes or at fearful crossroads (Faulkner's town, a "railroad division point" [162 / 191], is filled with "transients"), primitive man eased his worry over the journey by throwing a stick or stone on a cairn begun by earlier travelers or money in a well (small coins are thrown at people throughout the chapter). For instance, when Peruvian Indians climbed steep mountains, they would halt by cairns and, placing their stones on the others, "their weariness left them" (9.9). In fact, stone throwing was part of many scapegoat ceremonies (9.253–54), and Bobbie's status as scapegoat on whom all the evils of transience are heaped, passing in the midst of men who are—at the very least—casting aspersions, is made explicit in the scene in which Joe drags her into the woods.

Bobbie is also an appropriate receptacle of evil not only as prostitute but also because of her "periodical filth," for among primitive peoples, at the onset of menses, a girl must be isolated from the tribe under the care of an older woman (like the "carved lioness guarding a portal"), be kept covered with her head bowed, eyes lowered (like the "downlooking" Bobbie who, outside, wears a hat), and flogged to scourge her "sin" (like the beatings Joe administers). Although Bobbie is not the pubescent girl Joe believes her to be, her description suggests the primitive belief toward menses as corruption: "She was not only not tall, she was slight, almost childlike. But the adult look saw that the smallness was not due to any natural slenderness but to some inner corruption of the spirit itself: a slenderness which had never been young, in not one of whose curves anything youthful had ever lived or lingered" (161 / 189–90). The theme is reinforced by all the hiding places, from the loft with its hidden clothes, to the "back street" restaurant with its guarded portal, to "*the eyelid closing prisons within the eye's self*" (165 / 194), to the hidden valley, to the moonlit urns, to Bobbie's bureau with its flyspecked box of candy, to the hiding place in the wall where Joe keeps the rope and Mrs. McEachern keeps her cache of change, itself in a tin can. Although related to Jesus' teaching in the temple "treasury," where boxes were kept for charitable gifts, the theme of hidden treasure is widened by Frazer's discussions of women being isolated in separate huts in a kind of ritual humiliation (like the woman in the temple). For example, in southeast Africa, "when a girl thinks that the time of her nubility is near, she chooses an adoptive mother, perhaps in a neighboring village. When the symptoms appear . . . she is secluded with several other girls in the same condition for a month. They are shut up in a hut, and whenever they come outside they must wear a dirty greasy cloth over their faces as a veil" (10.29). Sometimes they are suspended between heaven and earth, because in their tabooed state, they are "endowed with the coveted yet burdensome gift of immortality" (10.99).[40] So Bobbie is Joe's secret treasure

---

40. The passage continues: "The wizened remains of the deathless Sibyl are said to have been preserved in a jar or urn which hung in a temple of Apollo at Cumae; and when a group of merry children . . . amused themselves by gathering underneath the familiar jar and calling out, 'Sibyl, what do you wish?' a hollow voice, like an echo, used to answer from the urn, 'I wish to die'" (10.99). Rather than Keats's

(even if one that can be had for small change), a child, who is also a member of the oldest profession.

We have still to discuss Bobbie's mythic counterpart. The disparity between the two pictures of her in chapters 8 and 9 suggests the similar confusion between the daughter-mother figures of the Eleusinian Mysteries, Persephone and Demeter, probably two stages of the corn (7.68).[41] Frazer's language suggests Joe's innocence in 8 or his puzzlement in 9, at her change in behavior: "It would hardly be strange if the muzzy mind of the Sicilian bumpkin, who looked with blind devotion to the Two Goddesses for his daily bread, totally failed to distinguish Demeter from the seed and Persephone from the ripe sheaves." "And if he had been closely questioned . . . Hodge might have scratched his head and confessed that it puzzled him to say where precisely, the one goddess ended and the other began" (7.59). Bobbie's smallness would make her the diminutive form of the two, at least in chapter 8.[42] After all, it is as if she, like Persephone, abducted by Pluto, had been carried off by Max, the "proprietor." And Mame would be Demeter, called "yellow" and "brass-rattling," since Mame is not only blonde, she also has "hard bright brassridged hair" (166 / 195), or is "brasshaired" (164 / 192).

The restaurant itself suggests the underworld, both mythic and modern, with its "dingy doorway between two dingy windows" (162 / 191), its "barren, somehow equivocal counter with the still, coldfaced violenthaired woman at one end as though guarding it" (165 / 194), with its constant smoke or "vicious frying sound" (167 / 196). The movements of Bobbie and Joe suggest the netherworld: he begins by descending among shadows and shades, which are "treacherous," to the "mouth of the lane" (160 / 188), and she is found "coming up out of the darkness" (175 / 205). The rape scene amid the furrows is traditional: Persephone's abduction in

---

Grecian urn, it seems likely that it was this repetition of "urn," used by Eliot as an epigraph to "The Waste Land," which influenced Faulkner's choice of the word.

41. Evidently the Demeter-Persephone myth was a favorite of Faulkner's. See Fowler for his use of the myth in *The Sound and the Fury* and Dickerson for his use of it in *As I Lay Dying.*

42. Slabey presents evidence for the connection between Bobbie and Persephone ("Myth" 331–32).

the fields was part of the Mysteries (7.66), enacted, as well, by Greek ploughmen (7.69).

Echoes of the Eleusinian initiations also appear: as initiate Joe would be subject to processions and all-night vigils (recall his nightly walks to meet Bobbie), which would include sitting veiled on stools, in silence or using scurrilous language, drinking "barley-water from a holy chalice" (7.38): on restaurant stools, Joe learns to drink, to wear his hat "cocked" and to call Bobbie his "whore."

In 9, on the other hand, the descriptions of Bobbie—"she writhed and threshed" (192 / 226), "her hair wild with the jerking and tossing of her head" (203 / 239)—suggest she has become Demeter at the Festival of the Threshingfloor, held in the full of the moon (featured in Faulkner's 9), when horseraces were held (like McEachern's and Joe's frantic rides), and women used ribald language (like Bobbie's "Me f——ing for nothing with a nigger son of a bitch" [204 / 240]).

Meantime, here in 8, because Bobbie appears to judge no man (she accepts Joe's innocence, his "flyspecked candy," his "nigger-blood") but rather seems to pass judgment on herself (always "downlooking," as is Jesus in the adulteress episode), the suggestion is that this stumbling, sacrificial animal is the acceptor of much passing evil. But in her own highly tabooed state, she transfers that evil to Joe, for she is performing forbidden services—undressing, serving food, using those too-big hands—all of which are considered polluting (10.49). The "passing in the midst" is itself dangerous: "According to the Talmud, if a woman at the beginning of her period passes between two men, she thereby kills one of them; if she passes between them towards the end of her period, she only causes them to quarrel violently" (10.83). Even the sight of such a woman may cause a man to be struck blind (10.29), as Joe will be shown to have been, in chapter 9. Indeed, after reading in 8 of Bobbie's acceptance of Joe ("maybe I like him," she says), we wonder if we have been blind when we read in 9 that it took two men to hold her, "she writhing and struggling, her hair shaken forward, her white face wrung and ugly beneath the splotches of savage paint, her mouth a small jagged hole filled with shrieking" (192 / 226).

Like Mrs. McEachern in chapter 7, Bobbie is here given a

"crown" (to be passed on to McEachern in 9): "the still and lowered crown of her head as she sat on the bed, her hands on her lap" (180 / 211). In chapter 9 that downlooking head, those poignant, too-big hands suddenly represent a grotesque unresponsiveness: "The waitress sat on the bed." "She sat with her face lowered, not even looking at the door when it opened, a cigarette burning in one still hand that looked almost monstrous in its immobility against the dark dress" (200 / 235). But then chapter 9 will present a number of visions and revisions.

Chapter 9: Moonstruck, the Blind Man Sees

Singularly unified, John's chapter 9 presents the healing of the blind man, who comes to see spiritually, while the Pharisees become increasingly blind. When the disciples wonder "who did sin, this man, or his parents, that he was born blind?" Jesus says neither: the blindness exists "that the works of God should be made manifest in him." To cure the man, Jesus "spat on the ground, and made clay of the spittle, and he anointed the eyes of the blind man with the clay," telling him to "wash in the pool of Siloam," which, John says, means "sent."

We do find the spit in Faulkner, used metaphorically: watching Joe sneak out, McEachern "felt something of that pure and impersonal outrage which a judge must feel were he to see a man on trial for his life lean and spit on the bailiff's sleeve" (189 / 122). But we should note that John's curative spit is made thoroughly offensive, and that although it does give the judge insight, still nobody is blind. Yet what about McEachern, whose reaction to a boy's sneaking out is likened to a judge, dealing with a man on trial for his life. Although this metaphor does not represent blindness, it does dramatize an attitudinal blindness.

As for the clay and the pool of Siloam which means "sent," the only possible liquids in Faulkner's 9 are again metaphoric. One involves the word *seethed* (meaning "to boil"), which could, with the "sluttishness" (or "dirt") represent the mud, when McEachern believes "himself to be standing just and rocklike and with neither haste nor anger while on all sides the sluttishness of weak human men [man (CT)] seethed in a long sigh of terror about the actual representative of the wrathful and retributive Throne" (191 / 225). Another is in the word *wake*, when it seems as if McEachern "had been guided and were now being propelled by some militant Michael Himself as he entered the room. Apparently his eyes were not even momentarily at fault with the sudden light and the motion as he thrust among bodies with turned heads as, followed by a wake of astonishment and incipient pandemonium, he ran toward the youth" (190 / 224). Here we should notice that, causing the "wake" (with its double meaning), McEachern is "propelled" and "guided," like one who is "sent," or like the attitudinal blindness of the "spit" passage.

Thus, if John presents blindness as a metaphor for the refusal to see, Faulkner presents the refusal to see as a metaphor for blindness.

So we find many examples of attitudinal blindness (and of being "sent"). Begin with McEachern in bed: "Within about thirty minutes of intensive thinking he knew almost as much of Joe's doings as Joe himself could have told him, with the exception of names and places. Very likely he would not have believed those even from Joe's mouth, since men of his kind usually have just as firmly fixed convictions about the mechanics, the theatring of evil as about those of good" (188–89 / 221–22). When he follows Joe, he is "walking fast, in that same pure and impersonal outrage, as if he believed so that he would be guided by some greater and purer outrage that he would not even need to doubt personal faculties" (189 / 222). He goes "straight as an arrow" to the horse which takes him "in some juggernautish simulation of terrific speed . . . as if in that cold and implacable and undeviating conviction of both omnipotence and clairvoyance of which they both partook known destination and speed were not necessary" (190 / 223). Repeatedly, he is guided by conviction, by some "militant Michael," rather than his own eyes.

But if he has been "blind," the "sight" he is finally given leads to "nothingness." Staring at Joe's face, McEachern "walked toward it in the furious and dreamlike exaltation of a martyr who has already been absolved, into the descending chair which Joe swung at his head, and into nothingness" (191–92 / 225).

Joe is also not-seeing and driven: He was "not aware of what he was saying nor of what was happening." Leaving the dance, he "could not have known where McEachern had left the horse, nor for certain if it was even there. Yet he ran straight to it, with something of his adopted father's complete faith in an infallibility in events." (194 / 227). At Bobbie's, he is also "oblivious," "in a quiet, dreamlike state" (203 / 238). And he experiences the same contradictory, blinding vision: "He just stared at her, at the face which he had never seen before, saying quietly (whether aloud or not, he could not have said) in a slow amazement: *Why, I committed murder for her. I even stole for her* as if he had just heard of it, thought of it, been told that he had done it" (204 / 239). And he ends in the same eye-opened nothingness: "He lay upon his back quite still. But he was not out because his eyes were still open, looking quietly up at them. There was nothing in his eyes at all, no pain, no surprise" (205 / 240).

In this pattern, something the characters see creates a "blind sight," whereupon they are driven (sent) to drive away others, only to be themselves cast into another blind sight, the nothingness. Seeing Joe's disobedience, McEachern is led to the dance, drives away Bobbie, swings at the face of Satan, and is cast into "nothingness." Seeing his virulence, Joe strikes down McEachern, sweeps aside Mrs. McEachern, "completely dismisses" the blonde woman, and ends on the floor, his eyes wide open to "nothing." Even Mrs. McEachern fits this pattern. When she sees Joe's face looking "as McEachern had seen it as the chair fell," she is driven "as if that implacable urgency which had carried her husband away had returned like a cloak on the shoulders of the boy and had been passed from him in turn to her." She runs after Joe "as though she were a phantom obeying the command sent back by the absent master" (195 / 229), and when Joe passes "out of sight," she passes into nothingness.

Returning to John, we might notice the difference between Jesus' "passing judgment" in chapter 8, and his ferocious words of judgment in chapter 9: "For judgment I am come into this world, that they which see not might see; and that they which see might be made blind." When the Pharisees ask, "Are we blind also?" Jesus says, "If ye were blind, ye should have no sin: but now ye say, We see; therefore your sin remaineth." In John, where we know the heroes and villains, this presents no problem. But when such irony, doubling back on itself, is applied to Faulkner, we might wonder about all this blindness, especially with Joe's apparent murder of his father and theft of his mother and the equally brutal behavior of others toward him.

But adding the Frazer perspective will help us understand some strange behavior, for it relates to the periodic expulsion of evil (the sin manifested in the blindness), which must be periodically routed in the form of embodied demons. In these ceremonies, the primitive will don masks or costumes and fight, scream, curse, beat with sticks, rush about, dance, run away or use ropes to slide down, pull away, or drive out evil. It is, in other words, a time of sanctioned "lunacy" (often in conjunction with the moon), during which old scores are settled and evils literally spat out, or scapegoat figures are chased or loaded with filth and abuse or money, put on "cars" and carried out of town. Sometimes the figures are inanimate. Around Easter, the gypsies of southern Europe carry a wooden vessel filled with herbs and the dried carcass of a reptile from tent to tent, so that all may spit into it before spells are said and it is thrown into running water (9.208).

Elsewhere the scapegoats are alive. Among the Mandan Indians, "a man, painted black to represent the devil," frightens the women until he is finally "chased from the village, the women pursuing him with hisses and gibes, beating him with sticks, and pelting him with dirt" (9.171). Or in Munich, "on the Eve of Ascension Day a man disguised as a devil was chased through the streets." "His pursuers were dressed as witches and wizards and provided with the indispensable crutches, brooms, and pitchforks which make up the outfit of these uncanny beings. While the devil fled before them, the troop of maskers made after him with wild whoops and halloos, and when they overtook him they ducked him in puddles or rolled him on dunghills" (9.214–15). When this scapegoat figure removed his costume, it was stuffed, "painted black, with a pair of horns and a lolling red tongue," and hung by a rope from the church tower window, before it was flung down and fought over by "the rabble" (9.215).

These ceremonial elements can be found throughout Faulkner's chapter. Begin with the insistent "moonfilled window," the "moondappled streets," the "moon shadows," the "refracted moonglow."[43] Masks and costumes appear in many forms: McEachern fumes that Joe would "don apparel which he would and could need only as some adjunct to sinning" (188 / 221); the faces at the dance "might have been masks" (193 / 227); McEachern's urgency is like a "cloak" (195 / 229); Max's voice is "like a shell, like something he carried before his face" (199 / 234); Bobbie has "a dead mouth in a dead face" (204 / 239); and like a scapegoat-idol, the blonde woman is "as immobile and completely finished and surfaced as a cast statue" (205 / 240). The chapter also has a high occurrence of *stick* and *knock*, with all the people striking at each other. Moreover, the particulars are significant. Joe beats the white horse with a broom, used in Christian Europe to drive away witches (9.157), here connected with vegetation, since it had been "driven into Mrs. McEachern's flower bed . . . for something to grow on" (196 / 230).

Appropriate, too, are the references to vanishing, the most singular being, when Joe runs up to his room, he laughed back: "He turned his head and his laughing, running on up the stairs, vanishing as he ran, vanishing upward from the head down as if he were running headfirst and laughing into something that was obliterating him like a picture in chalk being erased from a blackboard" (195 / 229). Not all expulsion ceremonies were purely ceremonial. Earlier, many kings simply disappeared. Among the Swahili on New Year's Day, "every man did as he pleased. Old quarrels were settled, men were found dead on the following day, and no inquiry was instituted" (9.226n). Actually, Frazer is arguing that most of these ceremonies are "civilized" whereas earlier, "ruder" versions

---

43. Kerr's exploration of Faulkner as a Gothic writer notes the dominance of the moon in this episode (110). Frazer writes that some believe "the transformation of were-wolves into their bestial shape takes place particularly at full moon" (10.314).

would kill the king's stead (animal or human scapegoat) and before that, the king himself, the dying god (7.22 ff.).

Besides echoing these ceremonies, Faulkner suggests that McEachern is the dying god and Joe is the scapegoat, who was often the king's own son. Said to be "crowned," McEachern would represent Old Mars of ancient Rome who "was led in procession through the streets of Rome, beaten with long white rods, and driven out of the city . . . on the day preceding the first full moon of the old Roman years." Originally a vegetation god, Mars had a horse sacrificed to him each October "to secure an abundant harvest." And since Joe is a "clodhopper" at the "clodhopper dance," with others who revealed "a heritage of patient brooding upon endless furrows and the slow buttocks of mules" (192 / 229), it is fitting that the blows to Old Mars were administered by the costumed "Brethren of the Ploughed Fields," the dancing priests, named for the dances they executed in annual religious ceremonies, just as "superstitious rustics are wont to dance and leap high in spring" to make the crops grow (9.229–34).

As for Joe as scapegoat-devil, if McEachern sees in him "the face of Satan," so does Joe: cantering home, he was "exulting perhaps at that moment as Faustus had, of having put behind now at once and for all the Shalt Not, of being free at last of honor and law. In the motion the sweet sharp sweat of the horse blew, sulphuric; the invisible wind flew past. He cried aloud, 'I have done it!'" (194 / 228). Several times, Joe's relationship to his "adopted" father—taking his place—is noted, as when he is struck down: "With something of the exaltation of his adopted father he sprang full and of his own accord into the stranger's fist. Perhaps he did not feel either blow, though the stranger struck him twice in the face before he reached the floor, where like the man whom he had struck down, he lay upon his back, quite still" (204–5 / 240). The references to Joe as a "child" and "kid" are appropriate because of this stand-in relationship to McEachern, and because Dionysus was called "Kid." One ceremony in Thrace, "a direct descendant of the Dionysian rites," includes "two men disguised in goatskins" with masks and thick padding on their shoulders, and characters such as a bride, a gypsy-man and his wife, a policeman, and an old woman carrying a seven months bastard who is supposed suddenly to grow up and "develop a huge appetite for meat and drink and to clamour for a wife." After a mock marriage, the "bridegroom" is shot with a bow and "falls down on his face like dead," after which he is supposedly skinned and prepared for burial, whereupon he comes to life again (7.26–28).

Many elements from this description are in Faulkner's final scene in which the two men who grab at Joe's shoulders "might have been brothers" (201 / 236); the blonde woman is "as implacable and calm as the white lifted glove of a policeman" (204 / 240); and Joe, called "bastard" and "kid," sees Bobbie's hand "as big and dead and pale as a piece of cooking meat" (202 / 237), licks his lip "as a child might lick a cooking spoon" (205 / 241), calls for his bride, and when knocked down, is "slashed" at by the stranger.[44]

Only now we see that Frazer's nonjudgmental context allows us to keep both views of characters from chapters 8 and 9, for it suggests that Bobbie's sluttishness, Joe's brutality, or McEachern's blind lunacy, is as temporary as the earlier, kinder, passing judgment. For example, when Bobbie screams and beats at Joe's face amid the "pandemonium" (190 / 224), she is only acting like those mummers whose noises and blows may "serve as a means of forcibly freeing the sufferers from the demons or other evil things that cling to them unseen" (9.252).

One other point. In the final italicized conversation over Joe's prostrate form, the word *one* is repeated five times:

> *He ought to stay away from bitches*
> *He cant help himself. He was born too close to one*
> *Is he really a nigger? He dont look like one*
> *That's what he told Bobbie one night. . . .*
> *We'll find out. We'll see if his blood is black. . . .*
> *That's enough. Let's get on to Memphis*
> *Just one more. . . .*
> *Sure. . . . This one is on the house too* (205–6 / 241)

Now this might be coincidence, but a Frazer passage suggests otherwise. When the Grand Lama of Lhasa, the Jalno, casts dice with

---

44. The manuscript includes, "But that was long ago. He had been a kid then, a child then" (Mms. 84).

the "half white, half black" King of the Years, before he is sent fleeing on a white horse, fortune favors the Jalno, who always throws sixes "while his opponent turns up only ones." But then "the Jalno's dice are marked with nothing but sixes and his adversary's with nothing but ones" (9.220).

Moreover, speculating further on the shift from sacrifice to vicarious sacrifice to the mere form of it, Frazer suggests a pattern like Faulkner's blindness, driven sight, and nothingness: "Such forms are no mere mushroom growths, springing up of themselves in a night. If they are now lifeless formalities, empty husks devoid of significance, we may be sure that they once had a life and a meaning; if at the present day they are blind alleys leading nowhere, we may be certain that in former days they were paths that led somewhere, if only to death" (9.221–22).

Chapter 10: The Entrance of the Good Shepherd

Faulkner's chapter 10, the shortest, covers the longest period, some fifteen years from the "final footfall" at Bobbie's house to Joe's arrival in Jefferson. It is circular, beginning with Joe's guiding himself out the door, saying, about his body, "It never would have opened a window and climbed through it" (210 / 245), and ending with his climbing so smoothly into Joanna's window that he seems to "flow."

Here is the opening of John 10: "Verily, verily, I say unto you, He that entereth not by the door into the sheepfold, but climbeth up some other way, the same is a thief and a robber. But he that entereth in by the door is the shepherd of the sheep." The parallel is reinforced in chapter 11, when, referring to his entering Joanna's house by the window, Joe is said to have felt "like a thief, a robber" (221 / 257).

Observe that the parallel with John is not by character but by characterization. Although Joe shepherds his body through the door at the beginning of the chapter, by chapter's end, he uses the window: "He could discern a door in the kitchen wall. He would have found it unlocked if he had tried it. But he did not. He passed it and paused beneath a window" (216 / 252).

Aside from other evidence, we might ask why this motif of doors versus windows could not apply to Faulkner's 8, in which Joe exits by the McEachern window and enters the guarded portal of the restaurant; or to chapter 9, in which he again exits by the window, reentering through the door to rob his mother.[45] The question has several answers. To begin with, there is some overlap in John; these three chapters are set at the Feast of Tabernacles, and language is repeated. Although 9 is the story of the blindman, it is in 10 that the Jews question, "Can a devil open the eyes of the blind?" Similarly, it is in Faulkner's 10 that Joe is actually called blind: "He went toward the door, his hands out before him like a blind man or a sleepwalker" (209 / 244). Then too, the language here refers to "entering," even when the action is exiting: in going out the door of Bobbie's house, Joe "entered the street which was to run for fifteen years" (210 / 246). Furthermore, although Jesus' metaphor does follow ordinary expectations—we do use doors unless we are robbers—Faulkner calls attention to the theme. Thus, we might not expect Mame to lock the door so Joe would have to climb through a window, and she does not. But Joe remarks on that fact. And as for Joe's entering Joanna's window, if Faulkner intended to show Joanna as unguarded and Joe as unstoppable, he might well have sent him boldly to the door, rather than merely tell us it was unlocked. After all, when Joe robs his mother, he does so, Faulkner notes, by the door.

Most interesting, Joe's use of the door versus the window reflects the theme of herding along "the way" in chapter 10. It begins, "Knowing not grieving remembers a thousand savage and lonely streets. They run from that night when he lay and heard the final footfall and then the final door" (207 / 242). Beneath the burning light, Joe lies on the floor, "an object" the others step over (the action will be important in Frazer), while Max and company act

---

45. Pitavy (41) and Ohashi (119–28) remark on the widespread motif of the window, from Lena's beginning to Joe's adventures to Lucas's departure to Hightower's end.

out John's parable of the porter opening the door, putting forth his own sheep, which he calls by name, going first while they follow. The conversation is without punctuation, as if the individual words had more meaning than their context; indeed, the language amusingly suggests the care and command of animals—*kid, chicken feed, keep, here, leave it, pick it up, get on, go on*—and even the use of their products: *knit and comb.* Here is a sample: *"Here bobbie here kid heres your comb you forgot it heres romeos chicken feed too jesus he must have tapped the sunday school till on the way out its bobbies now didnt you see him give it to her didnt you see old bighearted thats right pick it up kid you can keep it as an installment or a souvenir or something"* (207 / 242).

For Joe, these voices are all one until after the "final feet" and the "final door," after the "wireends knit." Hoping he is "moving toward the front door," he drinks some whiskey and, "with the slow, hot coiling and recoiling of his entrails," he guides his body along: "Now it was his head that was clear and his body that would not behave. He had to coax it along the hall, sliding it along one wall toward the front, thinking 'Come on, now; pull yourself together'" (209 / 245). He thinks, *"If I can just get it outside, into the air, the cool dark"* and watches his hands "fumbling at the door, trying to help them, to coax and control them" (210 / 245). He calls his body "it":

"Sweet Jesus, I could not have got out until morning then. It never would have opened a window and climbed through it." He opened the door at last and passed out and closed the door behind him, arguing again with his body which did not want to bother to close the door, having to be forced to close it. . . . He stepped from the dark porch, into the moonlight, and with his bloody head and his empty stomach hot, savage, and courageous with whiskey, he entered the street which was to run for fifteen years. (210 / 245–46)

The blank, animallike movement forward continues: "From that night the thousand streets ran as one street, with imperceptible corners and changes of scene, broken by intervals of begged and stolen rides, on trains and trucks, and on country wagons with he at twenty and twentyfive and thirty sitting on the seat with his still, hard face . . . the driver of the wagon not knowing who or what the passenger was and not daring to ask." (210–11 / 246). Describing the places Joe passes through, Faulkner suggests the "way" is itself the herder, whether "between the savage and spurious board fronts of oil towns" or "through yellow wheat fields waving beneath the fierce yellow days of labor and hard sleep in haystacks beneath the cold mad moon of September" or "through cities, through an identical and wellnigh interchangeable section of cities without remembered names, where beneath the dark and equivocal and symbolical archways of midnight he bedded with the women and paid them when he had the money, and when he did not have it he bedded anyway" (211 / 246–47). Up to his arrival in Jefferson, "he might have seen himself as in numberless avatars, in silence, doomed with motion, driven by the courage of flagged and spurred despair; by the despair of courage whose opportunities had to be flagged and spurred" (213 / 248–49).

As with terms such as *bedded* or *spurred*, which are commonly applied to animals, much of Joe's saga is based on sense experience. For example, he tries to become black by his sense of smell, living

> with a woman who resembled an ebony carving. At night he would lie in bed beside her, sleepless, beginning to breathe deep and hard. He would do it deliberately, feeling, even watching, his white chest arch deeper and deeper within his ribcage, trying to breathe into himself the dark odor, the dark and inscrutable thinking and being of negroes, with each suspiration trying to expel from himself the white blood and white thinking and being. And all the while his nostrils at the odor which he was trying to make his own would whiten and tauten, his whole being writhe and strain with physical outrage and spiritual denial. (212 / 248)

Although ingenious parallels to John might be found with individual passages—such as the "hireling" who cares not for the sheep, relating to the prostitutes—it may be more helpful to consider Frazer's accounts of shepherds' "Parilia," in honor of the god-goddess Pales, or the Festivals of St. George, the patron saint both of the herds and the wolves. Each spring, when sheep, goats, and cattle were first driven out to pasture, they were newly exposed to the hazards of wolves and witches, so that special protection was required. One widespread practice involved smells, namely, the burning of sulphur or heaps of straw, pungent wood, or flowers, and making the animals—and the shepherds—leap over the resulting "blue smoke" (2.327); recall Max and the others repeatedly stepping over Joe, "burned" by the "suspended globe." The festival was also an efficacious time for coupling animals, like Joe's "beddings." Many customs involved processions, begging from door to door, like Joe's "begged" rides. Or offerings were made, called "tail-money" (2.331), humorously like Joe's payments to the prostitutes. Even the twice-mentioned molasses relates to the dose of sulphur and molasses, given every spring.

The language of doors is appropriate, because they were often the first line of defense. Herdsmen would make crosses on the doors of stalls or of their homes and on gateposts (*Pales* means "stakes"), and they would lay sods with thorns stuck in them or various branches "deemed especially efficacious in banning fiends" (2.336). In Transylvania it was thought that "witches ride on the backs of the cows into the farmyard, if branches of wild rosebushes or other thorny shrubs are not stuck over the gate" (2.338).

Midway in John's chapter 10, the scene shifts to the Feast of the Dedication, where Jesus walks "in Solomon's porch" while the Jews question his identity: "How long dost thou make us to doubt? If thou be the Christ, tell us plainly."

In Faulkner, at the shift to Jefferson, Joe is circling Joanna's house, questioning the black boy too closely: "Colored folks look after her?" The response is another door image: "At once it was as if the boy had closed a door between himself and the man who questioned him" (214 / 250). Since this is the first time the "way" has been closed, we might suspect (we do anyway) that we should look on Joe differently from his earlier role of scapegoat. Somewhere along the way, he has become "catlike" (213 / 248); entering Joanna's house, he will be three times likened to a cat, a notorious witch-animal (10.316). And that Joe may represent both the herded animal of "numberless avatars," driven out at the beginning of the chapter and the possessed cat-thief, entering the fold at the end, is perfectly consistent with primitive belief, since witches or werewolves may take the form of any animal they wish (10.315n).

In any case, while Joe lies in the copse, he sees "the shadow of a moving person cross the further wall." Perhaps this "cross" is meant as protection, except that Joe is himself protected; feeling "the neversunned earth strike, slow and receptive, against him through his clothes: groin, hip, belly, breast, forearms" (215 / 251), he wisely has his arms "crossed" over his forehead, for the disguise of a witch-animal can best be penetrated with a stab "on the brow or between the eyes" (10.315).

There is a similar standoff in the relationship to come. Because grass is important in the shepherd's life, spring was also the time when "St. George arose and unlocked the earth, so that the grass grew" (2.333). Now we can see the dilemma of the unlocked door, the conflict between wanting to be open and fearing the entrance of fiends. Tyrolean processions, called "ringing out the grass," were meant both to make the grass grow and to disperse the St. George's Day evil spirits (2.344). Here is Joe, magically suspended above the grassy noises: "In the grass about his feet the crickets, which had ceased as he moved, keeping a little island of silence about him like thin yellow shadow of their small voices, began again, ceasing again when he moved with that tiny and alert suddenness" (216 / 252). Thus, Joe is a fiend who will yet bring new life.

Since the next chapter deals with the lady who will be raised from the dead, she first appears with a face that is "quiet" and "grave" and speaks "in a voice calm, a little deep, quite cold" (218 / 254), her candle lit, like the wise virgin. And in view of her coming dedication, it is appropriate that Joe first appears to her eating the field peas, as he says, "for sweet Jesus."

Chapter 11: Lazarus Raised; the Dead Unbound

It is the Joe-Joanna story of chapters 11 and 12 that leads to Joe's death, just as the Lazarus episode in John 11 and 12 leads to Jesus' crucifixion.[46] The thematic unity of Faulkner's chapters is signaled

46. The last verses of John 10 were probably the original ending of Jesus' public ministry, chapters 11 and 12 having been added to make the raising of Lazarus the

by clusters of the seemingly trivial word *all*, as in this passage at the beginning of 11: "Sometimes he could almost believe that they did not talk at all, that he didn't know her at all. It was as though there were two people: the one whom he saw . . . by day . . . while they spoke to one another with speech that told nothing at all; . . . the other with whom he lay at night and didn't even see, speak to, at all" (219 / 255). Or in this passage at the end of 12: "But the shadow of [the revolver] and of her arm and hand on the wall did not waver at all, the shadow of both monstrous, the cocked hammer monstrous, backhooked and viciously poised like the arched head of a snake; it did not waver at all. And her eyes did not waver at all. They were as still as the round black ring of the pistol muzzle. . . . They were calm and still as all pity and all despair and all conviction" (267 / 310).

Appropriate to the raising of the dead, the two chapters celebrate All Saints' and All Souls' days, November 1 and 2, which represent the church's domestication of the primitive belief that each year "the dead rise from their graves and flit about the neighbouring hills" (6.54). In their honor, doors are left open; lamps and candles are lit; garments or food such as "cakes and sweetmeats" are left in special rooms or cast on the floor; and people keep a vigil, telling stories of the dead or visiting their graves to weep or pray in their honor (6.51–83).

In addition to the diction of souls and saints, all of these customs appear in Faulkner's two chapters. The open doorway, just discussed, will continue in relation to Joe's access to the "house proper." The light for the dead will appear in many forms, from Joanna's candle, to the fireflies (themselves returning souls [3.67]) which "drifted and drifted," to the lamplight by which Joanna is killed. As for the food and clothing, Joe is regularly supplied with clean clothes, as are those in Joanna's tales, while the "cakes and sweetmeats" appear as "corn cakes" with "sweetening" or the dishes "set out for the nigger," which Joe climactically smashes.

---

precipitating cause of the crucifixion. Fadiman's study of the manuscript indicates that Faulkner wrote the two chapters as one, composing the Burden flashback separately, with present-time interruptions on base pages (87 & 109).

Most important, the dead are recalled in these tales, which include Joanna's visit to the grave, her prayers, and her tears.

In fact, several story elements from chapter 11 spill over into chapter 12. For example, regarding those tears, one notable feature of John 11 is the simple verse "Jesus wept." Here it is the four-year-old Joanna who weeps, but in the next chapter there is this paragraph-ending: "She cried, wept" (245 / 284).

In John's chapter 11, learning that Lazarus is ill, Jesus says his sickness is "not unto death but for the glory of God," yet after a typical Johannine misunderstanding in which the disciples take literally a metaphorical reference to Lazarus as "sleeping," Jesus says plainly Lazarus is dead. He goes to Bethany, where Lazarus' sisters greet him characteristically: Martha, active, questioning; Mary, passive, falling at his feet. Responding to each, Jesus has the stone taken from the cave, cries "Lazarus come forth," and "he that was dead came forth, bound hand and foot with graveclothes: and his face was bound about with a napkin," whereupon Jesus says, "Loose him, and let him go." Because of this miracle, the high priests determine and prophesy that Jesus should die for the nation, and Jesus goes into hiding, amid fresh questions about his movements.

Faulkner's chapter 11 is a typical time scramble.[47] It presents the first year of the Joe-Joanna relationship, she being like two people, the one part inviolable, even as Joe nightly tries to "despoil" her. When she finally surrenders, it is to tell the history of her abolitionist family, after which she and Joe question each other about their respective backgrounds.

Joanna is often spoken of in relation to death: she is "prepared for sleep" (like Jesus' metaphor); in her lawyer's safe "reposed" her will and her handwritten instructions "for the disposal of her body after death" (221 / 257); beneath Joe's hands, her "body might have been the body of a dead woman not yet stiffened" (223 / 259); and her surrender, when or if "despoiled," is of a "spiritual privacy,"

---

47. Reed (132) observes that in chapter 11 the "text is studded with references to particular times or periods of time and the relationships between one and the other, but order is gone."

likened, in chapter 12, to "the breaking down of a spiritual skeleton the very sound of whose snapping fibers could be heard almost by the physical ear" (242 / 281). Like Lazarus, she is spoken of in relation to her clothing, Joe often thinking "*Under her clothes she cant even be made so that it could have happened*" (222 / 258). Moreover, when she comes to the cabin, her hair is "loose," an echo of "Loose him, and let him go." This suggests she is the wrapped body being raised from the dead, an action prefigured by her father's words: "You must struggle, rise."

But Joe is also spoken of as surrendering, rising, and even floating: "It was as though, as soon as he found that his feet intended to go there, that he let go, seemed to float, surrendered" (225 / 260). Elsewhere he "seemed to swing faintly, as though in a drifting boat, upon the sound of her voice" (234 / 273).

Moreover, the language of clothing is linked to the dead characters of the past, describing Nathaniel's childhood, when "each Sunday . . . washed and clean, the children in calico or denim, the father in his broadcloth frockcoat bulging over the pistol in his hip pocket, and the collarless plaited shirt which the oldest girl laundered each Saturday as well as the dead mother ever had, they gathered in the clean crude parlor" (230 / 267). Or his first wedding, when "father's sisters worked, making Calvin's mother a wedding gown and veil. They made the gown out of flour sacks and the veil out of some mosquito netting that a saloon keeper had nailed over a picture behind the bar. They borrowed it from him. They even made some kind of suit for Calvin to wear. He was . . . to be the ringbearer" (237 / 276). Further, it is Grandfather Calvin who twice says, "I'll be bound" and whose "jaw slacked as if he had seen a ghost" when his new daughter-in-law "looked enough like his dead wife to have been her sister" (233 / 271). The "sister" motif, important in the Lazarus story, almost emerges in this look-alike of two generations, and, more strained, in Nathaniel's three sisters.

But the motif emerges elsewhere. If we set aside the notion that Joanna is the one raised from the dead, there is evidence that she represents a combined Martha and Mary, the active versus the passive, struggling within the same person. Joe says, "It was as though there were two people" (219 / 255), or he thinks of her as a "dual personality," (221 / 258); in chapter 12, she has two people "locked like sisters" (246 / 286) within her. Most important, Calvin is Joanna's brother, and he is actually buried, killed "not by one white man but by the curse which God put on a whole race" (239 / 278); if you make that "human" race, the line fits Christian theology.[48] Furthermore, to the four-year-old Joanna, he does appear frighteningly raised from the dead: "It was something about father." "A something . . . that he had put on the cedar grove, and that when I went into it, the grove would put on me so that I would never be able to forget it" (238–39 / 277). And finally, like Lazarus, Calvin never speaks.

But before we decide who is playing what role, we should also recall the parallel between Joanna and Diana and her sacred oak at Nemi. Because she cast Dianus into a shadow, Frazer believed that Diana must have stood for "the older principle of mother-kin, or the predominance of the wife in matters of inheritance over the husband" (5.45). In fact, the succession to the throne, central to the priesthood at Nemi, involved a runaway slave, a "member of an alien and barbarous race" (1.42). Frazer suggests that although the king generally ruled, both myth and tradition showed him taking over the throne by marriage rather than paternal inheritance; so that "among the Latins the women of royal blood always stayed at home and received as their consorts men of another stock, and often of another country." Under such conditions "where descent through the mother is everything . . . no objection will be felt to uniting girls of the highest rank to men of humble birth, even to aliens or slaves" (2.274).

Given this scenario, Joe's role as runaway slave could be one reason for the chapter's obsession with battles (see my chapter 4) and the talk of surrender, especially since the battle is symbolic, as if Joe "struggled physically with another man for an object of no actual value to either, and for which they struggled on principle alone" (222 / 258). Joe's "ordeal" is by "shock": "The first time

---

48. R. G. Collins (*"Light"* 106) suggests that the connection should be made, quoting Faulkner: "The curse is slavery. . . . The Negro is the white man's guilt manifested" (*Faulkner in the Univ.* 79).

that he deliberately looked again toward the house, he felt a shocking surge and fall of blood; then he knew that he had been afraid all the time that she would be in sight, that she had been watching him all the while with that perspicuous and still contempt; he felt a sensation of sweating, of having surmounted an ordeal. 'That's over,' he thought. 'I have done that now.' So that when one day he did see her, there was no shock" (226 / 263). Another reason would be that the succession to the throne often did depend on athletic contests, sometimes between suitors or sometimes with the king's daughter herself: Atalante made her suitors contend with herself in a footrace; usually the winner, she would cut off their heads and hang them along the racecourse (2.301). The Tartar king's daughter, Aijaruc, "outdid all the men in her father's realm in feats of strength. She vowed she would never marry till she found a man who could vanquish her in wrestling." Or the Queen of Iceland, Brunhild, "was only to be won in marriage by him who could beat her in three trials of strength" (2.306). Recall that Joanna "resisted fair, by the rules that decreed that upon a certain crisis one was defeated, whether the end of resistance had come or not" (222 / 259).

Besides being goddess and priest, Joanna is the tree itself. In chapter 12, Joe thinks "it was like trying to argue with a tree" (254 / 295) and her knot of hair looked "as savage and ugly as a wart on a diseased bough" (260 / 302). Amusingly appropriate is Joe's *"Under her clothes she cant even be made so that it could have happened"* (222 / 258). Indeed, when we read that men dress trees then tear the clothing from them (2.141), or they "go naked to the plantations by night, and there seek to fertilize the trees precisely as they would impregnate women" (2.100), we realize that the rape scene can be read as Joe's teaching the tree to be fertile. Observe Faulkner's use of the word *limbs:* "He found her in the dark exactly where the light had lost her, in the same attitude. He began to tear at her clothes. He was talking to her, in a tense, hard, low voice: 'I'll show you! I'll show the bitch!' She did not resist at all. It was almost as though she were helping him, with small changes of position of limbs when the ultimate need for help arose" (223 / 259).

This language of trees is also appropriate to the weddings of the heroic past, for throughout Europe the connection between the oak and the highest deities was celebrated in marriage ceremonies which could include a man or woman, a King or Queen of the Wood, being married to one another, or to a priest or priestess, or the appropriate deity, or the tree itself: the oak god Zeus was periodically joined to an oaken image of Hera; in Athens the wine god Dionysus was annually wedded to the queen; and the union of Janus (Dianus) and Diana (later, Jupiter-Juno) was celebrated with marriage processions (2.189–90).

Thus, the Burden flashback reinforces the chapter's central themes. That Joanna lights the candle, leaves out the food, suggests that Joe is returning from the dead. And he does, under her questioning, surrender up his dead past, his confusion over what he is. Yet Joanna is "the body that had died three years ago and had just now begun to live again" (273 / 317). That Grandfather Calvin says "I'll be bound" suggests he is the bound Lazarus, yet, as if echoing the binding of Lazarus' hand, foot and face, Nathaniel's marriage specifically includes "ringbearers," "spanish boots," and "mosquito netting." As usual, John's themes have been made to apply to many characters. For they all represent, if not brother, certainly brotherhood, the kinship of black and white or North and South, which must be raised from the dead, just as Joanna's father, looking "like people of two different races" (229 / 266), suggests she must when she has her frightening dream of "black shadows": "At last I told father . . . that I must escape, get away from under the shadow, or I would die. 'You cannot,' he said. 'You must struggle, rise. But in order to rise, you must raise the shadow with you'" (239–40 / 278–79). In the spinning out of the Joe-Joanna Ur-myth in the present time, ironically celebrated in the past with marriage, adornment, and feasting, we see that both predictions were true. Yes, she and the shadow must struggle and rise, and yes, they must die.

Chapter 12: Agony in the Garden: The Corn Must Fall

In Chapter 12, where we discover how Joe came to murder Joanna, the behavior of the characters is especially difficult to fathom. Of course, we do learn what the townspeople, blind on the simplistic level of race, could never have imagined, that she forced him to. But if we ask why, not only are we far from the cliché-ridden land of small-town bigotry, we are hardly in the range of explicable human behavior. Joanna seems to be mad or nymphomaniacal, as if any man, albeit black, would do. Joe's not leaving is mysteriously beyond his control. Up to the last moment, he can only repeat Joanna's imperative (in a setting like the Agony in the Garden) made all the more powerful by its irrationality: "As he sat in the shadows of the ruined garden on that August night . . . and heard the clock in the courthouse two miles away strike ten and then eleven, he believed with calm paradox that he was the volitionless servant of the fatality in which he believed that he did not believe. He was saying to himself *I had to do it* already in the past tense; *I had to do it. She said so herself*" (264 / 307). The furthest involvement Joe considers is physical security; the furthest Joanna considers is physical passion and both reject even these. So without any great love between them, Joe's final repeated words, "For her and for me," may puzzle us. Why did she and he think they must die?

The only apparent answer comes from Joanna's "mad" vision: somehow they are playing roles larger than themselves. For her, it is Joe as Negro, first as lover, then as high priest of the Cause, then as a path to salvation. Joe is, in fact, more of a black here than in any other chapter. Everywhere else there is doubt about his parentage. Here, although he begins thinking of himself as entering "that house which no white person save himself had entered in years" (245 / 284), soon he is whistling "something in minor, plaintive and negroid" (258 / 299), while Joanna calls him "Negro! Negro! Negro!"; speaks of his "bastard negro child"; determines he should become "a nigger lawyer"; or insists that he kneel and pray, the black savage.

For Joe, these larger roles appear in the three "phases": "During the first phase it had been as though he were outside a house where snow was on the ground, trying to get into the house; during the second phase he was at the bottom of a pit in the hot wild darkness; now he was in the middle of a plain where there was no house, not even snow, not even wind" (254–55 / 295–96). Correlating these metaphors with the Joe-Joanna myth, the first phase, described in chapter 11, was the binding of oak and mistletoe, which takes over the soul of winter's "dead" tree, their dead past. The other two phases here will involve rainmaking ceremonies, first to produce rain and then to stop it so that harvesting may begin.[49]

Consider first the rainmaking. When the primitive wishes to make rain, he imitates its look, feel, or noise. Thus, if a sacrificial animal is used, it will be black like storm clouds, and when it is beaten, its cries will signify the thunder and its tears or blood, the rain. East African tribes "sacrifice black fowls, black sheep, and black cattle at the graves of dead ancestors, and the rain-maker wears black clothes" (1.290–91). Elsewhere women will sprinkle or roll naked in water or mud, pray, weep, sing obscene songs, anoint some magical figure such as a stranger, "often taken for a deity" (1.277), or twins, thought to have magical power over rain (1.262). In Sumatra, "all the women of the village, scantily clad, go to the river, wade into it, and splash each other with the water. A black cat is thrown into the stream and . . . allowed to escape to the bank, pursued by the splashing of the women" (1.291). The women of Bengal make two images and carry them to the fields by night. "There they strip themselves naked, and dance round the images singing obscene songs," although, Frazer notes, the "link between ribaldry and rain is not obvious to the European mind" (1.284n). In Armenia, the children carry a figure from house to house, singing "Bring water to pour on her head / Bring butter to smear on her ear" (1.275). In India, "naked women drag a plough across a field by night while the men keep carefully out of the way, for their presence would break the spell" (1.282). On occasion, "they discharge volleys of abuse at the village officials," and even though Hindu women ordinarily "never engage in agricultural operations," yet "in drought it seems to be women of the highest or Brahman caste" (1.283). But then "noble matrons" of Rome "used to go with bare feet, streaming hair, and pure minds, up the long Capitoline slope, praying to Jupiter for rain" (2.362).

Notice these elements in Faulkner's chapter 12. For Joe, the second phase "was as though he had fallen into a sewer" (242 / 281),

49. Asals suggests the three phases represent the three temptations of Christ.

and dirty or corrupt liquids arise, from the "mud" in the opening paragraph, to Joanna's body, "ready to flow into putrefaction at a touch, like something growing in a swamp" (247–48 / 287), to the two sisters within that body, the one "damned" and the other "drowned," the water puns intended:

> [Joe] stayed, watching the two creatures that struggled in the one body like two moongleamed shapes struggling drowning in alternate throes upon the surface of a black thick pool beneath the last moon. Now it would be that still, cold, contained figure of the first phase who, even though lost and damned, remained somehow impervious and impregnable; then it would be the other, the second one, who in furious denial of that impregnability strove to drown in the black abyss of its own creating that physical purity which had been preserved too long now even to be lost. Now and then they would come to the black surface, locked like sisters; the black waters would drain away. (246 / 286)

Moreover, Joanna uses the "forbidden wordsymbols" and forces Joe to run through the house and woods at night, where he would "find her naked, or with her clothing half torn to ribbons upon her, in the wild throes of nymphomania, her body gleaming in the slow shifting from one to another of such formally erotic attitudes and gestures as a Beardsley of the time of Petronius might have drawn. She would be wild then, in the close, breathing halfdark without walls, with her wild hair, each strand of which would seem to come alive like octopus tentacles, and her wild hands and her breathing" (245 / 285). Recall Joanna's tears: "She cried, wept" (245 / 284). Repeatedly, their relationship is presented in terms of water, even floods:

> At first it had been a torrent; now it was a tide, with a flow and ebb. During its flood she could almost fool them both. It was as if out of her knowledge that it was just a flow that must presently react was born a wilder fury, a fierce denial that could flag itself and him into physical experimentation that transcended imagining, carried them as though by momentum alone, bearing them without volition or plan. . . . Then the tide would ebb. Then they would be stranded as behind a dying mistral, upon a spent and satiate beach. (248 / 288)

The third phase reflects the same desire for fecundity, but it involves ceremonies appropriate to excess rain. Then rain doctors will fast or eat dry food with unwashed hands, avoid waters of all kinds, and build a fire, itself a fertility symbol, which they never allow to go out (1.270–71). They also practice sexual continence, since it is widely held that "adultery or fornication has a powerful influence to injure the harvest" (2.107), as does incest or the seduction of a virgin (2.112). Believing "that the anger of the gods at incest or bestiality manifests itself in the form of violent storms, heavy rain, or long drought," one tribe controls the weather by killing a sow and a cock and burying the two in "intimate embrace" (2.113).

The manner of Joanna's death is itself a rain-fertility charm, related to harvesting the Corn Mother, a spirit "believed to be present in the handful of corn which is left standing last on the field; and with the cutting of this last handful she is caught, or driven away, or killed" (7.133).[50] As the Old Woman, the Great Mother, or Maiden, the last bound sheaf may be made into a puppet, adorned with flowers and ribbons, then beaten or drenched with water or thrown on a pyre and burned. And the spirit of the corn is transferred to the person who "gets her," the one who cuts or binds the last sheaf at threshing (7.204). Such a person is subject to rough treatment and taunts, like getting the Old Maid in cards. "He has the Old Woman and must keep her," the others jeer, blackening his face or binding him to the Old Woman and throwing them in the water.

The Corn Spirit may have a double form. When bride and bridegroom, "dancers pluck the bunches of oats one by one from the Oats-bridegroom while he struggles to keep them, till at last he is completely stript of them and stands bare, exposed to the laughter and jests of the company" (7.163). When mother and child, the harvesters call out to the woman who binds the last sheaf, "You are getting the child!" (7.151).

Still other avatars include the "neck," which all the reapers try

---

50. Amusingly, "short cut" and "cut short" appear frequently in this Faulkner chapter, including the odd "The blow cut his voice short off" (259 / 301).

to "cut through" (7.268); or the "cat", which makes the last reaper the "Tom-cat" (7.281); or the dog, which means he "has the White Bitch" (7.272). Another variant, the Stranger, involves a man or woman who, appearing at harvest time, is seized and wrapped in sheaves, in some places merely handled roughly, in others, killed, the head cut off, the body burned or drenched (7.216 ff.). Although some figures are shown reverence (7.211), generally the one who personifies the Corn Spirit has lost some competition (7.253) because the role forebodes marriage to an old person (7.139) or the birth of a baby (7.145); a misfortune (7.218) or even death (7.254).

As suggested, Joanna goes through numerous avatars. First she is found "hidden, in closets, in empty rooms, waiting, panting, her eyes in the dark glowing like the eyes of cats" (245 / 285); then she is the two sisters, the "damned" and the "drowned." Then she is the stranger, staring at Joe "with the wild, despairing face of a stranger" (247 / 286); then she is "with child," which proves to be as fanciful as "getting the child"; and then she is just the Old Hag, whom Joe beats: "He struck with his fist, then . . . the long wind of knowing rushed down upon him. 'You haven't got any baby,' he said. 'You never had one. There is not anything the matter with you except being old. You just got old and it happened to you and now you are not any good anymore'" (262 / 304–5).

But Joe, too, is bound to her every stage. As she is corrupt, in six months "she began to corrupt him." He is "like a man being sucked down into a bottomless morass" (246 / 285). He, too, is called the stranger, along with their supposed child: "He would go to her now with reluctance, a stranger, already backlooking; a stranger he would leave her after having sat with her in the dark bedroom, talking of still a third stranger." Yet they are married, bound together: "As though by premeditation, they met always in the bedroom, as though they were married" (249 / 289). Receiving her note, he "should have seen that he was bound just as tightly by that small square of still undivulging paper as though it were a lock and chain" (257 / 299). And specifically, he is bound by shame: "He would have died or murdered rather than have anyone, another man, learn what their relations had now become" (256 / 298). In other words, becoming the last to thresh or bind the Bitch, the Old

Woman, the Stranger, the Cat, Joe becomes the "Tom-cat" (259 / 301), the one who is dirtied, made black, thrown into the water, the one who must suffer the laughter and abuse of other men.

What has all this to do with John? These are the last hours before the betrayal. Like Joe's sense of "foreboding and premonition" and Joanna's "dawning of halfdeath," Jesus states this imminence using this metaphor: "Except a corn of wheat fall into the ground and die, it abideth alone: but if it die, it bringeth forth much fruit."

Now—remarkably—when we look back at John for specific parallels, we find it is possible to read his three stories not only as forecasts of death, but also (whether John knew it or not) as having connections with rainmaking. In the first, Mary anoints Jesus' feet with a costly ointment, which she wipes off with her unbound hair. But biblical commentators note that the anointing of the feet is odd. Usually the head is anointed, or the feet of the dead. Even odder is Mary's wiping off the ointment, and with her hair unbound, since loose hair would have been considered immodest.[51] Faulkner hints at the wiping off of feet in a metaphor regarding Joanna's surrender: "as when a defeated general on the day after the last battle, shaved overnight and with his boots cleaned of the mud of combat surrenders his sword to a committee" (242 / 281). But universalizing John's story, he also relates Mary's "loose" behavior to rainmaking rituals in the depiction of Joanna, behaving immodestly, like the high-caste Hindu women or the barefooted "noble matrons."

In John's next scene "Jesus, when he had found a young ass, sat thereon; as it is written, Fear not, daughter of Sion: behold, thy King cometh, sitting on an ass's colt." The original Old Testament passage reads like some kind of animal trick: "riding upon an ass, and upon a colt the foal of an ass" (Zech. 9:9). Faulkner hints at this oddity in the rather fanciful analogy of Joanna, looking animallike, "her plump body . . . more richly and softly animal than ever" (251 / 291), carrying the "trick," the "bastard negro child" within. But this story also has connections with rainmaking, for

51. In Luke's account, she is the "woman sinner" (7:37–38). The Anchor Bible suggests an oral cross-influence between Luke and John (451).

the people wave palm branches and cry, "Hosanna," a prayer for rain at Tabernacles (Anchor 457); the theme is explicit in Zechariah: "And his dominion shall be from sea even to sea and from the river even to the ends of the earth. As for thee also, by the blood of thy covenant I have sent forth thy prisoners out of the pit wherein is no water" (9:10–11).

In John's version of the Agony in the Garden, when Jesus prays, "Father, save me from this hour," he is answered by "a voice from heaven," which some thought was an angel, while others only "said that it thundered." The petitions are suggested in Joanna's "notes" to Joe, which bind him inexorably to her, and to her prayers, "talking to God as if He were a man in the room with two other men" (265 / 308). But both the petitioning and the thunder are weather controls, mock thunder being a rain charm (2.181).

To be sure, these "tricks" of Faulkner's words only reinforce his central purpose: to echo John's stern inevitability. In each scene Jesus takes the behavior at hand—the anointing, the entry, and the voice—and turns it into a forecast of death that operates like a command. This cup shall not be passed. So also for Joe and Joanna, the corruption, the carrying of the child, and the prayers: each forecasts their imminent death, binding them both to the "flat pattern" of tomorrow when their union of black and white must be harvested as a message to the town and as an imperative to all.

John closes with a quote from Isaiah (echoed in chapter 9): "He hath blinded their eyes, and hardened their heart; that they should not see with their eyes, nor understand with their heart, and be converted." Faulkner's closing scene also suggests that Joe, riding with the frightened youngsters after the murder, is both blind and deaf. Holding the gun, "he does not notice" it; when they hiss to each other, he was "completely unaware that he was riding directly behind desperate terror"; when they speak to him, "he was not even paying attention" (268 / 311–12). Yet he finally does come to see. After the car is gone, "he struck a match and examined the pistol in the puny dying glare. The match burned down and went out, yet he still seemed to see the ancient thing with its two loaded chambers: the one upon which the hammer had already fallen and which had not exploded, and the other upon which no hammer had yet fallen but upon which a hammer had been planned to fall." Even without the match, Joe sees, and then he hears: "His arm came back, and threw. He heard the pistol crash once through undergrowth. Then there was no sound again" (270 / 314). He understands that Joanna acted "for her and for me." If we apply John's text, Joe now sees something he had been blind to. Is it Joanna's love? Her desire for his salvation? At the very least, he might see that she was as bound to the Old Woman as he. At the very least, he might be experiencing pity.

His words, "for her and for me," now seem less puzzling. Joe's rootless condition had bound him, the passing stranger, to the Old Woman, but she has raised their spent lives to the level of myth. So the words which begin in understanding, become, in the repeating, like a pledge.

CHAPTER VI

The Book of Glory and Epilogue

Light in August, Chapters 13–21

Chapter 13: Familiars of the Air Dog the (Unclean) Heels

THE RATHER complicated events of 13 present a new beginning, back at Lena's arrival in Jefferson. Gathering around the fire, the crowd looks at Joanna's body until the sheriff arrives and questions the closest "nigger." After all return to town (passing Lena along the way), a reward flushes out Brown, who informs on Christmas. Tracking dogs are brought in, but they lead nowhere. Byron visits Hightower to ask advice, yet refutes him. Shopping, Hightower hears of Christmas's capture and returns home in a panic. Finally, Byron visits Hightower again, saying that he has moved Lena to Brown's cabin, despite the older man's disapproval.

Confusing. But unifying themes do emerge when we follow some of the chapter's odd tropes and images. For instance, the fire truck that pulls up, proud and gaudy (and useless), to Joanna's burning house has "mechanical ladders that sprang to prodigious heights at the touch of a hand, like opera hats" (272 / 316). Unremarkable in itself, but soon the dogs are baying "with the passionate abandon of two baritones singing Italian opera" (280 / 326).

Then Brown is "like a man that cant play a tune, blowing a horn right loud, hoping that in a minute it will begin to make music" (286 / 332). Then Hightower reads Tennyson as if "listening in a cathedral to a eunuch chanting in a language which he does not even need to not understand" (301 / 350). And all this music further combines with other strident noises: the bells and whistles of the fire engine; the "honking and blatting" of the cars; the train, "a thousand costly tons of intricate and curious metal glaring and crashing up and into an almost shocking silence filled with the puny sounds of men" (280 / 325); the "bell-like and abject wailing" of the dogs, the men shouting at them (282 / 327).

Although we might expect murder to prompt a hue and cry, why music or music becoming just plain noise?

Another odd metaphor reports the fire truck has "neat and virgin coils of hose evocative of telephone trust advertisements in the popular magazines" (272 / 316). American Tel and Tel did not call itself a "trust" in its advertisements of the twenties, but it did picture "virgin coils" and did speak of "trust." One ad with large coils of cable, although not very neat, speaks of "a nation-wide telephone service as a public trust." That the "trust" comes from the "service" is reflected in the caption: "5000 people whose sole job is bettering your service." Another ad, with a very neat coil of cable being unrolled, reads, "In the service of all the people." Another reads, "1800 conversations at once through a cable less than 3 inches thick" (see figs. 2 & 3).

Notice the metaphor involves something printed that sells trust and service and speaks of an amazing conduit for hundreds of voices in the air. Similar elements of trust and service in business join the printing in a long metaphor in which the crowd around the body on the sheet prefers vengeance because that made

> nice believing. Better than the shelves and the counters filled with longfamiliar objects bought, not because the owner desired them or admired them, could take any pleasure in the owning of them, but in order to cajole or trick other men into buying them at a profit; and who must now and then contemplate both the objects which had not yet sold and the men who could buy them but had not yet done so, with anger and maybe outrage and maybe despair too. Better

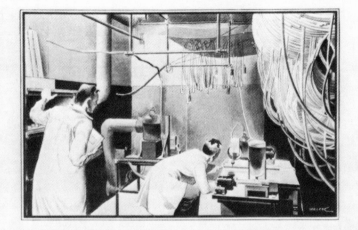

5000 people whose sole job is bettering your service

An Advertisement of the
American Telephone and Telegraph Company

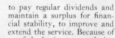

THE very nature of the telephone business necessitates a single inter-connected system. The American Telephone and Telegraph Company accepts its responsibility for a nation-wide telephone service as a public trust.

It also accepts responsibility for the safety of the funds invested in it by more than 420,000 persons in every walk of life. From the time of its organization it has never missed paying a regular dividend, so that investors rightly feel assurance in providing money for the growth of the business.

It is the policy of the company to use all income, beyond that necessary to pay regular dividends and maintain a surplus for financial stability, to improve and extend the service. Because of the nature of the business, speculative profits have no place in it.

The Bell System maintains in its research, engineering and business staffs and in the Bell Laboratories 5000 workers—in a total of 350,000 employees—whose sole occupation is to improve the telephone art and to make these improvements instantly available throughout the nation. These workers are a guaranty of continued progress in furnishing the public a constantly improving telephone service at the lowest possible cost.

240

FIGURE 2.   *Courtesy of AT&T Archives.*

BIG AND LITTLE, RICH AND POOR, CAN PROJECT THEIR PERSONALITIES OVER THE WIDE NETWORK OF ITS WIRES

In the service of all the people

An Advertisement of the
American Telephone and Telegraph Company

THE Bell System is owned by 450,000 stockholders and operated by more than 400,000 workers for the service of the people of the nation.

It is a democratic instrument of a democracy. Big and little, rich and poor, can project their personalities over the wide network of its wires. For friendship or business, pleasure or profit, the telephone is indispensable to our modern civilization.

This year the Bell System is erecting new telephone buildings in more than 200 cities. It is putting in thousands of miles of cable, thousands of sections of switchboard and hundreds of thousands of new telephones. Its expenditure for plant and improvements in service in 1929 will be more than 550 millions of dollars—half again as much as it cost to build the Panama Canal.

This program is part of the telephone ideal that anyone, anywhere, shall be able to talk quickly and at reasonable cost with anyone, anywhere else. There is no standing still in the Bell System.

254
December, 1929

FIGURE 3.   *Courtesy of AT&T Archives.*

than the musty offices where the lawyers waited lurking among ghosts of old lusts and lies, or where the doctors waited with sharp knives and sharp drugs, telling man . . . without resorting to printed admonishments, that they labored for that end whose ultimate attainment would leave them with nothing whatever to do. (273 / 317–18)

Or here is Hightower's "tricking sense" in the store:

He leaned forward against the counter, above his laden basket. He could feel the counter edge against his stomach. It felt solid, stable enough; it was more like the earth itself were rocking faintly, preparing to move. Then it seemed to move, like something released slowly and without haste, in an augmenting swoop, and cleverly, since the eye was tricked into believing that the dingy shelves ranked with flyspecked tins, and the merchant himself behind the counter, had not moved; outraging, tricking sense. (292 / 339)

Notice that the pattern depicts the familiar world (like that of business) being turned upside down, somehow reversed or tricked, by the world of familiars: the known, the domestic (family, servant, animal), and ghosts. When the crowd appears "as though out of thin air," they look at the body on the sheet "with that static and childlike amaze with which adults contemplate their own inescapable portraits" (271 / 315), or they look at the fire "with that same dull and static amaze which they had brought down from the old fetid caves where knowing began" (272 / 316). Or the sheriff has tricking ancestors: "He was not yet thinking of himself as having been frustrated by a human agent. It was the fire. It seemed to him that the fire had been selfborn for that end and purpose. It seemed to him that that by and because of which he had had ancestors long enough to come himself to be, had allied itself with crime" (274 / 318). In fact, two explicit statements invert the ordinary world. In one, the "heritage" of Joanna's quiet life and outrageous death had "supplied" the town "with an emotional barbecue, a Roman holiday" (273 / 317). In the other, with the arrival of "two gaunt and cringing phantoms," the dogs, "it was as if the very initial outrage of the murder carried in its wake and made of all subsequent actions something monstrous and paradoxical and wrong, in themselves against both reason and nature" (280 / 325).

This recalls a third odd metaphor, when the deputy looks "like a spaniel waiting to be told to spring into the water" (276 / 321). The chapter's list of high-frequency words reminds us that the dogs (also familiars) amusingly reverse roles: brought in to lead the men, they must be "dragged . . . away by main strength" from dead leads, or when they are turned loose, "thirty minutes later they were lost. Not the men lost the dogs; the dogs lost the men." When they are finally found, "their voices sounded almost like the voices of children" (281–82 / 327). Then there is a "dogeared" Tennyson, and a high occurrence of *dogged,* along with other words suggesting steadfastness. There is also a high frequency of *odor,* which suggests the relationship between the dogs, following the scent, and Hightower's "rank manodor," which makes the corners of Byron's nostrils "whiten and tauten" (282 / 328). Then there is an odd metaphor involving frustrated women who "print with a myriad small hard heels . . . periods such as perhaps *Is he still free!*" (273 / 318).

So, we have dogs, following manodor, which is the smell of feet, also called "dogs"; heels leaving prints; familiars acting like "heels" or dogs not "heeling," not following their masters; all of them going astray, just as Byron (wrongly) assumes "as though by inspiration, divination" that Hightower's smell "is the odor of goodness. Of course it would smell bad to us that are bad and sinful" (282 / 328); just as those fire truck ladders lead nowhere; just as that noise is not quite music.

When we follow the heels into John 13, where Jesus says, "He that eateth bread with me hath lifted up his heel against me," we find the same theme of the familiar world turned upside down. The central action of Jesus' washing the feet of the disciples, reflects precisely this reversal of Master and Servant.

Notice that Faulkner has not paralleled the specific action of washing feet; indeed, one of the chapter's high-frequency words is *unwashed,* from Hightower's "stale linen" and "static overflesh," which is "not often enough bathed." Although we do find words like *water, wave, tub, swim,* or *wake,* all of them are jokes: the water is for the spaniel; the sheriff is a "tub" of a man; the street "swims" from Hightower's sweat; or the "sapless trees and dehydrated lusts" being to "swim" when Hightower reads. Instead, Faulkner focuses on the thematic unity in John.

When Jesus asks to wash Peter's feet, the disciple suddenly challenges the Master: "Lord, doest thou wash my feet?" Jesus answers that Peter cannot now know his purpose, whereupon Peter retorts, "Thou shalt never wash my feet." Not until Jesus says, "If I wash thee not, thou hast no part with me," does Peter submit: "Lord, not my feet only but also my hands and my head." Then follows the Last Supper, during which Jesus announces that one at the table will betray him and gives the sop to Judas. Since "to give such a morsel at a meal was an ordinary mark of goodwill" (Cambridge 268), which instead marks a betrayal, the action is itself something of a trick, a marking of the unclean: "ye are clean, but not all," says Jesus, knowing "who should betray him."[1] Moreover, after the sop is given, Satan enters Judas and he leaves, the disciples thinking that he is going to buy food or give to the poor, another combination of business, services, and tricks against belief. And the theme of reversal by the familiar is climaxed when, after Peter vows he would lay down his life for him, Jesus says, "The cock shall not crow, till thou hast denied me thrice." Which brings us back to the noise.

Just as the metaphors in Faulkner's 13 suggest the world of familiars is reversing the familiar world, so do the episodes. The men who come "with pistols already in their pockets," looking "for someone to crucify" need only be "shown several different places where the sheet had lain" (272 / 316) to take up the cause of the "outlander," when, as "children (some of their fathers had done it too) they had called after her on the street, 'Nigger lover!'" (275 / 320), more voices in the air. Questioned, the black man knows nothing until he reverses himself, and what he finally reports is no more than what one of the white men himself knows, another reversal, and both of them worthless.

In the most treacherous reversal—the betrayal of "the master,"

In chapter 20, Hightower "sees himself offer as a sop" his martyrdom (463 / 540).

Christmas, by "the disciple," Brown—we find this amusing play with the word *turn* (and following a scent):

> "You want to turn state's evidence?" the sheriff asked him.
>
> "I dont want to turn nothing," Brown said, harsh, hoarse, a little wild in the face. "I know who done it and when I get my reward, I'll tell."
>
> "You catch the fellow that done it, and you'll get the reward," the sheriff said. So they took Brown to the jail for safekeeping. "Only, I reckon . . . as long as that thousand dollars is where he can smell it, you couldn't run him away from here." (279 / 324)

In the most benign reversal—between Hightower and Byron— we find both men are stubborn. Although Byron has come for guidance, when Hightower advises him to send Lena home, Byron reacts, "I reckon not," and he says it "immediately, with immediate finality, as if he has been waiting . . . for this to be said" (285–86 / 332). Or later, when Byron says he is only "trying to do the right thing," Hightower thinks, " 'And that . . . is the first lie he ever told me. Ever told anyone, man or woman, perhaps including himself.' He looks across the desk at the stubborn, dogged, sober face that has not yet looked at him" (289 / 336). Then Hightower abruptly changes tone, tricking:

> "Well." He speaks now with a kind of spurious brusqueness which, flabbyjowled and darkcaverneyed, his face belies. "That is settled, then. You'll take her out there, to his house, . . . then you'll tell that man—Bunch [Burch (*CT*)], Brown—that she is here."
>
> "And he'll run," Byron says. He does not look up, yet through him there seems to go a wave [wave, (*CT*)] of exultation, of triumph, before he can curb and hide it, when it is too late to try. For the moment he does not attempt to curb it; backthrust too in his hard chair, looking for the first time at the minister, with a face confident and bold and suffused. . . .
>
> "Is that what you want him to do? . . ."
>
> Byron has caught himself. His face is no longer triumphant. But he looks steadily at the older man.
>
> . . . . .
>
> "No," Hightower says. "You dont need my help. You are already being helped. . . ."

... "Helped by who?"
"By the devil," Hightower says. (289–91 / 336–38)

And this, we can assume, is an echo of Satan entering Judas, especially since when Byron returns—from shopping—he enters without stumbling, with a "new air born somewhere between assurance and defiance" (295 / 343).

Yet as usual, the theme of betrayal applies broadly. Byron betrays his master, but he also betrays himself, believing he is acting unselfishly. And when Hightower betrays Byron, tricking him into exposing that self-interest, he too betrays himself. Leaving the "odorous and cluttered store," he must "cozen" himself from the "nimbus quality" of the "familiar buildings," the "mirage," by muttering, "I have bought immunity." "I paid for it. I didn't quibble about the price." As the street "shimmers and swims," it is as if "sweat, heat, mirage, all, rushes [rush (*CT*)] fused into a finality which abrogates all logic and justification and obliterates it like fire would" (293-94 / 341).

The final odd metaphor is that fire. Not surprisingly, fire is mentioned frequently here, but so is heat, and that "emotional barbecue." But fire is central to primitive methods of purifying oneself in the presence of the dead. In language echoed by Faulkner's metaphors, Frazer explains that for the savage

> the world still teems with those motley beings whom a more sober philosophy has discarded. Fairies and goblins, ghosts and demons, still hover about him both waking and sleeping. They dog his footsteps, dazzle his senses, enter into him, harass and deceive and torment him in a thousand freakish and mischievous ways. The mishaps that befall him, the losses he sustains, the pains he has to endure, he commonly sets down, if not to the magic of his enemies, to the spite or anger or caprice of the spirits. (9.73)

Such spirits are "never bent on good." Among other tricks, they "lure hunting dogs from the trail" or "drive men crazy or into fits" (9.84). The native can trust no one, "for who knows whether his nearest neighbor, his professedly best friend, is not plotting to bring trouble, sickness, and even death on him by means of magic? Everywhere he sees snares set for him, everywhere he scents treachery and guile" (9.83). Because the air is so thick with spirits "you cannot stir without striking against one of them" (9.85), at times the native "turns fiercely on his persecutors and makes a desperate effort to chase the whole pack of them from the land, to clear the air of their swarming multitudes, that he may breathe more freely and go on his way unmolested, at least for a time. [This] clean sweep of all their troubles generally takes the form of a grand hunting out and expulsion of devils or ghosts" (9.73). In ceremonies similar to the expulsion of embodied evils (described in chapter 9), the people make a great noise, form processions, build fires, but centrally, they have a Saturnalia, in which traditional Master-Servant roles are reversed (a feature of the Roman Saturnalia [9.307]), or free speech is licensed, dogs are unchained, or the people engage in mock mourning, craving pardon to and for the dead.

Begin with the strident noises. In China, because "they believe that a beheaded man wanders about a headless spectre in the World of Shades," when "an execution takes place, the people fire crackers to frighten the headless ghost away," and the executioner is carried "over a fire lighted on the pavement," because "disembodied spirits are afraid of fire" and the living can thus shake off "the ghost who is supposed to dog their steps" (11.17). Especially helpful are bells and gongs, known from classical times to be demon-dispelling (9.246n).

Recall the sheriff's, "Turn them dogs loose" (281); on May Day in Central Europe, "Men and boys make a racket with whips, bells, pots, and pans; the women carry censers; the dogs are unchained and run barking and yelping about" (9.158–59). Recall Hightower in the "shimmering streets" with "stale linen" which is "not often enough bathed." In Frazer's discussions of washing, we read of the Incas' method of washing: "All the people, great and small, came to the doors of their houses, and with great shouts of joy and gladness shook their clothes as if they were shaking off dust, while they cried, 'Let the evils be gone.' [Then] they passed their hands over their heads, faces, arms and legs, as if in the act of washing" (9.130). Recall Byron's new, defiant air; in the annual expulsion among the people of Guinea, "a perfect lampooning liberty is allowed, and scandal so highly exalted, that they may freely sing of all the faults, villanies [*sic*], and frauds of their superiors as well as inferiors, without punishment" (9.131).

Most important is the fire. Threatened with evil, primitive man will begin again (as Faulkner's book does) by extinguishing all existing fires and ceremoniously starting one anew. Called "need-fires," they explain the chapter's high incidence of the word *need* and the otherwise unnecessary double name of *Joe* (Christmas and Brown), the fire setters, since it was thought that those who kindle the need-fire must bear the same Christian name (10.277). In fact, the old fires were extinguished and the new begun with sacred materials in the belief that the purifying fire will come "from the air," from a sacred source, like the mysteriousness of Faulkner's fire as "selfborn" (274 / 318) or "unsourceless" (275 / 320). But this "emotional barbecue" is needed not only because "the body on the sheet" must be placated, but also because the body in "stale linen" must be denied.

Chapter 14: Abiding in Many Mansions along the Way

Although it is the most "written" of the four gospels. John does have textual problems, especially in the discourses. The beginning of chapter 13, "when Jesus knew that his hour was come," signals a new narrative thrust, up to the arrest in 18, but this section includes problems such as the close of 14, where Jesus apparently ends the Last Supper, saying "Arise, let us go hence," yet continues to talk for three more chapters; or in 13 and 14, where the disciples ask, "Lord, whither goest thou?" yet in 16, Jesus complains, "None of you asketh me, Whither goest thou?" Some scholars have linguistic explanations: regarding the *quo vadis* problem, emphasizing the present tense suggests, "You *no longer* ask 'Whither goest thou'" (Anchor 710). Others have naturalistic explanations: regarding Jesus' signal to end the meal, although all arise from the table, the discourses may have been spoken before they leave or at some halting place on the way to Gethsemane (Cambridge 285–86). Others have literary or historical explanations: regarding the organization, it may incorporate material throughout Jesus' ministry suitable to this final address to the disciples (Anchor 582).

There are even stylistic explanations. For example, the convoluted organization of chapter 14 may be "an instance of the Johannine technique of overlapping, where the conclusion of one unit is the beginning of the next" (Anchor 623).

Yet such a style could reflect the chapter's theme of the Perousia, or Second Coming. Although Jesus is going away, he will return in the form of the Comforter or Advocate, when the differences between here and there will be erased: "In my father's house are many mansions," or "dwelling places" (the Latin root is closer to the French, *maison*). The places are circumscribed by the Second Coming and the singular way. Time and place collapse into one another: "In my Father's house are many mansions." "I go to prepare a place for you." "And whither I go ye know and the way ye know. . . . I am the way, the truth, and the life. . . . the words that I speak [are of] the Father that dwelleth in me. . . . he shall give you another Comforter, that he may abide with you for ever; . . . ye know him; for he dwelleth with you and shall be in you. . . . At that day ye shall know that I am in my Father, and ye in me, and I in you." Throughout the chapter, the "way" becomes a state of mind; the "place," an indwelling. The commandment is to abide, meaning both to dwell in and wait for the return, "at that day."

When we turn to the manuscript study of *Light in August*, Fadiman reports that this chapter has more paste-on slips per page than any other, and that the pages have no canceled numbers (47), which suggest the "episodes were originally written chronologically and then purposely reshuffled to create the hazy quality of Joe's trancelike state in which each day blurs into another" (49). Yet this confusion of time affects more than Joe.[2] To begin with, the first three episodes, in which the sheriff discovers Lena is living in Joe's cabin, occur well after the next eight, in which Joe appears

2. See Ficken ("Critical" 374–84) for a complete chronological listing of the events in *Light in August*.

at the church and the hunt begins. In fact, we have the phenomenon of the deputy's thinking about Brown, "If he dont get that reward, he will just die" (309 / 359), some five pages *after* he speaks
his thought to the sheriff: "If he dont get that thousand dollars, I
reckon he will just die," who promptly scuttles that notion with "I
reckon he wont" (304 / 354) before it is thought of. Actually, the
pattern in this is the circle—like the theme of the Second Coming.
Many of the episodes are circular. For example, the deputy goes to
Lena and reports back, or the sheriff trails Joe's scent to the negro
cabin and must loop back to the cottonhouse.

Such a pattern is consistent with the chapter's similar profusion
of place, for the "many mansions" include Lena's cabin, the
church, the sheriff's house, his office, the cottonhouse, the farm-
house, and the negro cabin. Still other places are mentioned gra-
tuitously: the deputy says Byron is "camped in a tent about as far
from the cabin as from here to the post-office" (302 / 351); the
sheriff says it "aint none of my house" (304 / 353); Joe remembers
"somewhere a house, a cabin. House or cabin, white or black. . . .
'It was a cabin that time'" (316–17 / 368–69). Appropriate to the
circle motif, many of the places are "rings": "The churchyard was
a pallid crescent of trampled and beaten earth, shaped and enclosed
by undergrowth and trees" (308 / 357). Or the sheriff squelches
Brown: " 'You try to keep that from slipping your mind again, then,'
he said. 'If you got any mind to even slip on you.' They were ringed
about with quiet, interested faces" (310 / 360). Then there is the
circle of Joe's whole life: "I have been further in these seven days
than in all the thirty years." "But I have never got outside that
circle. I have never broken out of the ring of what I have already
done and cannot ever undo" (321 / 373–74).

Increasingly, as that image suggests, the dwelling becomes a
state of mind, an indwelling. Joe is in "the coma state" (317 / 369).
He will be "hunted by white men at last into the black abyss"
(313 / 364). He muses on the place some children had fled from,
"as though to him they had in moving merely walked out of two
shells" (318 / 370). Indeed, he has lived his life, like the "unswimming sailor," in a closed system, which is both familiar and foreign: "It is as though he desires to see his native earth in all its

phases for the first or the last time. He had grown to manhood in the country, where like the unswimming sailor his physical shape and his thought had been molded by its compulsions without his learning anything about its actual shape and feel. For a week now he has lurked and crept among its secret places, yet he remained a foreigner to the very immutable laws which earth must obey" (320 / 372). And increasingly, as *that* powerful image suggests, the elements of time and place collapse into each other: "When he thinks about time, it seems to him now that for thirty years he has lived inside an orderly parade of named and numbered days like fence pickets, and that one night he went to sleep and when he waked up he was outside of them" (313–14 / 364–65). "Time, the spaces of light and dark, had long since lost orderliness. It would be either one now, seemingly at an instant, between two movements of the eyelids, without warning" (315 / 367). Although we might expect a hunted man to worry about place, Joe is obsessed with determining the day, like "that day": "That night a strange thing came into his mind. . . . He found that he was trying to calculate the day of the week. It was as though now and at last he had an actual and urgent need to strike off the accomplished days toward some purpose, some definite day or act, without either falling short or overshooting" (317 / 369). Time has become Joe's environment, and when the days are "accomplished," he will get back to the road, the way, which leads to his return.[3]

Relating this to *The Golden Bough*, we find Joe is here in a condition for which Faulkner would find apt material in primitive societies. Because he has committed a murder, he is tabooed. Just as chapter 13 dealt with communal purification rites, here we find individual purification rites for mourners, manslayers and handlers of the dead and even those who, as strangers, carry the spirits of the dead. First and foremost, the tabooed person must be kept apart from the community, living in the woods or fields or special huts; he has special strictures about feeding himself or eating with oth-

---

3. That Joe's surrender to the role of scapegoat represents a "return" to the human race is reflected in Faulkner's comment that because Joe had never known what he was, he was forced "to repudiate mankind, to live outside the human race. And he tried to do that but nobody would let him, the human race itself wouldn't let him" (*Faulkner in the Univ.* 118).

ers; and he may return to the community only after he has purified himself by lighting firebrands, taking emetics, washing in streams, or shaving.

Often such rites begin with the sound of a gun: opening the church door, Joe "apparently grasped it by the knob and hurled it back into the wall so that the sound crashed into the blended voices like a pistol shot" (305 / 354). The violence is justified because Joe is entering as a stranger into the negro world, and for one tribe, headhunters entering enemy territory "may not eat any fruits which the foe has planted nor any animal which he has reared until they have first committed an act of hostility" (3.111). Similarly, it is to neutralize the spirits of the dead that the woman runs toward Joe, screaming, "It's the devil"; that Joe knocks the church leaders about; that he leaps into the pulpit, cursing and yelling; and that he lights a cigarette and waves it toward the circle of blacks in the brush. A tribe in New Guinea, at the appearance of a strange ship, "shook and knocked their idols about in order to ward off ill-luck" (3.104), while among the Eskimos, "when a stranger arrives at an encampment, the sorcerer goes out to meet him. The stranger folds his arms and inclines his head to one side, so as to expose his cheek, upon which the magician deals a terrific blow, sometimes felling him to the ground. Next the sorcerer in his turn presents his cheek to the smiter and receives a buffet from the stranger." (3.108). Travelers among some Indian tribes reported that the medicine man, "standing in the middle of the circle of lodges," would suddenly confront them and yell "in a sing-song, nasal tone, a string of unintelligible words" (3.105). And Joe's cigarette may be fancifully imagined in one description of the tribe's "devil-man," who puts "a small green twig into his mouth" and then draws it "from his mouth—this was extracting the evil spirit—after which he blew violently, as if to speed it away" (3.104–5). Or it could reflect the custom in Australia when one tribe visits another, "the strangers carry lighted bark or burning sticks in their hands, for the purpose, they say, of clearing and purifying the air" (3.109).[4]

---

4. Slatoff (185), Cottrell (209), and Holman (160) all relate Joe's behavior in the church to Christ's cleansing of the temple. Indeed, the Christian context also suggests that the old gods must be knocked about upon the entrance of the new.

Another parallel arises with the "shell" image, especially Joe's *"I am tired of running of having to carry my life like it was a basket of eggs"* (319 / 371). Among the Kayans of Borneo, local demons are propitiated by making "an offering of fowls' eggs, which . . . are carried from the house, sometimes for distances so long that the devotion of the travellers is more apparent than their presents to the spirits of the land" (3.110).

Most important, these customs are also appropriate to those tabooed by contact with the recent dead. For example, "among the Maoris any one who had handled a corpse, helped to convey it to the grave, or touched a dead man's bones, was cut off from all intercourse and almost all communication with mankind. He could not enter any house, or come into contact with any person or thing, without utterly bedevilling them" (3.138). Kept for society's defiling tasks, this man was like an Untouchable: "Twice a day a dole of food would be thrown on the ground before him to munch . . . without the use of his hands; and at night, huddling his greasy tatters about him, he would crawl into some miserable lair of leaves and refuse, where, dirty, cold, and hungry, he passed, in broken ghost-haunted slumbers, a wretched night as a prelude to another wretched day" (3.139). Similarly, the widower in New Guinea "becomes a social outcast, an object of fear and horror, shunned by all. He may not cultivate a garden, nor shew himself in public, nor traverse the village, nor walk on the roads and paths. Like a wild beast he must skulk in the long grass and the bushes; and if he sees or hears any one coming, especially a woman, he must hide behind a tree or a thicket" (3.144). Like Joe, carrying his razor, this man must carry a weapon "to defend himself, not only against wild boars in the jungle, but against the dreaded spirit of his departed spouse, who would do him an ill turn if she could (3.144–45).

Since the primitive warrior is in "spiritual quarantine" both before and after victory (3.157), Joe will behave here as in chapter 5, where he was preparing to kill. He will live in the brush, just as returning Ovambo warriors of southern Africa must first spend the night in the open fields (3.176). Or he will have food placed before him, "appearing suddenly between long, limber black hands fleeing too in the act of setting down the dishes" (317 / 368), just as the Pima warrior will be "waited on by an old woman, who brings him his scanty dole of food" (3.182).

Almost universally, the end of the quarantine is signaled by a cleansing. For some, this involves taking emetics. Like Joe's eating "the rotten fruit, the hard corn, chewing it slowly, tasting nothing . . . with resultant crises of bleeding flux" (316 / 368), so a killer from a British East African tribe "must purify himself by taking a strong purge made from the bark of the segetet tree and by drinking goat's milk mixed with blood" (3.175). Or like Joe's washing and shaving in the stream before he turns himself in,[5] so among certain peoples of Assam, the family of a deceased, must, after three days, bathe, shave, and be sprinkled with holy water (3.285).

Also common is the use of circles. With some, the tribe encircles the offender (3.182); with others, the offenders crouch in a circle to be purified (3.176); in still others, the manslayer must return "to bathe as near as possible to the spot where the man was killed" (3.179). This probably reflects the widespread belief that a ring acts as both a spiritual fetter and a spiritual bar, so that some mourners creep through rings of brush to leave behind the dangerous spirits of the dead (11.177n). Yet if Joe has never broken out of the ring, he may be the subject of this "return": "To bring back a runaway slave an Arab . . . will trace a magic circle on the ground, stick a nail in the middle of it, and attach a beetle by a thread to the nail, taking care that the sex of the beetle is that of the fugitive. As the beetle crawls round and round, it will coil the thread about the nail, thus shortening its tether and drawing nearer to the centre at every circuit. So by virtue of homeopathic magic the runaway slave will be drawn back to his master" (1.152).

In any case, purification rites belong to most societies. It is no coincidence that Joe's movements in this chapter 14 suggest the fourteen stations of the cross for the church penitent. Biblical commentators note several traditions behind the "many mansions." In one, they correspond to "different degrees of human merit," so in the next world there will be many abodes, "good for the good; evil

5. That this is a cleansing ritual was observed by Roberts (147) and Kerr (122).

for evil" (International 531). In another, they represent heavenly resting places for the just, as opposed to "the souls of the wicked who cannot enter into habitations and must wander" (Anchor 625).

Thus, Joe's strange behavior in this chapter is not only justifiable, it is worthy. He has been given the role of fallen man, seeking salvation, performing the fourteen stations of the cross, in a pre-Cross, circular world. But having made his peace with God, Joe will reenter the world of man, now prepared to reenact Christ's break into linear time.

Meanwhile, even the close of his wanderings is described in circular terms. With the end of the Last Supper ("Arise, let us go hence"), signaled by Joe's last day, when he "rises" (317 / 369), at peace, because he "dont have to bother about having to eat anymore" (320 / 372),[6] the "ineradicable" gauge, the "black tide" is now "creeping up his legs, moving from his feet upward as death moves" (321 / 374).

Chapter 15: Firstfruit Processions from the True Vine

As part of her theory that the Christmas flashback was conceived after the present-time narrative, Fadiman shows that the manuscript chapters 15 through 18 were originally ordered and grouped differently.[7] She believes that the changes may account for the book's "inconsistencies and contradictions," which were not deliberate, although the book's "ambiguities" were, and she reconciles Faulkner's "scrupulous attention to the most minute detail" with his overlooking "several minor discrepancies on the novel's factual level" (193), by suggesting that fact is not fiction, which is of a higher order.

But it is possible that Faulkner's attention to detail would have

6. R. G. Collins ("*Light*" 107–8), suggests that the food served Joe in the Negro cabin may have represented the Last Supper, as does Slatoff (186), who also links Joe's being "at peace."

7. Fadiman (191). She suggests that originally 15 was joined with 16 (55) and followed 12 (130), and that 17 and 18 were once units (201).

included a blurring of facts, particularly in this discourse section, where, in John, "different subjects are not kept apart, but are continually crossing and entangling one another" (Cambridge 173). That Faulkner was responding to this "entangling" can be seen in his repetition of John's theme of bearing, discussed in my chapter 4.

The same discussion showed Faulkner using dictional clues to make precise distinctions among chapters, especially in the various nicknames given Hines. Here we should note that "Hines," an early form of *hind*, meant "farm steward," before it meant "rustic," and that "Eupheus" means "well-grown." Hearing these names first in chapter 15 is appropriate because John 15 begins: "I am the true vine, and my Father is the husbandman. Every branch in me that beareth not fruit he taketh away: and every branch that beareth fruit, he purgeth it, that it may bring forth more fruit. . . . I am the vine, ye are the branches: He that abideth in me, and I in him, the same bringeth forth much fruit." "If a man abide not in me, he is cast forth as a branch, and is withered; and men gather them, and cast them into the fire, and they are burned."

Although this theme emphasizes the organic relationship of Jesus with his disciples (Moffatt 287), the husbanding metaphor shifts, and the chapter has been the source of much discussion, especially Jesus' promise that he will send the Comforter, or "the Spirit of truth, which proceedeth from the Father." Known as "the Eternal Procession" (from the Latin *procedere*, meaning "to go forward"), these words have prompted "the much-debated question of the 'procession' of the Spirit from the Father, or Son, or both" (Moffatt 294), a major difference between the Roman and the Eastern churches.

Faulkner gives us processions, and he makes Hines both the vine, Joe's source, and the husbandman, who will seek to purge it, attacking Joe with a "withered branch": a "heavy piece of hand-peeled hickory" (324 / 377). Hines is both the source of Joe's tragedy and its outcome; the problem Hines fathered is the father of his own madness, of his whole obsessive life. Examining the chapter's themes will illuminate this dual relationship.

Although the themes of smallness and craziness were begun in chapter 6, where Hines was introduced, in 15 they come together in some remarkable ways. The Hineses are "a little touched—lonely, gray in color, a little smaller than most other men and women" (322 / 375). "He is "a frail little old man with the light, frail bones of a child" (326 / 380), and "a little crazed" (322 / 375), or "pure crazy," "like somebody that had done slipped away from a crazy house" (332 / 387), or "crazy, touched by God," or even like God, "His doings also a little inexplicable" (325 / 379). Hearing that Hines was "a little upset," the heat "a little too much for him," is Mrs. Hines, who is "low built," a "dumpy, fat little woman" (327 / 381), "just tall enough to see over the counter, so that she didn't look like she had any body at all" "like the Katzenjammer kids in the funny paper" (335 / 390). But the Hineses inhabit a diminutive world: besides living in a "small bungalow" (322 / 375), they sit on "little stools" (340 / 396) at the "little cafe" (339 / 395), and even the sheriff's voice, at one point, sounds "little, like a doll's voice" (336 / 392).

The union of these chapters comes from Frazer. In chapter 6, because John's theme is feeding the multitude, Faulkner's material from Frazer deals with the sacramental firstfruit ceremonies in which, at harvest, bread may be shaped into little figures and eaten sacramentally. In chapter 15, because John's theme is purging or husbanding the first fruit of the vine, Faulkner's material from Frazer deals with sacrificial firstfruit ceremonies in which, also at harvest, offerings are made to little gods or to ancestor figures themselves. Although Frazer says "it is not always possible to draw a sharp line between the sacrament and the sacrifice of first fruits" (8.109), the distinction Faulkner made follows John. John 6 presents the feeding of the multitude; John 15 presents the "Eternal Processions." So Faulkner's 6 emphasizes eucharistic eating, while 15 emphasizes offertory processions.

Offertory processions occur in the present and the past. Just as "Hines went on foot about the county, holding revival services in negro churches," so "negro women carrying what were obviously dishes of food would be seen entering from the rear the house where the couple lived, and emerging emptyhanded." And this act of "charity" the town would "slough"—the repeated word suggests pruning—even though "some of the dishes and pans had in all like-lihood been borne intact from white kitchens where the women cooked" (323 / 376). Then various people must "hold" or "tote" Uncle Doc, as "prisoner" or like "a small threshing hose in which the pressure is too great for its size" (326 / 380). And when he is carried home, the men "lifted him bodily from the car and carried him through the gate and up the walk of rotting bricks and shards of concrete, to the steps" (327 / 380–81). His wife leads him to a chair, indeed, leads him throughout the rest of the chapter ("Uncle Doc following her like a dog would" [339 / 395]), after she finds him downtown again, bludgeoning "the captive" with his "big walking stick," and after she has "dressed up" and put the plume on her head, which the folks of the town, telling the story, follow by eye, even at night in the train station. And of course, the main procession involves the twice-told story of the "captive," Joe Christmas, who is led through the lines of townspeople and briefly confronted by the plumed Mrs. Hines. Moreover, a manuscript fragment, evidently written and lost before the extant complete one, includes still more repetitions of these motifs of processions, smallness, and particularly of sticks.[8]

---

8. "It was his right, he claimed. They couldn't make anything out of what he was [saying] trying to say, what he meant: a little old dirty man shaking that big walking stick like he would hit them the same as he had tried to hit that nigger and crazy in the face as a bedbug, until there was some talk about locking him up [too] with the nigger; when that woman came up. Nobody knowed who she was at first. They didn't even know it was his wife. Except for them nigger women they say carry pans of food into their back door, there wasn't a dozen folks in Mottstown that ever saw her until she come up behind old Doc where he was [waving that] shouting and waving that stick; and we turned and saw that little old woman in a sunbonnet and an umbrella. She walked up and she says, 'Eupheus'. Like that. 'Eupheus.' And him turning on her with his mouth still open and his eyes looking like two little wheels and that stick lifted like he was going to hit her too. And she walked up to him and took him by the arm and led him to a chair that was in the door of Bird's store and set him in it like a baby. 'You stay here,' she says, not loud; not louder than if she was talking to herself, and she went on without looking back. She went right to the jail and walked right in and says, 'I want to see him.' She wouldn't tell them what for nor nothing. And she wouldn't go away and she didn't seem mad nor nothing. She just said, 'I want to see him,' and they said, '[*cancelled word*] Do you know him?' But she wouldn't say, and so they let her go up and she went to the cell door and looked thru the grating at him. He was setting on the cot, and she just looked

Now consider Frazer's descriptions of firstfruit sacrifices to ancestor gods. Repeatedly, the ancestors are represented by images or puppets, often dressed up as little men and women; or by miniature houses, small pieces of land, or little altars, on which offerings are burnt. The A-Kamba of British East Africa "build miniature huts at the foot of the trees for the accommodation of the ghosts" (8.113). Or in Malay, the ancestors are "household deities; some of them reside in pots in the corners of the houses; and miniature houses, standing near the family dwelling, are especially sacred to them" (8.124). In the East Indies, one harvest festival includes placing food before two figures dressed to represent the ancestors in the clothes of a man and a woman (8.122). Or in the Tonga Islands, a small piece of land is fenced in to grow yams for the firstfruit ceremonies, during which men and women, "ornamented with red ribbons" and "armed with spears and clubs," stay up all night before they bring their offerings in procession (8.129–32). Also appropriate is the killing of divine ancestor animals, especially birds and bears, as the Hineses are called (339 / 395 & 348 / 406), with honoring processions (8.192), caging, decorating with feathers (8.207–8) and with sacred sticks (8.189).

Remember, Jesus speaks of burning the withered branches. One Faulkner passage mentions smoke and matches and a traditional offering: vowing to protect Christmas, the sheriff says, "You better smoke that for a while," whereupon someone shouts, "He aint worth any thousand dollars to us. He aint worth a thousand dead matches to us," all of them knowing that no one would "see enough of that thousand dollars to fat a calf" (336 / 391–92). Fire sticks are part of many firstfruit ceremonies. In Gaudalcanar, after processions to the beach, "half-a-dozen tiny altars" were made from dry sticks on which were placed offerings (8.126). Fire sticks can themselves be ancestor deities; the Herero make "holy fires" from two sacred sticks representing the male ancestor and his wife (2.223–24).

---

in at him [w] a minute, not saying nothing. Then she turned and come on away. She come on back to Bird's store, where Doc was still setting in the chair like she had left him. She didn't even stop. She just says, 'Come on home,' and he got up and followed her." (Deborah Thompson 479–80)

Furthermore, all of these ancestral ceremonies go back to the most primitive firstfruit offertory, reflected in Hines's insistent, "Kill the Bastard!" namely, the widespread practice of offering "all male firstlings, whether of man or beast" (4.172), in the belief that, as with pruning, the first growth must be cut so that the whole plant will be stronger. We will read more on this in chapter 19, when the "captive" is actually killed.

But what about the craziness, the theme that went with the smallness? In fact, the two themes join in the Manii, discussed briefly in chapter 6. That the Roman *maniae*, the firstfruit loaves baked in the shape of men, were connected to the proverb about Diana's grove, "There are many Manii at Aricia," had puzzled Frazer in his opening pages. One tradition said the founder was Manius Egerius, linked as well to the grove's lesser divinity, Egeria (whose name means "to vomit" or "discharge"), goddess of a profaned "dark cavern" (1.18), whose function was to succor "women in travail" (1.41). Another referred to the "ugly and deformed people at Aricia, and they derived the name Manius from *Mania*, a bogey or bugbear to frighten children," while a Roman satirist thought it referred to "the beggars who lay in wait for pilgrims in the Arician slopes" (1.22). Eight volumes later, in a chapter on "Eating the God," Frazer conjectures that the proverb belongs to an earlier, ruder time: *Mania* (the Latin for "ashes of the dead") is also the name of the "Mother or Grandmother of Ghosts" to whom effigies were hung on doors for "ghosts of the dead," hoping that, "either out of good nature or through simple inadvertence, they would carry off the effigies at the door instead of the living people in the house" (8.94–95).

The connections with these themes are striking. In 6, Hines is living in a "backwater" (118 / 139), while here the Hineses live "in the slack backwater of their lonely isolation" (323 / 377) or in "that little house dark and small and rankly-odored as a cave" (329 / 383). Mrs. Hines, "with a face like that of a drowned corpse" (330 / 384) or "like dirty and unovened dough" (327 / 381), succoring both Milly and Lena in their "travail," would be the Mother or Grandmother of Ghosts, while Hines always at the "sootgrimed doorway" (118 / 139), is like a bugbear to the child, Joe. In chapter

16, both become effigies, even dead ones, as we shall see. Meantime, here, Faulkner is up to his old modernist tricks, making the *mania* into the maniac (as Hines is called) and his crazy wife.

Chapter 16: Bearing the Dead to the Comforter and Judge

"They shall put you out of the synagogues: yea, the time cometh, that whosoever killeth you will think that he doeth God service." This dramatic opening to John 16, foretelling persecution unto death, contrasts with similar passages in the synoptics, which mention only beatings.[9] John's closing verses also speak of persecution and of Jesus' rejection: "Ye shall be scattered, every man to his own, and shall leave me alone."

In Faulkner's chapter 16, Hightower, himself turned out of the church, hears its music of "crucifixions" and "death," then the stories of Hines's persecution unto death of Joe's father and mother, and he ends up rejecting Byron's petition, screaming, "Get out of my house!"

John likens the persecution to a woman delivering a child: "Ye shall be sorrowful, but your sorrow shall be turned into joy. A woman when she is in travail hath sorrow, because her hour is come: but as soon as she is delivered of the child, she remembereth no more the anguish, for joy that a man is born into the world." In light of this metaphor, Faulkner might have used chapter 16 to recount the birth of Lena's child; the word *travail* will be used in 17, in connection with her labor (384 / 448). Instead he separates her *travail* (meaning "work") from the *suffering* (a frequent word here) caused by the births in this chapter. Centrally, there is Milly's bearing Joe, which causes Hines to say, "My wife has bore me a whore" (356 / 416), calling her a "whore's dam" (358 / 417). And

---

9. "For they will deliver you up to the councils, and they will scourge you in their synagogues" (Matthew 10:17). "For they shall deliver you up to the councils; and in the synagogues ye shall be beaten" (Mark 13:9). "They shall lay their hands on you, and persecute you, delivering you up to the synagogues, and into prisons" (Luke 21:12).

then Hightower thinks of the Sunday service as purging the week's disasters before "the next week and its whatever disasters not yet born" (346–47 / 404). Listening to the music, he hears "the apotheosis of . . . his own environed blood: that people from which he sprang" (347 / 405). Then Byron tells him, "You were given your choice before I was born, and you took it before I or her or him either was born" (345 / 402). Then Mrs. Hines says, "Eupheus, it's the devil . . . that's quicking you" (352 / 411). But the ideas of suffering and giving birth in the word *bearing* are most dramatic in her description of what she has borne: "For more than fifty years . . . I have suffered it. . . . On the very night that Milly was born, he was locked up in jail for fighting. That's what I have bore and suffered. . . . I told him . . . the devil was in him. . . . after Milly was born . . . that him being locked up in a jail on the very hour and minute of his daughter's birth was the Lord's own token" (352 / 410).

In John, the theme of bearing relating to Jesus' death ("I have yet many things to say unto you, but ye cannot bear them now") is also linked with the coming of the Comforter, who will judge and guide the disciples "into all truth." Likewise, in Faulkner, the theme of bearing is linked with death, and with a guide and comforter who will bring all to truth and judgment. The themes come together in his use of Frazer.

There are two kindred European ceremonies simulating the death of a divine being: Burying the Carnival on Shrove Tuesday and Carrying Out Death on "Dead Sunday." In both, to the accompaniment of music or weeping, crowds, often begging, carry or lead through the streets some sort of straw or puppet effigy which they then burn, bury, or toss in water. In Normandy, "a squalid effigy scantily clothed in rags, a battered old hat crushed down on his dirty face, his great round paunch stuffed with straw, represented the disreputable old rake who after a long course of dissipation was now about to suffer for his sins." To the drumming of pots and blowing of horns, this effigy was promenaded, occasionally halting while "a champion of morality accused the broken-down old sinner of all the excesses he had committed and for which he was now about to be burned alive." Or at Saint-Lô, before it was thrown in the local river, "the ragged effigy of Shrove Tuesday was followed by his widow, a big burly lout dressed as a woman with a crape veil, who emitted sounds of lamentation and woe in a stentorian voice" (4.228). Or in Provence, an effigy was led by a procession of judges, barristers, and mourners: "After a formal trial he is sentenced to death amid the groans of the mob; the barrister who defended him embraces his client for the last time: the officers of justice do their duty: the condemned is set with his back to a wall and hurried into eternity under a shower of stones. The sea or a river receives his mangled remains" (4.226). The Swabian form of this custom involved "a straw-man, called the Shrovetide Bear" (4.230), similar to the Wurmlingen "Carnival Fool," a man in straw, who is led about the village by a rope as a bear, dancing to a flute, before he is "carried out of the village to the sound of drums and mournful music and buried in a field" (4.231–32). In another version, called "Sawing the Old Woman," an old woman

> was drawn through the streets on a cart, attended by two men dressed [to resemble a] religious order whose function it was to attend and console prisoners condemned to death. A scaffold was erected in a public square; the old woman mounted it, and two mock executioners proceeded, amid a storm of huzzas and hand-clapping, to saw through her neck, or rather through a bladder of blood which had been previously fitted to it. The blood gushed out and the old woman pretended to swoon and die. (4.240)

Elsewhere "a man dressed as a woman in black clothes is carried on a litter or bier by four men; he is lamented over by men disguised as women in black clothes, then thrown down before the village dung-heap, drenched with water, buried in the dung-heap, and covered with straw" (4.231). Finally, the modern form of this custom, the New Orleans Mardi Gras or "fat Tuesday" (central to *Pylon*), includes mechanized effigies from which come loud, recorded voices.

This mechanization, the squalid effigies (bear or straw), the music and lamentations, the bearing of the dead, the begging petitions, and rejections, the moral harangue and trial, even the final burying, sawing, and dousing, all may be found in Faulkner's chapter 16, and as usual, in some surprising ways.

Consider the effigies, mechanical or not. To Hightower, the Hineses look "interchangeable . . . like two bears." They enter "with something puppetlike about them, as if they were operated by clumsy springwork. The woman appears to be the more assured, or at least the more conscious, of the two of them. It is as though, for all her frozen and mechanically moved inertia, she had come for some definite purpose" (348–49 / 406–7). The image is explicit when Gavin Stevens later says that she was "like an effigy with a mechanical voice being hauled about on a cart by that fellow Bunch and made to speak when he gave the signal" (422 / 492–93). And Hines is actually straw: "I think she came here just to watch that old man, lest he be the straw that started the hurricane" (421 / 491).

For both, the mechanization and the puppetry are associated with their speaking. When Mrs. Hines pauses, her "harsh, droning voice dies" (the various forms of "dying" occur here with high frequency), after which "the still, stonefaced woman . . . begins to speak again, without moving, almost without lip movement, as if she were a puppet and the voice that of a ventriloquist in the next room" (359 / 418). From a "dead voice" comes sudden noises: "Her voice is sudden and deep, almost harsh, though not loud. It is as though she had not expected to make so much noise when she spoke. . . . Again the voice ceases, dies harshly though still not raised, as though of its own astonishment. It is as if the three words were some automatic impediment which her voice cannot pass" (350 / 408). When Mrs. Hines stops, her voice "is on a falling inflection, as if the machine had run down in midrecord" (353 / 411). Likewise, Hines interrupts with "startling suddenness," and when he stops, "his tone does not drop at all. His voice just stops, exactly like when the needle is lifted from a phonograph record by the hand of someone who is not listening to the record" (351 / 409).

The music itself becomes one of many petitions in the chapter, this one for crucifixion and death:

> The organ strains come rich and resonant . . . with that quality of abjectness and sublimation, as if the freed voices themselves were assuming the shapes and attitudes of crucifixions, ecstatic, solemn, and profound in gathering volume. Yet even then the music has still

a quality stern and implacable, deliberate and without passion so much as immolation, pleading, asking, for not love, not life, forbidding it to others, demanding in sonorous tones death as though death were the boon, like all Protestant music. (347 / 404–5)

Thinking of their pleasure-denied lives, Hightower asks, "*Why should not their religion drive them to crucifixion of themselves and one another?*" In the music he hears "the declaration and dedication of that which they know that on the morrow they will have to do" (347–48 / 405), and the "morrow's" crucifixion involves both a drenching and a "dying salute": "It seems to him that the past week has rushed like a torrent and that the week to come, which will begin tomorrow, is the abyss, and that now on the brink of cataract the stream has raised a single blended and sonorous and austere cry, not for justification but as a dying salute before its own plunge, and not to any god but to the doomed man in the barred cell within hearing of them and of the two other churches, and in whose crucifixion they too will raise a cross" (348 / 405–6).

The actual bearing of the dead takes many forms. In the opening description, Byron sees "a canvas deck chair, mended and faded and sagged so long to the shape of Hightower's body that even when empty it seems to hold still in ghostly embrace the owner's obese shapelessness; approaching, Byron thinks how the mute chair evocative of disuse and supineness and shabby remoteness from the world, is somehow the symbol and the being too of the man himself" (342 / 399). Extraordinarily, Hightower's face is described as if his nose were carrying something sagging and dead: "His mouth is open, the loose and flabby flesh sagging away from the round orifice in which the stained lower teeth show, and from the still fine nose which alone age, the defeat of sheer years, has not changed. Looking down at the unconscious face, it seems to Byron as though the whole man were fleeing away from the nose which holds invincibly to something yet of pride and courage above the sluttishness of vanquishment like a forgotten flag above a ruined fortress" (343 / 400). When Hightower listens to the gathering crowd of churchgoers, among them is the dead Miss Carruthers: "*Now they are gathering, approaching along streets [along the street (CT)] slowly and turning in, greeting one another: the*

groups, the couples, the single ones. There is a little informal talk-
ing in the church itself, lowtoned, the ladies constant and a little
sibilant with fans, nodding to arriving friends as they pass in the
aisle. Miss Carruthers (she was his organist and she has been dead
almost twenty years) *is among them; soon she will rise and enter*
the organloft" (346 / 403–4). But the most significant bearing of
the dead comes from Byron and the Hineses, carrying the stories
of Joe's dead parents. That Joe's father was from the circus makes
him a Carnival figure; when he is killed, he is cast down into the
mud. Even this "real" death is promptly made symbolic, for when
Byron finishes speaking, at once Mrs. Hines speaks "in the same
dead, level tone: the two voices in monotonous strophe and antis-
trophe: two bodiless voices recounting dreamily something performed in a region without dimension by people without blood"
(355 / 414–15).

The moral harangues from Hines are obvious. Besides his ser-
mons at the prayer meetings and the orphanage, Hines lectures
Milly and his wife, reading to her "out of the Bible, loud, without
nobody there to hear it but me, reading and hollering loud out of
the Bible like he believed I didn't believe what it said" (360 / 420).
But others also lecture. Crying, Hightower lectures Byron, calling
him "the guardian of public weal and morality. The gainer, the in-
heritor of rewards" (344 / 401). Byron lectures Hightower: "But you
are a man of God. You cant dodge that" (344 / 402), while Hightower's reply (setting aside the confusing pronouns) encapsulates the
theme of persecution in God's service: "I am not a man of God.
And not through my own desire. Remember that. Not of my own
choice that I am no longer a man of God. It was by the will, the
more than behest, of them like you and like her and like him in
the jail yonder and like them who put him there to do their will
upon, as they did upon me, with insult and violence upon those
who like them were created by the same God and were driven by
them to do that which they now turn and rend them for having
done it" (345 / 402).

To be sure, it is difficult to know how some motifs should be
applied. For instance, stones and rocks are found here widely. Mrs.
Hines is "glacierlike, like something made of stone and painted"

(349 / 407), and she is "immobile," or "stone-faced," or she has the "stonevisaged patience of a waiting rock" (365), while all but the old man are, at one point, still as "three rocks above a beach, above ebbtide" (361 / 421). Although stones have many primitive uses, since these are usually "patient" or "waiting," they may refer to the New Caledonians' painted stones, "kept in the burial-grounds, as if to saturate them with the powerful influence of the ancestors; they are brought from the cemetery to be buried in the fields or at the foot of trees for the sake of quickening the fruits of the earth, and they are restored to the cemetery when they have discharged this duty" (1.163–64).

Consider now what happens to these characters. Since, by chapter's end, "Byron alone seems to possess life" (366 / 426), the other three characters, dead, are all representations of the Carnival and must suffer some ritual death. Hines is exploded or burned: after he begins his harangue with "a quality latent and explosive" (349 / 407), he has "a spent quality like a charred wick of a candle from which the flame has been violently blown away" (365–66 / 426). Mrs. Hines begins as "immobile" or "stonefaced," and since her story is followed by Hines, who seems to "flux" between alertness and coma, who is "incredibly old, incredibly dirty" and whose harangue about the Lord's will a-working is about "outrage" and "abomination" and "desecration" and "polluting the earth," she must be the ancestral stone that is buried in his dung.

We might have expected her to parallel the sawn Old Woman, yet, amusingly perverse, Faulkner saved this for Hightower. First of all, as the others "sit facing him; almost like a jury," he looks "like an awkward beast tricked and befooled of the need for flight, brought now to bay by those who tricked and fooled it" (365 / 426). Second, Byron thinks, *You'd think they had done got swapped somewhere. Like it was him that had a nigger grandson waiting to be hung*" (367 / 428), as if Hightower is taking the old woman's place. Then Byron becomes his consoler, as Hightower complains: "Ah. Commiseration?. . . Commiseration for me, or for Byron? Come; out with it. . . . I have known that all along. Ah, Byron, Byron. What a dramatist you would have made" (368 / 429). "Or maybe you mean a drummer," says Byron, meaning "salesman," but he uses a word suitable to the ceremonies.

Now appropriate to his being a sacrificial victim, which must evidence the indwelling god (1.384), Hightower starts to quiver and shake, while Byron begins doing something stranger. He sits with his hand on his lap, "the thumb and forefinger of which rub slowly together with a kneading motion" (366 / 426). Even when he stands, leaning on the desk, his "slow hand . . . moves, preoccupied and trivial. . . . slow and ceaseless" (369 / 430). Moreover, while Hightower's voice is sharp, high, or shrill, Mrs. Hines's voice is "rusty," and what she says is "I never *saw* him when he could walk and talk. Not for thirty years I never *saw* him" (367 / 428, italics mine). But the most convincing evidence that these details are meant to suggest that some part of Hightower is being sawn away by a combination of Byron's urging and Mrs. Hines's immobility is that when Byron's hand stops, Hightower's awful self-awareness is signaled by falling flesh: Byron thinks, *"It aint me he is shouting at. It's like he knows there is something nearer him than me to convince of that* Because now Hightower is shouting 'I wont do it! I wont!' with his hands raised and clenched, his face sweating, his lip lifted upon his clenched and rotting teeth from about which the long sagging of flabby and puttycolored flesh falls away" (370 / 431). Such a suggestion is valid only because it supports the story itself: by marking Hightower as "just an old man who has been fortunate enough to grow old without having to learn the despair of love" (369–70 / 431), Byron and Mrs. Hines painfully expose why this man is like Death. And so, appropriately, the chapter ends with his drenching. Sweating, Hightower falls forward, "his bald head and his extended and clench-fisted arms lying full in the pool of light from the shaded lamp," while all outdoors continues the music: "Beyond the open window the sound of the insects has not ceased, not faltered."

Chapter 17: Naming the Beast by Priestly Prayer

In chapter 16 the ceremony of Carrying Out Death ended with a burial or drenching to promote fecundity. Naming the dead or telling their story (as the Hineses do) accomplishes the same purpose. Many tribes "whirl bullroarers in the fields and call out the names of the dead" to make the crops thrive (7.104). Among the Kai, "when the newly planted fruits are budding," legends are told and the types of yams are mentioned, along with the names of "the powerful beings who first created the fruits of the earth" (7.102–3). So the narratives in 16 (with Hines as bullroarer) will help to bring in the new life which opens chapter 17, the birth of Lena's baby.

But in contrast to the beneficent naming in 16, in 17 we are in such sacred areas that naming will be dodged, misspoken, or ta-booed. The birth of Lena's baby at dawn is a paradigm for a number of "dawnings." For the Hineses, it is the rebirth of Joey, amid much "dumb and furious terror" (380 / 444). For Hightower, it is a rebirth "of purpose and pride" (383 / 447), along with the ability to pray when he realizes Byron has left; while to Lena this same moment represents the dawning knowledge that she wants Byron to stay. As for Byron, it is only at the birth of Lena's baby that he fully realizes that Lena is not a virgin, that Lucas is the true father. Such "dawn-ings" are painful; insights do not come easily nor are they always welcome. Primitive man supposes they come only to the divine or "incarnate human gods."

As Frazer conceptualizes it, primitive man starts in a spiritual democracy in which all are governed by sympathetic magic: like cause produces like effect. But as knowledge grows, man begins to realize "the vastness of nature and his own littleness," and "as his old sense of equality with the gods slowly vanishes, he resigns at the same time the hope of directing the course of nature by his own unaided resources, that is, by magic, and looks more and more to the gods." During this stage, "sacrifice and prayer are the re-source of the pious and enlightened portion of the community, while magic is the refuge of the superstitious and ignorant." But as man comes to see the world as a "system of impersonal forces act-ing in accordance with fixed and invariable laws" (an idea which had not "dawned or darkened" his life), magic is reborn because it shares with science the belief in cause and effect (1.373–74).[10]

Incarnate human gods belong to the first stage of religion in

10. Regarding this schematization, Frazer says "doubtless" this course of devel-opment has "varied greatly in different societies" (1.421).

which gods, men, and animals are still beings of the same order. Anyone could be god-possessed. When the incarnation is temporary, the person has supernatural knowledge rather than supernatural power, meaning he or she can perform "divination and prophecy rather than miracles." But "when the divine spirit has permanently taken up its abode in a human body, the god-man is usually expected to vindicate his character by working miracles," although "miracles are not yet considered breaches of natural law. Not conceiving the existence of natural law, primitive man cannot conceive a breach of it. A miracle is to him merely an unusually striking manifestation of a common power" (1.376–77).

When possession comes about, the human personality "lies in abeyance, the presence of the spirit is revealed by convulsive shiverings and shakings of the man's whole body, by wild gestures and excited looks" (1.377). One eyewitness reported that "when the priestess sat beside the sick man, with her head covered by a cloth, she began to quiver and shake and to sing in a strident tone, at which someone [said] 'Now her own spirit is leaving her body and a god is taking its place.' On removing the cloth from her head she was no longer a woman but a heavenly spirit, and gazed about her with an astonished air" (1.379). Another manifestation of possession is the "shrill cries, and violent and often indistinct sounds" (1.377). After inhaling incense, one woman "falls into a sort of trance accompanied by shrieks, grimaces, and violent spasms. The spirit is now supposed to have entered into her, and when she grows calmer her words are regarded as oracular" (1.384). Or among the Gallas, "when a woman grows tired of the cares of housekeeping, she begins to talk incoherently." Her husband takes this as a "sign of the descent of the holy spirit Callo upon her" and frees her from "domestic duties" (1.395–96).

Since a god-possessed sovereign is sacred, his name and the words referring to his person are sacred. The king of Siam has "a special language devoted to his sacred person and attributes." "Even the natives have difficulty in mastering this peculiar vocabulary. The hairs of the monarch's head, the soles of his feet, and breath of his body, indeed every single detail of his person both outward and inward, have particular names" (1.401).

Some possessions are hereditary. For instance, the "gods of Samoa generally appeared in animal form, but sometimes they were permanently incarnate in men, who gave oracles, received offerings . . . , healed the sick, [or] answered prayers" (1.389). Usually such sacred persons live "in mystic seclusion" (1.386). One missionary reported that the local god "was a very old man who lived in a large house within an enclosure. . . . No one entered the enclosure except the persons dedicated to the service of the god; only on days when human victims were sacrificed might ordinary people penetrate into the precinct" (1.387). Likewise, the Grand Lama, identified by his knowledge of ancestor gods, "lived withdrawn from the business of this passing world in the recesses of his palace." His worshippers bribed attendants for "a little of the natural secretions of his divine person" to ward off illness (1.411–12). Then there was "the elephantheaded god Gunputty" of western India: "Seven successive incarnations, transmitted from father to son, manifested the light of Gunputty to a dark world. The last of the direct line [was] a heavy-looking god with very weak eyes" (1.405).

Much of this points to Hightower, the "eastern idol" (83 / 98 & 298 / 346), dim-sighted, sweating, weeping, fat, with "puttycolored flesh" which quivers and shakes, who is sent for to act as "doctor," here a high-occurrence word. Indeed, all in this chapter will have some priestly role. But what in John prompted Faulkner to select this material from Frazer?

Called the "Priestly Prayer," John 17 has the only recorded long prayer by Jesus (International 558). Superlatives abound in the comments here: one calls it "one of the most majestic moments in the Fourth Gospel" (Anchor 744); another, "the simplest in language, the profoundest in meaning, in the whole Bible" (Cambridge 307). Partly, this is because of the many refrains. Some form of "thou hast sent me" occurs six times, or a single word, such as *given* may occur as often as sixteen times. Whole passages are repeated: "That they all may be one; as thou, Father, art in me, and I in thee, that they also may be one in us: that the world may believe that thou hast sent me." "That they may be one, even as we are one: I in them and thou in me, that they may be perfect in one, and that the world may know that thou hast sent me" (17.21–23).

The chapter says that Jesus has been sent; the work is finished; the moment is come for him to be glorified, even as he glorified his Father. "I am no more in the world," he says, asking that his disciples be protected by God's name: "Holy Father, keep through thine own name those whom thou hast given me, that they may be one, as we are." The passage is read as God's giving his name to Christ (Cambridge 311), a power Jesus claims nowhere else (International 569). The naming is important, for anti-Christian legends conclude that Jesus' "magical power" came from his having "gained possession of the divine name" (Anchor 755). This is reinforced by the anomaly (unique in John) of Jesus' referring to himself by name: "that they might know thee the only true God, and Jesus Christ, whom thou hast sent."

Thus, both John and Frazer discuss someone chosen, a holy man, apart from the world, possessed by a god, according to Frazer, at one with God, according to John, who has the priestly roles of petitioner, guardian, healer, or prophet, all through God's word and particularly God's name. In both, this name is taboo: Jesus never pronounces it, although he does use the solemn I-Am formulation discussed in chapter 6.

Returning to *Light in August,* this same I-Am formula occurs when Byron seeks Hightower in his sanctum, snoring "profoundly": "There was a quality of profound and complete surrender in it. Not of exhaustion, but surrender, as though he had given over and relinquished completely that grip upon that blending of pride and hope and vanity and fear, that strength to cling to either defeat or victory, which is the I-Am, and the relinquishment of which is usually death" (372 / 434).

There are many instances of significant naming or odd language. Hightower thinks about Lena's child: *"I have no namesake. But I have known them before this to be named by a grateful mother for the doctor who officiated. But then, there is Byron. Byron of course will take the pas* [pas *(CT)*] *of me"* (384 / 448).[11] Many avoid

---

11. Ficken's analysis of the typescript of *Light in August* shows that *pas* was originally left without underscore, so that "Faulkner is using the French word for 'right of precedence'" ("Critical" 315).

words or note another's language. Byron thinks, "I reckon he has not slept much." " 'Even if he aint playing—playing—' He could not think of the word midwife, which he knew that Hightower would use. 'I reckon I dont have to think of it,' he thought" (371 / 433). Or, overleaf, Byron "went almost as straight to the right door as if he knew, or could see, or were being led. 'That's what he'd call it,' he thought, in the fumbling and hurried dark. 'And she would too.' He meant Lena, lying yonder in the cabin, already beginning to labor. 'Only they would both have a different name for whoever did the leading' " (372 / 434). Later Hightower congratulates himself: "Life comes to the old man yet, while they get there too late. They get there for his leavings, as Byron would say" (383 / 446). Or he queries Lena: "You wont say the word?" (389 / 454).

The most amusing manifestation of tabooed language is in the odd methods of communication, including snoring, jerking the head, whispering, moaning, whimpering, clicking, winking, wailing, and speaking in tongues. Hightower snores "profoundly," making Byron realize that "he aint so much upset, after all" (372 / 434). Or his musing is "like the peaceful whining of a querulous woman who is not even listening to herself" or he clicks his tongue "as though in displeasure" (382 / 446). Hines "talks funny," "winking," "squinting," and "squinching." His wife jerks her head, whispers, and questions Hightower "with a gaze dumb, inarticulate, baffled" (376 / 439). At the child's cry, she "seemed to answer it, also in no known tongue, savage and triumphant" (381 / 444). Glaring at Hightower, she is like an animal in the manager scene: "dumb, beastlike, as though she did not understand English." She makes "a hoarse, whimpering noise" and nods, "pawing lightly at the child" (381 / 445).

Lena herself speaks in tongues. Byron hears "a moaning wail, loud, with a quality at once passionate and abject, that seemed to be speaking clearly to something in a tongue which he knew was not his tongue nor that of any man" (377–78 / 441). He sees her "looking down at the shape of her body beneath the sheet with wailing and hopeless terror" (376–77 /439). She complains of being "mixed up" by Mrs. Hines: "She keeps on talking about him like his pa was that . . . the [that——the (CT)] one in jail, that Mr

Christmas. She keeps on, and then I get mixed up and it's like sometimes I cant—like I am mixed up too and I think that his pa is that Mr—Mr Christmas too. . . . And I am afraid she might get me mixed up, like they say how you might cross your eyes and then you cant uncross" (387–88 / 452–53).

However, the most striking instance of special communication involves Byron "borning a baby." When he hears the child cry, "something terrible happened to him" (376 / 439). "He knew now what it was that seemed to lurk clawed and waiting" (377 / 440). The "blow fell and the clawed thing overtook him from behind" (379 / 443). What is the "clawed thing"? The naming of himself, of Lena, and of the true father, Lucas Burch:

> With stern and austere astonishment he thought *It was like it was not until Mrs Hines called me and I heard her and saw her face and knew that Byron Bunch was nothing in this world to her right then, that I found out that she is not a virgin* And he thought that that was terrible, but that was not all. There was something else. His head was not bowed. He stood quite still in the augmenting dawn, while thinking went quietly *And this too is reserved for me, as Reverend Hightower says. I'll have to tell him now. I'll have to tell Lucas Burch. . . . Why I didn't even believe until now that he was so. It was like me, and her, and all the other folks that I had to get mixed up in it, were just a lot of words that never even stood for anything, were not even us, while all the time what was us was going on and going on without even missing the lack of words. Yes. It aint until now that I ever believed that he is Lucas Burch. That there ever was a Lucas Burch.* (380 / 443–44)

As in John and Frazer, it is the knowing, the naming, which makes one the high priest. And this chapter is full of those who bring the Magi's gifts of prophecy. Hightower is most obvious. Cloistered in a room Byron had never before penetrated (372 / 434), called upon to take his book, Hightower acts as medicine man, prophet, and confessor. As the divine, he is able to conjure up the past: "He can see, feel, about him the ghosts of rich fields, and of the rich fecund black life of the quarters, the mellow shouts, the presence of fecund women, the prolific naked children in the dust before the doors; and the big house again, noisy, loud with the treble shouts of the generations" (385 / 449). And for once, he is able to prophesy the future: Lena *"will have to have others. . . . Many more. That will be her life, her destiny. The good stock peopling in tranquil obedience to it the good earth; from these hearty loins without hurry or haste descending mother and daughter. But by Byron engendered next"* (384 / 448). Hightower even manages to squeeze out a prayer (four times "naming" God) over Lena's bowed head: "He rises and stands over her with his hand on her bowed head, thinking *Thank God, God help me. Thank God, God help me"* (391 / 456).

The beastlike Hineses are god-possessed animals, pawing over the child, a new incarnation of Joe.[12] Lena is possessed, moaning, speaking in tongues, surprised at her own convulsing body. Hightower recalls her as if she had something within: "the young strong body from out whose travail even there shone something tranquil and unafraid" (384 / 448), something which he manages to drain: when she looks at his hard gaze, "suddenly her face is quite empty, as though something which gave it actual solidity and firmness were beginning to drain out of it" (390 / 455). And once this solidity is gone, she cannot foretell her future with Byron: "And you worry me about if I said No or not and I already said No and you worry me and worry me and now he is already gone. I will never see him again" (390 / 455–56).

As for Byron, the possession comes through the knowing and naming the beast within. Recall that Frazer's movement from magic to religion to science depended on an increase of knowledge, when the "invariable laws" had "dawned" on man and he realized "his own littleness." The language is echoed in Byron's moment of self-knowledge, appropriately, at dawn, when "he knew. Dawn was making fast. He stood quietly in the chill peace, the waking quiet—small, nondescript, whom no man or woman had ever turned to look at twice anywhere. He knew now that there had been something all the while which had protected him against believing, with the believing protected him" (379–80 / 443). So he

---

12. Hirshleifer (229) observed that "the child at Lena's breast" reflects Joe's role as hanged god in that it is seen as a face "which seems to hang suspended."

stands, head unbowed, knowing now, and with that knowing promptly comes the priestly dedication: he must bring Lucas to Lena, finish his work, and depart this world of Jefferson.

But evidently his value as priest has not been limited to this one moment. When we recall the repeated word *given* in John, it is significant that Hightower's closing words both acknowledge what Byron has given, and, in keeping with his own now-gone possession, prophesy falsely: "So he departed without coming to tell me goodbye. After all he has done for me. Fetched to me. Ay; given, restored, to me. It would seem that this too was reserved for me. And this must be all." But Hightower is wrong. As Faulkner says, "There is one thing more reserved for him" (392 / 457).

Chapter 18: Are You the King? Trials and Denials

While John's three-chapter version of the Passion is fragmented by time, Faulkner tells the Passion story from three different perspectives, Father, Son, and Holy Ghost.[13] Using material from Frazer, in 18 he traces the trial of the Father (Brown and Bunch), in 19 the killing of the Son (Joe Christmas), while in 20 he depicts the resurrection of the Holy Ghost, Gail Hightower—note the initials, reversed.

Pilate's first words to Jesus are "Art thou the King of the Jews?" Although the question can express honor, irony, or mere curiosity, scholars emphasize the pronoun, so that "pity is mingled with contempt" (Moffatt 335). Both the question and the identification are paradigms, for John's chapter includes the identification of Jesus to the soldiers of the high priest; of Peter as Jesus' disciple; and of Jesus' doctrines before the authorities. The chapter even ends with a question and an identification. When Pilate asks if Jesus should be released as part of the Passover amnesty, and the Jews cry, "Not this man, but Barabbas," John closes, "Now Barabbas was a robber."

---

13. Rice (387) observed several unifying themes in these three chapters. For example: "Like Hightower's vicarious sword brandishing, Byron's mule-mounted gallop for revenge is a comic foreshadowing of Percy Grimm's relentless pursuit of Christmas."

But notice that each identification leads to a denial. When Jesus asks the armed men, "Whom seek ye?" and they say, "Jesus of Nazareth," as soon as he says "I am he," they fall to the ground, so he must ask again, "Whom seek ye?" Or when Peter is thrice asked if he is Jesus' disciple, he thrice denies it. Or when Jesus is asked if he is king of the Jews, he replies, "My kingdom is not of this world." And Barabbas is never mentioned again.

What is the truth of these identifications? In the first instance, Jesus is more than Jesus of Nazareth. His response, which can be translated without the "he," suggests the I-AM of God (Cambridge 320), that powerful naming previously discussed. In the second instance, Peter's denials suggest he *has* fallen from discipleship. In the third, the intended contempt in Jesus-as-king becomes heavy with irony. The more it is said, the truer it becomes. As for Barabbas, since the name means "Son of the Father," he may be identified with Jesus.[14]

Similar identifications, which lead to denials of self (and self-denials) may be found in Faulkner. Chapter 18 begins with Byron standing in the square, "a small man" who no longer cares if others identify him, "though a week ago" "he would not have stood here, where any man could look at him and perhaps recognise him." But now, he identifies himself—four times saying *Byron Bunch*—in his despairing thoughts (394 / 459). Then there are his conversations with Mrs. Beard and the sheriff about his and Lena's notoriety. Mrs. Beard's, "Well . . . it's Mister Byron Bunch. Mister Byron Bunch," triggers this identification and denial: " 'Yessum,' he said, thinking, 'Only a fat lady that never had much trouble than a mopping pail would hold ought not to try to be . . .' " (395 / 461). Teasing him when he is unable to state his business, she finally says, "You men." "You cant even know your own limits for devilment. Which aint more than I can measure on a pin, at that. I reckon if it wasn't for getting some woman mixed up in it to help you, you'd ever one of you be drug hollering into heaven before you was ten" (396 / 462), which prompts Byron's, "I reckon you aint got any call

14. Anchor 856 (although to what purpose cannot be determined).

to say anything against her." This mild defense of Lena is Byron's most direct moment, for the rest of the conversation could be called "Byron Holds His Tongue" or "Mrs. Beard Saves Byron's Face," for either he yesses her or she pretends he had meant anyway to leave Jefferson, like any "footloose" man (398 / 463).

A similar exchange goes on with the sheriff, both men lying about the joys of unencumbered city life:

> "What do you aim to do now, Byron?"
>
> ". . . I been thinking about going up to Memphis. Been thinking about it for a couple of years. I might do that. There aint nothing in these little towns."
>
> "Sho. Memphis aint a bad town, for them that like city life. Of course, you aint got any family to have to drag around and hamper you. I reckon if I had been a single man ten years ago I'd have done that too. Been better off, maybe." (398–99 / 464–65)

While these sensitive exchanges—denying self and self-denying—are far from the tone of Brown's identifications and denials, his ordeals also represent a denial of self (his fatherhood) and a self-denial (his reward). Taunting, the deputy says they are going "visiting":

> "I dont want to visit nobody here. I'm a stranger here."
>
> "You'd be strange anywhere you was at," the deputy said. "Even at home. Come on."
>
> "I'm a American citizen. . . . I reckon I got my rights, even if I dont wear no tin star on my galluses."
>
> "Sho," the deputy said. "That's what I am doing now: helping you get your rights." (403–4 / 470–71)

When Brown stands identified before Lena, his face displays "shock, astonishment, outrage, and then downright terror" (406 / 473), while his words indicate all that is being denied:"Well, well, well. . . . If it aint Lena. Yes, sir. So you got my message. Soon as I got here I sent you a message last month as soon as I got settled down and I thought it had got lost—It was a fellow I didn't know what his name was but he said he would take—He didn't look reliable but I had to trust him" (406 / 473–74). Watching the "two terrified beasts" of his eyes, Lena thinks her own suppressed thoughts: "*He is going to make out like he was not afraid,*" and "*He will have no more shame than to lie about being afraid, just as he had no more shame than to be afraid because he lied*" (407 / 474). As he talks, his eyes are "bland, alert, secret, yet behind them there lurked still that quality harried and desperate" (408 / 475). When he is finally "released" (like the robber, Barabbas), Lena saying "I reckon you are right busy now," Brown says, "For a fact, I am," using the god-identifying formula. His last words as he leaves through the window are an identification which suppresses everything: "It's a man outside. In front, waiting for me" (409 / 477). Even the signature on his note to the sheriff amusingly reflects this theme: "*Not Sined but All rigt You no who*" (413 / 481).

These "interrogations" of Byron and Brown occur at the same time as the hearings of the Grand Jury, the term often used to describe Jesus' interrogations before the Sanhedrin. Yet Christmas's story is in the background. As with John, who here emphasizes the political charges (Moffatt 335), Faulkner here emphasizes the succession to the kingship, or who will win Lena's hand.[15]

One cluster of images, augurs of change, includes talk of revolutions, reports, explosions, or signs from the heaven such as meteors. Repeatedly Brown rages against those "bastards" (an illegitimate succession), who "try to beat me," who wear the "little tin star," who "tromple" on his "rights" as "a American citizen," until, after the "sorry dregs of his pride revolted" (409 / 477), he says, "I be dog if it aint enough to make a man turn downright bowlsheyvick" (415 / 484). Twice, he is stripped "naked" (407 / 474 & 409 / 477). And while his face "lighted: it was a flash" (404 / 471), Byron imagines himself a stick of dynamite: "He could feel himself breathing deep, as if each time his insides were afraid that next breath they would not be able to give far enough, . . . and that all the time he could look down at himself breathing, at his chest, and see no movement at all, like when dynamite first begins, gathers itself for the now Now NOW, the shape of the outside of the

---

15. Kerr (128) noted the parallel here with the "courtly love combats over a lady," as did Fadiman (65).

stick does not change" (394–95 / 460). Or consider this "rising" of Byron:

> The hill rises, cresting. He has never seen the sea, and so he thinks, "It is like the edge of nothing. Like once I passed it I would just ride right off into nothing. Where trees would look like and be called by something else except trees, and men would look like and be called by something else except folks. And Byron Bunch he wouldn't even have to be or not be Byron Bunch. Byron Bunch and his mule not anything with falling fast, until they would take fire like the Reverend Hightower says about them rocks running so fast in space that they take fire and burn up and there aint even a cinder to have hit the ground." (401 / 467–68)

Byron rightly exclaims "Great God in the mountain" when he and Brown pass "as though on opposite orbits and with an effect as of phantoms or apparitions" (417 / 487), since Brown represents the passing god. As Frazer says, since gods were thought to die, their representatives on earth were killed at the first sign of weakness or, to avoid the catastrophe weakness engenders, at the end of a fixed term. Sometimes this meant watching the heavens for signs like a "star in the East"; falling stars signalled the death of some sorcerer, enemy, or chief (4.60–8). Every eight years Greek magistrates watched a moonless sky for a meteor or shooting star, a sign "that the king had sinned against the deity" (4.58).

Usually these eight-year cycles were celebrated by games and physical trials such as races or wrestling (like Joe's contests with Joanna in 11 to win the bride). Different reasons are given for this connection between games and the overthrow of kings. Some believe festivals such as the Olympics were originally to claim the kingship, while others believe they were funeral games, to placate or honor the dead, probably the dead king. The contests in Faulkner range from the "trials" to the children's games (402 / 469, 414 / 483, 416 / 485), appropriate since "often with the decay of old faiths the serious rites and pageants of grown people have degenerated into the sports of children" (4.77). But the more serious contests include Byron's race to catch Brown, Brown's "last desperate cast in a game already lost" (410 / 478), their battle itself, and, going on at the same time in chapter 19, the hunt for and killing of Joe Christmas under the aegis of the Player.

The chapter also includes "rewards," a high-occurrence word, mainly because, from Brown's perspective, staying around for the thousand-dollar reward means he also "wins" Lena's hand. Such offers to marry the princess would have been given to strangers (4.135) (one of Brown's self-identifications [403 / 470]), and were often refused because the sovereignty might be "brief and fatal" (4.115). In one of Lancelot's adventures, he refuses the throne for "he had no mind to die so soon," whereupon a dwarf and a fair damsel accept the honor (4.120–22), which might suggests Byron and Lena.[16] Or in one Indian legend, because the kings of Ujjain were fed to an arch-fiend, a hero puts himself in the victim's stead and "after a terrific combat the fiend capitulated and agreed to quit the city" (4.123), which might suggest Brown.

Actually, the Greek octennial festivals included "the slaying of a great water-dragon by a god or hero" (4.78), probably for rain (4.107). In one creation story "the strong and valiant god Indra conquered a great dragon or serpent . . . which had obstructed the waters so that they could not flow. He slew the monster with his bolt, and then the pent-up springs gushed in rivers to the sea" (4.106). And Brown's vanishing "like a long snake" (409 / 477), does open the floodgates: for Byron, the "moving wall of dingy cars" becomes a "dyke beyond which the world, time, hope unbelievable and certainty incontrovertible, waited," so "when the last car passes, moving fast now, the world rushes down on him like a flood, a tidal wave" (417–18 / 487).

Several other details in this rich Johannine chapter bear examination. When the soldiers take Jesus, Peter cuts off the ear of the high priest's servant. Disconcertingly, nothing more is made of this other than Jesus' admonition: "Put up thy sword into the sheath: the cup which my Father hath given me, shall I not drink it?" Another particular is the binding and striking of Jesus, milder in John than in the synoptics. A third is the crowing of the cock following Peter's denials, although scholars question the presence of fowls, considered unclean, in Jerusalem (Cambridge 327). One conjectures this refers to the trumpet call at the end of the third watch

16. Baker (159) characterized Byron as "the good young man devoted to serving and saving, sweeping up the loose carbon from the streets after the dark, fire-breathing dragons have passed by."

known as *gallicinium* or "cockcrow" (International 604). In any case, cocks would have been allowed in Jefferson, and Faulkner could have put one in. He does include the Americanism "galluses," or suspenders, which neatly combines "cock" (from the Latin *gallus*) and "gallows," meaning "cross." But he had also used this term in *Mosquitoes* (244).

As usual, it is prudent to suggest that Faulkner submerged the physical act in favor of the act's import. Consider the binding. Along with the hearing itself, this is reflected in the metaphor describing Lena's hold over Brown during his "trial": "It was as though she held him, forcing him to, trying him with, that final lie at which even his sorry dregs of pride revolted; held him neither with rods nor cords but with something against which his lying blew trivial as leaves or trash" (409 / 477).

Or regarding Peter and the crowing of the cock, Byron's denial of his discipleship to Lena is signaled in his thoughts as he self-denyingly leaves her to Brown: "*All right. You say you suffer. All right. But in the first place, all we got is your naked word for it. And in the second place, you just say that you are Byron Bunch. And in the third place, you are just the one that calls yourself Byron Bunch today, now*" (402 / 468). In fact, this is the moment when Brown, himself "stripped naked . . . of verbiage and deceit" (409 / 477), snakes out Lena's window, for as Byron turns and looks across the "shallow bowl" (the cup) of the valley, he sees the silent figure of Brown running away. And while within the cabin, Lena hears Brown's "single faint sound" (409 / 477), for Byron, up on the hill, "a cold, hard wind seems to blow through him. It is at once violent and peaceful, blowing hard away like chaff or trash or dead leaves all the desire and the despair and the hopelessness and the tragic and vain imagining too. With the very blast of it he seems to feel himself rush back and empty again, without anything in him now which had not been there two weeks ago, before he ever saw her" (402–3 / 469). If Faulkner did not mean that "blast" to be the trumpet, he might have figured Byron's instant vainglorious resolve to "whip" Brown is the crowing of the cock.[17]

17. Schoenberg (87) suggests that Faulkner has created an analogue of Peter's denials in the dormitory setting of *Absalom, Absalom!* where, to Shreve's repeated "Jesus!" Quentin denies knowledge of incestuous love. "The surprise is that the

A similar submerging of Johannine detail into image or essence lies in the echoes of the severed ear. To begin with, the chapter's "hearings" have resulted chiefly in denials. Then, the word *ear* appears in this image describing Brown's denials, during which his "heartiness, like the timbre, seemed to be as impermanent as the sound of the words, vanishing, leaving nothing, not even a definitely stated thought in the ear or the belief" (407 / 475). The image is so slight, we might doubt the connection, except that several battles similarly leave people unable to hear. Confronting the black "Aunty," Brown's "rage and impotence" make him seem "to muse now upon a sort of timeless and beautiful infallibility in his unpredictable frustrations. As though somehow the very fact that he should be so consistently supplied with them elevates him somehow above the petty human hopes and desires which they abrogate and negative. Hence the negress has to shout twice at him before he hears and turns" (411–12 / 480). Having battled with Brown, Byron's thoughts rush back to Lena "as though he has already and long since outstripped himself" (418 / 487), so that a "voice" must "speak again" to give him the news of what has happened.

As for what has happened, it will happen again in chapter 19: the passing of another god, Joe Christmas.

Chapter 19: Suspending Rules at the Post

In every other chapter, we may have trouble accepting Joe Christmas as a parallel to Jesus Christ, but not in this chapter. Here we find Joe central to the chapter's many particulars of the Passion: Mrs. Hines wants him "decently hung by a Force," while Stevens explains that his "black blood . . . swept him up into that ecstasy out of a black jungle where . . . death is desire and fulfillment" (425 / 496). Indeed, Stevens's endless discussions of Joe's black blood versus his white blood may reflect the lengthy speculations

---

third denial is not immediately followed by the crowing of a cock (as, indeed, it is if you want to consider Shreve cocky or cocksure)."

by biblical scholars on the "blood and water" that pour from Jesus' side. Regarding Jesus' words on the cross, "I thirst," Joe's past "left him at last high and dry in a barred cell with the shape of an incipient executioner everywhere he looked" (424 / 494–95). Regarding the casting of lots by the soldiers, the many games include the poker game by Joe's adversaries, Grimm's men, playing soldier. Regarding the "five wounds," Joe receives five gunshot wounds. Regarding Golgotha, the place of skulls, Joe dies in a "dead and empty small house" (293 / 341), which holds Hightower's bandaged "skull" (464 / 541). But especially at chapter's end, we are invited to see Joe in Christ's role when the "pent black blood" from his savage castration seems "to rush like a released breath," "like the rush of sparks from a rising rocket," and "upon that black blast the man seemed to rise soaring into their memories forever and ever" (440 / 513), as if one could only respond, "Amen."[18]

Faulkner has found another way to make a central motif of John 19 apply to others in his chapter. Biblical scholars say that unlike customary representations of the road to Calvary, Jesus probably carried only the crosspiece, a post, which was then affixed to a stationary post. In fact, the various meanings of the word *post* are everywhere in John 19. Consider its many meanings. Without suggesting that this was John's intention,[19] all of the events in his chapter have associations to this word: in the scourging, Jesus is fastened to a post; dressed in purple, crowned with thorns, Jesus is given the post of king; the post as a phallic symbol is suggested in Pilate's "Behold the Man"; the post as an ancient symbol of gods is suggested in the crowd's complaint that Jesus "made himself Son of God"; that the post is a doorway is appropriate to the hour, "the preparation of the Passover" when blood was smeared on the doorpost; to be like a "post," or unresponsive, is appropriate to Jesus' refusal to answer; a post is a fixed route or road for carriers, like the road to Golgotha; as mentioned, it is the cross itself; a post is

18. Recall that the particulars of the Passion in this chapter include Pilate's sign over the cross, with Faulkner suggesting parallels to John's use of Greek, Latin, and the local Hebrew. See my chapter 4.

19. It should be recalled, however, that a distinguishing feature of John's gospel is wordplay.

a sign or placard, like the one on which is written "King of the Jews"; a post is a station for soldiers like those posted at the cross; it is even a game, like the soldiers casting lots for the seamless coat; to post means "to relay," and Jesus does give over his mother to the Beloved Disciple; a post is a starting or winning stand, and Jesus' last words are "It is finished"; to post is to hurry or call for haste: because of the Sabbath, the soldiers hurry to break the legs of all, only to discover that Jesus is already dead; a post is a thin lance, like the one used to pierce Jesus' side; a posting is a book entry: John repeats that these events fulfill scripture; and finally, the prefix *post,* meaning "after," reflects John's "and after this" when Jesus' body is laid in a garden sepulcher.

Even discounting the symbolic examples, it is striking how often this word applies. The fact that Faulkner's own chapter reflects the multiple meanings of the word *post* suggests his awareness of this odd phenomenon. Indeed, the main thrust of Faulkner's chapter is precisely on the symbolic elements: the position of authority, the meaning of manhood, and the inexorability of blood when the authority and manhood are given over. In other words, John's story is not just about the victim, Christ; it is also about those forces that destroy Christ. To personify these forces, Faulkner introduces a brand new character, Percy Grimm, whose name in Latin (Percival) means "valley-piercer" or in Greek (Perseus) "destroyer." But like "Prufrock," which can be read either "Proof rock" or "Pru frock," Percy's name also reflects the southern idiom for "sissy" or "pansy," as we shall see.

But what kind of destroyer is this killer and castrator of Joe Christmas? He is said to represent Youth (he wishes he had been old enough to fight in World War I); Jingoism (he feel he represents "the protection of America and Americans"); Racism (he believes "the white race is superior" to all other races); or Fate (he appears to be moved by the Player). What are we to make of this multiplicity of issues?

The same problem arises in John. Who or what kills Jesus Christ? The Jews, say both tradition and, heavily, John. Pilate says he finds no fault in Jesus, but the Jews continue to cry for his crucifixion. Even the scourging and the mocking may have been vain attempts to awaken the crowd's pity. Now, while anti-Semitic modernist writers like Pound and Eliot might have seized on this issue, Faulkner, to his credit, focused instead on John's observations that Pilate does give over his authority; that the events move swiftly because Passover is at hand; and that they move inexorably: everything occurs as it is written.

This emphasis in John on Passover and the suspension of authority led Faulkner to a wealth of material in Frazer, for the same question arises out of the primitive tradition behind Passover. When the Angel of Death passed over the Israelites, killing the firstborn sons of the Egyptians, who or what was that Angel? Frazer relates the Passover story to the ancient, widespread practice of killing the king's firstborn (the firstfruit) as a substitute for the king.

The sacrifice of such redeemers was widespread. Among the Semites, especially in times of danger, the king would "give his beloved son to die for the whole people, as a ransom offered to the avenging demons" to be "slain with mystic rites" (4.166). The ancient kings of Boeotia were regularly bound to sacrifice their firstborn, although in time, a ram might be substituted, provided the prince kept away from the sacrificial hall (4.165).

Among the Hebrews, Passover may mark an early turn from infanticide: after the Jews' firstlings are saved by the lamb's blood on the door posts, henceforth "God ordained that all the firstborn of man and beast among the Israelites should be sacred to him" (4.175). Even the practice of circumcision may represent a custom "to save the life of the child by giving the deity a substitute for it" (4.181).

Much of this may be understood in Freudian terms. The institution of Passover can be seen as a societal control of conflicting impulses, the father's desire to perpetuate himself in his own form versus the form of his son, the body renewed. For Frazer, these psychological questions do not arise.[20] He saw the young god's death as a primitive attempt to revive the land. But perhaps the two traditions together suggest that the king's sacrifice represents his be-

20. Frazer's first edition was completed by 1890, some ten years before Freud's *Interpretation of Dreams.*

lief that he or his most precious member (his son, his penis) is so important that God and all life depends on its being proffered.[21]

But gradually (and not surprisingly) it came to be thought that both losses could be avoided if a deputy would take on the role of king: wearing the kingly costume and having kingly sway would give one the mantle of the divine (4.160). In Java, suicide for the sultan's sake was witnessed by a fourteenth century traveler, who said that although the deceased's family was given liberal pensions, apparently the act reflected his desire "to immolate himself out of affection for the sovereign" as his father and as his grandfather had done (4.53–54). Frazer "explains" this sacrificial phenomenon with his usual nineteenth-century hokum, suggesting that, unlike the English or other civilized races, many people have an "indifference or apathy" (4.136) toward death, partly because of a comfortable, pre-Christian belief in the pleasantness of afterlife, and partly because of "the less delicate nervous system of the negro" (4.138). Thus, heathens often "laid down their lives without a murmur or a struggle" (4.139). Nevertheless, with the coming of civilization (and some inkling of Christian Hell), these customs were reduced to symbols. For example, in Cambodia, the "office of temporary king was hereditary in a family distantly connected with the royal house." Briefly in power, the mock king wore special costumes and was escorted in processions around the city, until a mock execution was carried out on the third day (4.148). So also in Siam, the temporary king enjoyed royal prerogatives until, on the third day, he was forced to stand on one foot for three hours, but not before he had demonstrated the connection to agricultural fertility by tracing nine furrows with a gaily decorated plough and oxen (4.149).

But the symbolic sacrifice of the son may be more dramatically

---

21. Noting that in Matthew 19:12, Christ says, "There be eunuchs, which have made themselves eunuchs for the kingdom of heaven's sake," Irwin (153–54) says that "the principle of [Christ's] sacrifice is the same as that of self-castration—the giving up of a part to save the whole, and in both sacrifice and self-castration the part is given up to save the whole from the wrath of the father." Thus, "the essence of Christ's sacrifice [is that] the subject is both the agent and the victim, at once active and passive, a conjunction of masculine and feminine."

blood-on-the-post. During the Spring Festivals of Attis and Cybele, particularly on the third day, the high priest of the Galli offered blood drawn from his arm, while the lesser priests, stirred by the music "of clashing cymbals, rumbling drums, droning horns, and screaming flutes . . . gashed their bodies with potsherds or slashed them with knives in order to bespatter the altar and the sacred tree with their flowing blood" (5.268). Moreover, Frazer believes that "it was on the same Day of Blood . . . that the novices sacrificed their virility. Wrought up to the highest pitch of religious excitement they dashed the severed portions of themselves against the image of the cruel goddess. These broken instruments of fertility were afterwards reverently wrapt up and buried in the earth or in subterranean chambers sacred to Cybele" (5.268). And this mode of sacrifice is likened to the festival of the Syrian goddess, Astarte:

> While the flutes played, the drums beat, and the eunuch priests slashed themselves with knives, the religious excitement gradually spread like a wave among the crowd of onlookers, and many a one did that which he little thought to do when he came as a holiday spectator to the festival. For man after man, his veins throbbing with the music, his eyes fascinated by the sight of the streaming blood, flung his garments from him, leaped forth with a shout, and seizing one of the swords which stood ready for the purpose castrated himself on the spot. Then he ran through the city, holding the bloody pieces in his hand, till he threw them into one of the houses which he passed in his mad career. The household thus honored had to furnish him with a suit of female attire and female ornaments, which he wore for the rest of his life. (5.270).

If the Passover Angel of Death may be generalized to include these related traditions—the infanticides of the firstborn, the suicides or executions for the sake of the king, and the priestly castrations in the worship of the Mother Goddess—it can be seen as the destructive consequence of giving over authority to Caesar or to other false gods, exemplified in John by the Jews' cry, "We have no king but Caesar," and in Faulkner by all the false values held by Percy Grimm. So Faulkner's point in featuring Grimm is not so much his villainy as the absence or the suspension of rule that he—as mock king or castrated priest—represents.[22]

Reflecting these discussions in Frazer, the theme of a suicidal sacrifice of the scapegoat emerges in many forms in Faulkner's chapter 19. Of course, Joe Christmas is said to have "made his plans to passively commit suicide" (419 / 489). But then Grimm's articles of faith include knowing "that all that would ever be required of him . . . would be his own life" (427 / 498), while during his brief ascension in the town's affairs, called a "suttee of volition's surrender," his men feel that "they might die for him, if occasion rose" (432 / 504). And noting Frazer's generations of self-sacrificing slaves, their survivors cared for by generations of grateful kings, we find Stevens, whose "ancestors owned slaves" (420 / 489–90), caring for the Hineses, "the voluntary slaves and sworn bondsmen of prayer" (423 / 493).

Although the expiatory deaths in this chapter range from the ridiculous to the sublime, Frazer himself notes that many dramas of death and resurrection "originated in a rustic mummers' play," such as "English yokels on Plough Monday" (7.33). Faulkner's Monday is a "holiday," a "parade," with "a throng of people thick as on Fair Day" (433 / 506), and some tense scenes are filled with agricultural diction. Running among faces "empty and immobile as the faces of cows" (433 / 505) is Grimm, "the black, blunt, huge automatic opening a way for him like a plow." In the throng "was the inevitable hulking youth in the uniform of the Western Union, leading his bicycle by the horns like a docile cow." The bicycle Percy grabs "possessed neither horn nor bell" (434 / 507), while his men are twice called "sheepish" (431 / 503).

Notice too, all the "running," like the running Priests of Attis. Everyone runs here, along the streets, the alley, the rutted lane, the ditch, and the ravine. They even run metaphorically: Stevens says, "There was too much running with [Christmas], stride for stride with him. Not pursuers: but himself: years, acts, deeds omitted and committed, keeping pace with him, stride for stride, breath for breath, thud for thud of the heart, using a single heart" (424 / 495).

The running also reflects John's rush of events and the inexora-

---

22. As Millgate remarks (129), the occasion of Joe's crucifixion "permitted the worst elements in Jefferson to emerge and take command."

ble fulfillment of scripture: Joe rushes "into the embrace of a chimera, [chimaera *(CT)*] a blind faith in something read in a printed Book" (425 / 495); for Mrs. Hines, the events "had already been written and worded for her on the night when she bore his mother" (423 / 494). But particularly Percy Grimm has "something about him irresistible and prophetlike" (428 / 500), as if he is "served by certitude, the blind and untroubled faith in the rightness and infallibility of his actions" (434 / 507); he moves "as though under the protection of a magic or a providence" (437 / 510) or "with the delicate swiftness of an apparition, the implacable undeviation of Juggernaut or Fate" (435 / 508).

Indeed, Percy Grimm and his men at the execution (four all together, like the four soldiers in John) are like the inexorable Angel of Death itself. Rushing into Hightower's house, they are haloed, bringing "something of the savage summer sunlight which they had just left. It was upon them, of them: its shameless savageness. Out of it their faces seemed to glare with bodiless suspension as though from haloes" (438 / 511). Similarly, above the automatic, Grimm's face "had that serene, unearthly luminousness of angels in church windows" (437 / 510).

Even calling the pistol an "automatic" suggests the theme of irresistibility, as if its firing were not just easy but inevitable. Similarly, Joe's "bolts," in all senses of the term, are responsible for his death. When he bolts, his manacled hands, with "glint" and "glare" from the sun as if "on fire," or "like the flash of a heliograph" (436 / 509), empower him "like lightning bolts, so that he resembled a vengeful and furious god pronouncing a doom" (438 / 511). Yet his "bright and glittering hands" on the edge of the overturned table also bolt him to, mark him for, death.

But the most elaborate use of Frazer to illuminate a pattern in John relates to the mock king wearing the kingly clothes. John particularizes Jesus' clothing to show that it includes the purple robe, worn by kings, the seamless coat, worn by the high priest, and the linen clothes, wound round the dead.[23]

23. Cambridge (345). All three are combined in the description of Mrs. Hines as "beneath a nodding and soiled white plume, shapeless in a silk dress of an outmoded shape and in color regal and moribund" (420 / 490). Brylowski remarks that Mrs. Hines's dress is "suitable to the passion" (112).

Faulkner has made elegant use of this theme of clothing, which, invested with authority, becomes sacred—seamless—and therefore capable of winding the dead. Recall that Percy Grimm wears the scars of his battle with the "exsoldier" "as proudly as he was later to wear the uniform itself for which he had blindly fought" (426 / 497). With the civilian-military act, his new "burden" is "as bright and weightless and martial as his insignatory brass" (426 / 498). Arguing with the legion commander, Percy speaks of "we, as soldiers, that have worn the uniform" (427 / 499), and when the commander refuses to "use the Post," Percy retorts, "Yet you wore the uniform once" (428 / 499). Moreover, refusing Percy's request for side arms, the sheriff calls it, "Fifteen or twenty folks milling around the square with pistols in their pants" (430 / 502).

In fact, the growing authority of Percy's "army" is evinced by the metaphor of clothing which finally becomes one—seamless:

> So quickly is man unwittingly and unpredictably moved that without knowing that they were thinking it, the town had suddenly accepted Grimm with respect and perhaps a little awe and a deal of actual faith and confidence, as though somehow his vision and patriotism and pride in the town, the occasion, had been quicker and truer than theirs. His men anyway assumed and accepted this. . . .
> They now moved in a grave and slightly aweinspiring reflected light which was almost as palpable as the khaki would have been which Grimm wished them to wear, wished that they wore, as though each time they returned to the orderly room they dressed themselves anew in suave and austerely splendid scraps of his dream. (432 / 504)

As their game continues, the "caution, the surreptitiousness, which had clothed it was now gone." By Monday morning, "the platoon was again intact. And they now wore uniforms. It was their faces" (432 / 505), the *it* referring to the wearing of uniforms. But the theme is capped when Percy cries like a "young priest": "Jesus Christ!" "Has every preacher and old maid in Jefferson taken their pants down to the yellowbellied son of a bitch?" (439 / 512); when he slashes Joe's "garments about his hips and loins" (440 / 513); and when his five (gunshot) wounds are later covered with one, presumably seamless (and possibly linen) handkerchief.

Appropriate to the castrating priests of Attis, Grimm has been characterized as "a mixture of a Spanish Jesuit and a primitive priest of a blood cult" (R. G. Collins, *"Light"* 142). In fact, the language of that castrating blood cult is pervasive in the chapter, with words for the operation *(cut, break, detach, slashed, dropped, hacked)*; the thing cut *(post, picket, stake, horn, plow, pistol, poker, bar, bolt)*; the priests "leaping" or "springing" or discarding *(fling, pitch, cast, shot, thrown)*; and the scar left *(orifice, gape, hole, rut, fault, ditch)*. But before he ever brings Christmas to earth, it is Percy who has "lost a point" (437 / 510). He wears the "scars" of his tussle with the "exsoldier." And like the unmanned priests, often seen on the streets in costumes "with little images suspended on their breasts" (5.266), Percy is often found downtown in his uniform, displaying his marksman's badge and his bars with "the selfconscious pride of a boy" (427 / 498). And boy or youth or "young priest" he remains, as when the sheriff calls, "Come here, boy," and pats him familiarly on the hip (430 / 502). With inspired irony, Faulkner suggests that this "Percy" is no man; that he has no authority, other than the uniform of uniformity. Instead, the Grimm castrator has himself been castrated on the altar of his phony beliefs.

Most important, in depicting Grimm's ability to gain the town's "respect and perhaps a little awe and a deal of actual faith and confidence" (432 / 504), Faulkner demonstrates that the good people of this earth—Christian or not, past or present—always have the potential for savagery. Religion not only cannot save us from this savagery; religion can be the cause of it. When we allow ourselves to be clothed in flags, when our faces become seamless with fanaticism, we have indeed wound ourselves round with the linen of the dead, for we have lost our humanity. Ironically, sadly, it may only be restored by the distant mirroring memory of the Joe Christmases we have slain.

Chapter 20: Doubting Thomas Handles the Dead

In John 20, Mary Magdalene comes to the sepulcher and, seeing that the stone (which would have been wheel-shaped [Anchor 982]) has been rolled away, runs for Peter and the Beloved Disciple, who enters the tomb and, seeing the linen clothes, "believed." After they leave, Mary sees two angels, who ask why she is weeping; then she sees Jesus who identifies himself and says "Touch me not." That evening, when the disciples are behind locked doors, Jesus appears, showing them his hands and side. But the absent Thomas later says, "Except I shall see in his hands the print of the nails, and put my finger into the print of the nails, and thrust my hand into this side, I will not believe." Eight days later, Jesus reappears, saying, "Reach hither thy finger, and behold my hand; and reach hither thy hand, and thrust it into my side." When Thomas declares his belief, Jesus says, "because thou hast seen me, thou hast believed: blessed are they that have not seen, and yet have believed."

These strange events, which repeat the theme of seeing and believing, have many explanations. For example, what is seen in the grave that quickens belief? Some say that the wrappings, left flat, demonstrate the resurrection because "grave robbers would not have taken the time to unwrap the body, thus giving themselves the burden of carrying a stiff, naked corpse around" (Anchor 1007); others say it is the position or form of the clothes, either flat or "stiffly erect after the body had passed through them" (Anchor 1008). Or, why would Jesus admonish Mary not to touch him and then invite Thomas to thrust his hand into his side? Some speak of Jesus' nakedness before Mary (although, says one, "the eye of love clothes the vision in familiar garments" [International 666]); others say the translation should read, "Don't cling to me," as if Mary must be told not to try and hold Jesus (Anchor 992). Regarding the angels, some suggest they symbolize the two robbers on the cross; others suggest they indicate an accretion of apologetic legends (Anchor 989 & 975).

Faulkner's 20th chapter is likewise obsessed with the dead, who are likewise recognized by sense perceptions: hearing, smelling, touching, and particularly seeing. The chapter begins in "the final copper light," "like a dying yellow fall of trumpets dying into an interval of silence and waiting," and ends in "the dying thunder of hooves." When Hightower opens the trunk to the smell of "the moist grieving of the October earth," he is "almost overpowered by the evocation of his dead mother's hands which lingered among the folds" (443 / 516–17), and the stiff folds, which cause the coat to tumble forward, evoke a life resurrected like the empty linen of the tomb. The patch of Yankee blue on the coat "stopped his very heart," giving his face "an expression as of the Pit itself" (444 / 517–18).

Himself "little better than a phantom" (452 / 526), Hightower "grew to manhood among phantoms, and side by side with a ghost" (449 / 523). The one phantom was his father, who returns from the war a doctor, practicing "on the bodies of friend and foe alike" (447 / 521), while others "returned home with their eyes stubbornly reverted toward what they refused to believe was dead" (449 / 523).

The second phantom was his mother: "If on the day of her death he had been told that he had ever seen her otherwise than in bed, he would not have believed it." He thought of her "as without legs, feet; as being only that thin face and the two eyes which seemed daily to grow bigger and bigger, as though about to embrace all seeing, all life, with one last terrible glare of frustration and suffering and foreknowledge, and that when that finally happened, he would hear it: it would be a sound, like a cry" (449–50 / 524).

The third phantom was Cinthy, his grandfather's slave, who returned after his death "convinced at last that she would never more see either him or her husband (450 / 525). She had refused to believe the rumor of her husband's death, as he had refused to believe the rumor of his master's death, forcing a Yankee to shoot him although Cinthy claimed he would not have known a Yankee "if he wuz to see um" (451 / 526).

The "ghost" was the grandfather who had "gone to a war whar his business was killin' Yankees" (459 / 535), about whom the grandson asks, "How many Yankees did he kill?" (445 / 518), although "he found no terror in the knowledge that his grandfather . . . had killed men 'by the hundreds' as he was told and believed, or in the fact that the negro Pomp had been trying to kill a man when he died. No horror here because they were just ghosts, never seen in the flesh, heroic, simple, warm; while the father which he knew and feared was a phantom which would never die" (452 / 526–27). And about that night when his grandfather was "killed with a shotgun in a peaceful henhouse, in a temporary hiatus of his own avocation of killing" (462 / 539), Hightower says,

> They didn't know who fired the shot. . . . It may have been a woman, likely enough the wife of a Confederate soldier. I like to think so. It's fine so. Any soldier can be killed by the enemy in the heat of battle, by a weapon approved by the arbiters and rulemakers of warfare. Or by a woman in a bedroom. But not with a shotgun, a fowling piece, in a henhouse. And so is it any wonder that this world is peopled principally by the dead? Surely, when God looks about at their successors, He cannot be loath to share His own with us. (459 / 535)

As for Hightower himself, sitting "in the failing dusk, his head in its white bandage looming bigger and more ghostly than ever" (453 / 528), he had returned "to the place to die where my life had already ceased before it began" "because my life died there, was shot from the saddle of a galloping horse in a Jefferson street one night twenty years before it was ever born" (452 / 527).

But then every subject Hightower touches on concerns the dead. Marriage was "a dead state carried over into and existing still among the living like two shadows chained together with the shadow of a chain" (454 / 529). The church is "like one of those barricades of the middleages planted with dead and sharpened stakes, against truth and against that peace in which to sin and be forgiven which is the life of man" (461 / 538). His sin is a "sentence" (a double entendre) which "seems to stand fullsprung across his skull": "Then . . . if I am the instrument of her despair and death, then I am in turn instrument of someone outside myself. And I know that for fifty years I have not even been clay: I have been a single instant of darkness in which a horse galloped and a gun crashed. And if I am my dead grandfather on the instant of his death, then my wife, his grandson's wife . . . the debaucher and murderer of my grandson's wife, since I could neither let my grandson live or die" (465 / 541–42). And the final vision of haloed faces, Christmas and Grimm, makes him think, "I am dying" (466 / 543).

Notice the concurrent themes of doubting and believing: the rumors of death, the stories of war, the methods of escape, the emotions of others, all are believed or not. The "doings of heroes border so close upon the unbelievable that it is no wonder that their doings must emerge now and then like gunflashes in the smoke, and that their very physical passing becomes rumor with a thousand faces before breath is out of them, lest paradoxical truth outrage itself" (458 / 533–34). When his wife speaks of escaping, Hightower "believed at once that she was right" "He believed at once that his own belief about the seminary had been wrong all the while. Not seriously wrong, but false, incorrect. Perhaps he had already begun to doubt himself" (455 / 530). But this theme, although appropriate to the doubting Thomas chapter, has emerged in previous chapters, notably in chapter 3, where Hightower's story is first told.

This brings up a unique quality about chapter 20. Faulkner's chapter themes are usually identified by the odd metaphors or repetitions, although since some motifs recur in John or Frazer, they can recur in different chapters in Faulkner. For example, music features in the periodic expulsion of evil spirits and in the annual Carrying Out Death. So Faulkner's chapter 13 has music in the form of fire sirens, howling dogs, and opera singers, while in chapter 16, the choir gathers and sings steadily until the insects outside the window take up the chorus. But usually particular sections of Frazer can be applied to particular chapters in Faulkner because, along with the mutual themes, there are differences: the Frazer material echoed in 13 comes from *The Scapegoat*, where the ceremonies include a saturnalia and the music is strident; the Frazer material echoed in 16 comes from *The Dying God*, where the ceremonies include petitioning and the music is mournful.

But chapter 20's thematic clusters, more plentiful than elsewhere, all sound familiar, as if they have been resurrected from earlier chapters.[24] For example, one of chapter 16's themes is drama, yet such language also occurs here. The scene outside the window is framed "like a stage" (441 / 514), or Hightower paraphrases *Hamlet* (on ghosts) (453 / 528), or he sees himself as "a figure antic as a showman . . . a charlatan preaching worse than heresy, in utter disregard of that whose very stage he preempted"

---

24. Ficken ("Critical" 229) observes that Faulkner "carefully establishes numerous parallels in this chapter to other events or characters in the novel," and Baldanza (67–78) notes bookwide thematic parallels.

(462 / 539), or Cinthy's face is "the mask of a black tragedy between scenes (450 / 525). But that "mask," given also to Hightower and his wife (455 / 530 & 464 / 540), along with the costumes and the ghosts themselves, are reminders of chapter 13's expulsion of evil. Similarly, "naming" was important in chapters 15 through 17, particularly in the priestly taboos of 17. Here we find taboos against naming the dead, for Hightower's father, mother, and wife are never named; rather elaborate name-avoidances are used, such as " 'But sanctity is not the word for him' the son's son in turn thinks" (448 / 522), or his wife is "woman. *The* woman. Woman . . . the Passive and Anonymous whom God had created" (441–42 / 514). That we learn the *grandfather's* name is permitted, for with time, the names of heroes are handed down so their bravery will pass into the descendant through the ghost, awakened by name (3.349–74).

Similarly, chapter 3 presented scribal themes in the form of books, printing, and photographs, yet here Hightower thinks "how false the most profound book turns out to be when applied to life" (455 / 531), or that love only lives in books (456 / 531), or he calls himself the "author" of his wife's shame, or recalls that they left notes for one another in a hollow tree, an idea which he had got "from a book" (454 / 529). Here also is the hymnbook behind which he hid while the photograph was being snapped, while his father is said to have wanted "somebody that can sing alto out of a Presbyterian hymnbook, where even the good Lord Himself couldn't squeeze in any music" (446 / 520).

These themes involve more than Hightower. We find the motifs of rainmaking (blackness and corruption, especially of the grave, and floods versus dry sand), which arose in chapter 12. The motifs of giants and heroic races to honor the dead arose in chapter 18, yet when Hightower discovers his father's "somber frock coat," it looked "as though made for a giant; as though merely from having been worn by one of them, the cloth itself had assumed the properties of those phantoms who loomed heroic and tremendous against a background of thunder and smoke and torn flags" (443–44 / 517). And that cloth, worn by phantoms, along with references to food and clusters of the word *all* (Hightower's wife says she wants to escape "All of it! All! All!" [455 / 530]), recall the All

Souls' offerings in chapters 11 and 12. Or the motifs of smell, the Pit and the hands are part of chapter 5, where Joe Christmas is attempting to cure his "disease of the skin," while hands are also featured in 8, where Bobbie is in the tabooed state of menstruation. Of course, John's chapter 20 recounts the touching of Christ's wounds, so the theme is pronounced: the coat Hightower finds "had been arranged by hands that were now dead"; his dead mother had "blue, still, almost skeleton hands"; his father believed in the literal "layingon of hands" (449 / 523); the church members waited with hands raised (461 / 538); or put the church "into his hands" (460 / 537); and out of a "handful of men" (457 / 532), his grandfather is killed "wid a han'ful of feathers" (459 / 535). In fact, amid language of erection and eruption, Hightower's final action is to masturbate with those twin blobs of his hands:

> The wheel turns on ... leaving his body empty and lighter than a forgotten leaf and even more trivial than flotsam lying spent and still upon the window ledge which has no solidity beneath hands that have no weight; so that it can be now Now
>
> It is as though they had merely waited until he could find something to pant with. ... He hears above his heart the thunder increase, myriad and drumming. Like a long sighing of wind in trees it begins, then they sweep into sight, borne now upon a cloud of phantom dust. They rush past, forwardleaning in the saddles, with brandished arms, beneath whipping ribbons from slanted and eager lances; with tumult and soundless yelling they sweep past like a tide whose crest is jagged with wild heads of horses and the brandished arms of men like the crater of the world in explosion. They rush past, are gone; the dust swirls skyward sucking, fades away into the night which has fully come. (466–67 / 543–44)

Besides the "ghostly echo," several theories suggest themselves for this harkening back to previous chapters. The most obvious one is aesthetic: it is pleasant to find themes repeated.[25] But another theory relates to the symbols themselves. All of them concern what Frazer considered the most powerful shaper of man's social evolution, death and the dead (8.36).[26]

---

25. Chapter 10 of *Ulysses*, also unique, provides a scale model for the book as a whole.

26. Here is a partial list of the motifs in chapter 20: breath: the soul that escapes

Thus, while Faulkner drew on separate sections of Frazer in pre-vious chapters, here we find patterns resurrected. There are even echoes of Frazer's own summaries:

> For ages the army of spirits, once so near, has been receding further and further from us, banished by the magic wand of science. . . . The spirits are gone even from their last stronghold in the sky, whose blue arch no longer passes, except with children, for the screen that hides from mortal eyes the glories of the celestial world. Only in poets' dreams or impassioned flights of oratory is it given to catch a glimpse of the last flutter of the standards of the retreating host, to hear the beat of their invisible wings, the sound of their mocking laughter, or the swell of angel music dying away in the distance. (9.72–73)

But for the native, the spirits still reign: "Sky and earth, mountain, forest, trees and beasts . . . all is filled with living spiritual beings, who are either friendly or hostile to mankind. Unseen or embodied in visible form, hosts of spirits surround and hover about human habitations—bestial or misshapen goblins, souls of dead friends and souls of foes, sometimes as kindly guardians, oftener as mis-chiefmakers, bringing disease and misfortune, sucking the blood and strength of the living" (9.90). With most peoples, these spirits divide into good and bad, the bad being subordinate and yet more powerful on earth. Although the ancient Egyptians believed in both good and bad spirits, "the *Book of the Dead* practically ig-nores the former" (9.103). The ancient Slavs "believed in a white

---

at death (4.198); caves/vases: sacred holders of the dead (2.201); fire: can burn away evil influence of the dead (9.320); food/clothing: set out for the dead at All Souls (6.51); games: horse races, contests to placate the dead (4.92); garden: place of sep-ulcher, symbol of resurrection (5.236); hands: tabooed after contact with the dead (3.167); masks/costumes: to depict or frighten the dead (2.178, 9.123); names: of the dead, tabooed or efficacious (3.354); noise/music: to dispel the dead (9.109) or signal rebirth (7.15); notes: can communicate with the dead (2.36); pictures/photographs: holders of the soul (3.96); prayers/stories: can placate the dead (8.112); sickness: caused by the dead (8.100); smells: bodily corruption, spices drive away the dead (9.112); stakes/sticks: keep out spirits of the dead (9.96); suspension: the hanging god, intermediary spirit (5.288); thunder: spirits of the dead at war (2.183); truth-telling/seeing: inspired prophecy from the dead (6.13); wheel: with "death" at-tached, set afire and drowned (4.247).

god and a black god, but paid adoration to the last alone," having "nothing to apprehend from the beneficence of the first or white deity" (9.92).

Such passages apply to Hightower, from the god-making fears of his sickly childhood (spirits in Indochina appear as "gigantic animals and cause terrible stomach troubles" [9.98]), to his haunted adulthood, where his thoughts on ghosts operate like "a mediaeval torture instrument" (465 / 541). The raiding spirits are echoed by the childish prank of Hightower's ghostly chicken stealers, as are the stories of his wife, since spirits also have the power to make women demented (9.78), or barren (9.93), or to tear them from their husbands (9.103). But notice, although Frazer suggests that the army of spirits retreating from civilization rode under the banner of religion, Hightower's haunts carry the banner of the South's chauvinism. In fact, had Faulkner wanted to suggest that Christianity was the root of Hightower's (and, by extension, the South's) problem, he could have easily transposed the calvary of the townspeople with the cavalry of the young seminarian.

Actually, Hightower embodies Faulkner's scorn for failure of commitment. Throughout, the minister has been extraordinarily in tune with the changes around him, from the news of Joanna's murder, to Joe as "nigger," to the Hineses' petition, to Byron's defection, to the sunset, the moment when he apparently reaches his nightly climax. Repeatedly, Faulkner has suggested he is like Frazer's Public Magician, who draws his power from nature: "His whole being, body and soul, is so delicately attuned to the harmony of the world that a touch of his hand or a turn of his head may send a thrill vibrating through the universal framework of things; and conversely his divine organism is acutely sensitive to such changes of environment as would leave ordinary mortals wholly unaffected" (1.245).

Furthermore, in chapter 20, Hightower knows everything; like the doubting Thomas, he is shown everything. In one cluster of the word *all* (as the wheel rolls away the block to his understanding), Hightower clearly sees the need for charity "with all air, all heaven, filled with the lost and unheeded crying of all the living who ever lived, wailing still like lost children among the cold and terrible stars" (466 / 543). And while the *Book of the Dead* states that the soul of the departed must swear "that he had not oppressed his fellow-men, that he had made none to weep, that he had done no murder, neither committed fornication nor borne false witness, that he had not falsified the balance, that he had not taken the milk from the mouths of babes," he must also swear "that he had given bread to the hungry and water to the thirsty and had clothed the naked" (6.13). Thus, Hightower finally knows that in saying he has done nothing, that claim is itself an indictment.

Indeed, Hightower would have special obligations, for Frazer claims that once the Public Magician, as "the more sagacious" of society (1.215), has attained his natural ambitions of wealth and honor, he is then capable of great good: "The rise of one man to supreme power enables him to carry through changes in a single lifetime which previously many generations might not have sufficed to effect" (1.217). This Carlylian or Nietzschean view of the Great Man gives a special poignancy to Hightower's denial of responsibility, and may explain why his final vision is not of the victim, Joe Christmas, but of the victimizer, Percy Grimm, as if Hightower realizes that his failure was, like Pilate's, in not asserting his leadership,[27] so the void was filled by the new War Chief, a change of fetish from southern to American jingoism. [28]

It should be noted that, although Hightower's dead have been shown to be hungry and naked, one and all, they refuse sustenance: Hightower's father "would neither eat food grown and cooked by . . . a negro slave" (442 / 515), nor would he taste the Bourbon whiskey with which he is nightly saluted by his father. He marries the child of a "genteel couple" who used the church as a "substitute for that which lacked upon the dinnertable" (446 / 520), then goes off to war, leaving his wife to starve, insisting she refuse the help of neighbors. The negro woman refuses not only the son's provisions but her own freedom. Hightower, the child,

---

27. Cottrell (210–11) argues that Hightower should be linked with Pontius Pilate.

28. Referring to Faulkner's theological concerns, Davis (70) uses similar words, when he says that what Grimm has done is "to substitute for the one abstraction [Calvinism] another abstraction, America."

"would be unable to eat," and grown, enters the church where "truth could walk naked," where "the hampered and garment-worried spirit could learn anew serenity to contemplate without horror or alarm its own nakedness" (453 / 528). His marriage, his wife's "escape," should have clothed "the desperation naked in her face" (457 / 532), and it should have eased his own hunger. Yet as he says, "In the moment when I revealed to her not only the depth of my hunger," he also reveals "that never and never would she have any part in the assuaging of it" (462 / 538). His only offering to the people who met him at the station "with eagerness and hunger" (465 / 542) is "casting his sops as though he were flinging rotten fruit before a drove of hogs" (463 / 540). Even the chicken stealing represents sustenance repudiated:

> Hungry, gaunt, yelling, setting fire to the store depots . . . and riding out again. No looting at all: no stopping for even shoes, tobacco. I tell you, they were not men after spoils and glory; they were boys riding the sheer tremendous tidal wave of desperate living. . . . I think that they did it deliberately, as boys who had set fire to an enemy's barn, without taking so much as a shingle or a door hasp, might pause in flight to steal a few apples from a neighbor, a friend. Mind you, they were hungry. They had been hungry for three years. Perhaps they were used to that. Anyway, they had just set fire to tons of food and clothing and tobacco and liquors, taking nothing though there had not been issued any order against looting. (457–58 / 533–34)

These ghostly repudiations of sustenance reflect the difference between Jesus' appearance in John and that in Luke, where he proves his physicality by eating (Luke 24:41 ff.). Conversely, Faulkner's ghosts prove their physicality not by eating but by their renunciation of food. When they are caught "wid a han'ful of feathers," it is the wild improbability of their appearance (in the henhouse), the clumsy humanity of it, "riding the sheer tidal wave of desperate living," that makes them come to life.

Of course, Hightower will live on, a repository of the dead, his whole life trivial as dust.[29] Although he holds knowledge of the

---

29. Benson (548) says that because Hightower "shapes his own destiny by acts of

dead, this changes nothing for him. For all his sensitivity and insight, he can call himself murderer and return to his onanism, passing from "a consternation which is about to be actual horror" back to the "phantom dust" and the "soundless yelling." Ironically, he knows that his ancestral gods have more substance than he, for it is their thorough engagement in life, their willingness (like Christ) to suffer life's physicality, that makes their dead lives, risen, more real than their grave, the empty tomb of Hightower's bandaged skull.[30] This chapter on the resurrection suggests that if you look into the tomb, the shape of life will be at once dolorous, and droll.

Chapter 21: *The Hangdog, Peter, Restored*

Since the last shall be first, it is time for Byron Bunch to be placed in our pantheon of gods. He turns out to be our ironic Adonis. He is early recognized as a fellow yeargod by Christmas-Dionysus— who treats him "as if he were another post" (30 / 37). But Adonis was often confused with Osiris (5.32), and Lena-Isis, looking for Burch-Osiris, is sent to a fellow named Bunch. Moreover, "Byron," which suggests Lord Byron, is apt because Adonis means "Lord," and "Bunch" is apt because there were once "as many Adonises as there were trees and shrubs" (5.233).[31]

One version of Adonis, Tammuz, meaning "true son," had annually to be rescued by his mother-wife from the "house of darkness, where dust lies on door and bolt" (5.8). We might note that Byron, who has been rescued by Lena from Hightower's house of the dead, is here repeatedly depicted as a child: his face is "all shined up like a kid" (472 / 549), he is a *"durn little cuss that already looked like he had reached the point where he could bust out crying like another baby"* (476 / 555), or he is put "back outside on the ground like . . . that baby if it had been about six years

will," he is "morally accountable for his choices," unlike Christmas, who is "shaped by exterior forces and attitudes."

30. Krieger (335) notes the connection between the setting of Christmas's death, with its resurrection metaphor, and the resurrected events of Hightower's life.

31. For further discussions on Byron's name, see McCamy.

old" (477 / 555).[32] In fact, Lena's crying in chapter 17 because Byron is "gone" and she "will never see him again" (390 / 456), suggests the Lament for Tammuz:

> *At his vanishing away she lifts up a lament,*
> *"Oh my child!" at his vanishing away she lifts up a lament;*
> *"My Damu!" at his vanishing away she lifts up a lament.*
> *"My enchanter and priest!" (5.9)*

Another version of Adonis was David himself, because the origin
of his name, Dodo ("beloved one") may have been a babyism for
Tammuz (5.19n), and because the city of David, Bethlehem, or
"House of Bread," was anciently a grove dedicated to the grain
spirit, Adonis (5.257). David, the giant-slayer, recalls Byron's battle
with the "Great God" Brown in 18; certainly links with the House
of David, the paternal line of Jesus, would be appropriate to our
Faulkner character; for if Lena is a Mary figure, then Byron is Joseph.

The god's rites included carrying the images of Aphrodite and
Adonis "on two couches" with ripe fruits and cakes and plants in
bowers beside them in celebration of their marriage (5.224). All of
this lushness has been transformed in Faulkner's chapter 21 to the
theme of "furniture" and "accommodations." In their "flight into
Egypt," Byron and Lena ride with a "furniture repairer and dealer
who recently made a trip into Tennessee to get some old pieces of
furniture." The truck, carrying "camping equipment," "had a
housed-in body with a door at the rear" (468 / 545), which Byron
calls a "truck house" (471 / 548). To Byron's repeated, "It would be
a accommodation" (469 / 546), they discuss the seat up front or
that bed in the back, Lena riding on "a kind of cushion with the
folded blanket" (478 / 556–57). When they spread their blankets,
sleeping the night on the "bags and sacks," Byron acts as if he aims
"to settle down permanent in this truck and set up housekeeping"
(472 / 549). Moreover, the setting for the last chapter is the bed of
the furniture dealer, engaged in sly talk with his wife, who *"dont*

---

32. Brooks (69) says that Lena saves Byron from a "pallid half-life." Rosenzweig
(97) amusingly observes that since Byron becomes a child, "Lena is correct when
she predicts that she will have twins."

mind" being *"showed again"* if he *"dont"* (472 / 550). But the prime example of the young god being carried in procession with the Mother Goddess amid lush, ripe fruit and fertility symbols is that baby at Lena's breast, "that hadn't never stopped eating, that had been eating breakfast now for about ten miles, like one of these dining cars on the train, and her looking out and watching the telephone poles and the fences passing like it was a circus parade," with Lena saying, "My, my. A body does get around" (480 / 559).

Other language in the chapter supports similar ceremonies connected with May Day, which featured begging processions of the Lady (Lena is "a lady with a Saturday night family" [475 / 553], while the furniture man's wife says he mustn't talk that way *"before a lady"* [470 / 547]). They also featured the Lord ("Like if the Lord aimed for me to say it, I would say it, and if the Lord aimed for him to go to a hotel . . . he would do that too" [471 / 548]). But Frazer says the May Day Lord was just as suspect, because it was reported that "yung men and maides, olde men and wives, run gadding over night to the woods, groves, hils, and mountains, where they spend all the night in plesant pastimes . . . a great Lord present amongst them, as superintendent and Lord over their pastimes and sportes, namely, Sathan, prince of hel" (2.66).

Naturally, May poles were featured (Lena sits with Byron on a log "with her back to a tree" [473 / 551]) or rides *"looking out like she hadn't ever seen country—roads and trees and fields and telephone poles—before in her life"* (479 / 557). But also eggs (Byron helps Lena "like she and the kid were made out of glass or eggs" [472 / 550], or he walks "like he had eggs under his feet" [476 / 554]), and fires (Byron builds a fire with "enough wood to barbecue a steer," which people danced around (like "those two Frenchmen that were always bowing and scraping at the other one to go first" [473 / 551]) (2.59 ff.).

As in myth, where Adonis' wedding includes both the sorrow of his death and the joy of this rebirth, so May Day ceremonies suggested both the cutting down of the tree and its raising. Likewise in Faulkner, his ending is a beginning, and his language suggests the vanishing and reappearing of the hanged god. The hanging, linked as it is with "dog," suggests the Joycean trick of reading "dog" backwards for "god." Certainly Byron is hanged: "I be dog if I didn't want to find the hole and crawl into it with him. . . . And him standing there where she had set him down. The fire had burned down good now and I couldn't hardly see him at all. But I knew about how I would have been standing and feeling if I was him. And that would have been with my head bowed, waiting for the Judge to say, 'Take him out of here and hang him quick'" (477 / 555–56). And certainly he disappears, whether into that "hole" or into the "bushes." Moreover, the next day, when he reappears, "*standing at the side of the road*," he is again "*standing there* [like the Maypole], *face and no face, hangdog and determined and calm too, like he had done desperated himself up for the last time, to take the last chance, and that now he knew he wouldn't ever have to desperate himself again.*" "I be dog," he says, "if I'm going to quit now," whereupon Lena says, "Aint nobody never said for you to quit" (479 / 558). So they proceed to Saulsbury, "Saul" suggesting the new time of Paul the Apostle.

Which brings us to the biblical connection. The 21st chapter of John opens with a fishing scene, the disciples having no luck, when Jesus appears, unrecognized (although this is his third appearance), tells the "children," the disciples, to cast their nets on the right side of the ship, whereupon they cannot draw in their nets "for the multitude of fishes." When Peter hears it is "the Lord," he girds up his coat and throws himself into the water, eager to reach Jesus. On shore, they see "a fire of coals there, and fish laid thereon, and bread" by which Jesus feeds them. Then Jesus asks Peter three times if he loves him and three times Peter says he does, each time Jesus responding, "Feed my lambs" (or sheep) and finally commanding Peter to follow him. The gospel ends with the hyperbole "And there are also many other things which Jesus did, the which, if they should be written every one, I suppose that even the world itself could not contain the books that should be written. A-men."

Most scholars agree that this last chapter—especially the "fish story"—was written by a redactor or perhaps by a much older John. They cite language, grammar, and shift of emphasis. For example,

Jesus calls the disciples "children" (or "lads" [International 696]) using a colloquialism not found elsewhere in John. Or the final sentence involves both non-Johannine expressions (such as the hesitant "I suppose") and awkward Greek (translated as "many other things").

Most significant is the shift of emphasis from Jesus' appearance to the reestablishment of Peter's eminence, important to his position in church authority. In other words, many read the almost liturgical question-and-answer passages in which Peter is "grieved" by Jesus' questions as the symbolic repairing of Peter's three denials.

I have used the word *repairing* deliberately because Faulkner's chapter 21 introduces a furniture repairer (who would also restore). Yet this theme can be justified more widely. After all, the central story here is one of Byron trying to repair his relationship to Lena, establishing his future authority. And if Lena treats him like a child, this is no more than Jesus does his disciples, calling them "lads," feeding them, and making Peter respond to the same embarrassing question three times over. Recall also that John's grammatical problems are reflected in Faulkner's 21, where he uses a style that is not always the fault of the furniture dealer, who "told his wife of an experience which he had had on the road, which interested him at the time and which he considered amusing enough to repeat. Perhaps the reason why he found it interesting and that he felt that he could make it interesting in the retelling is that he and his wife are not old either, besides his having been away from home (due to the very moderate speed which he felt it wise to restrict himself to) for more than a week" (468 / 545). The "moderate speed" of this passage of "interestings" and "whiches" matches John's closing on "many other things which Jesus did, the which," or his slow opening: "After these things Jesus shewed himself again to the disciples at the sea of Tiberias; and on this wise shewed he himself." As for Faulkner's unusual language, out of many colloquialisms, the most significant may be the "desperated up," referring to Byron, and the repeated, "I knowed," referring to the furniture dealer himself, since these two represent the difference between Peter and the Beloved Disciple, generally thought of as John the Apostle. Although both were "unlearned" (Acts 4:13), Peter was "first to act," while John was "first to apprehend" (Cambridge 369); or Peter had the "greater ardour," while John had the "keener insight" (Moffatt 371). In Faulkner, our sense of Byron as a man who does rather than knows can be observed in his uncharacteristically clumsy assault on Lena. In fact, in contrast to our first meeting with him, where "Byron Bunch knows this" (27 / 33), here Byron knows nothing. Sappy with love, he does not know where he and Lena are going, that Lena is planning to accept him, or even how to behave himself. Yet the furniture dealer (who, like the Beloved Disciple, is known only by his title), beginning with no information, promptly knows a lot: he will say, "You aint had that chap no eight weeks." "Not if I know color" (470 / 547); or "I knowed what he wanted me to say" (471 / 548); or "I learned that quick" (474 / 552); or "I knew that he hadn't give up" (475 / 553). And his last speculations are entirely congenial with our own view of Lena:

> Yes, sir. You cant beat a woman. Because do you know what I think? I think she was just travelling. I dont think she had any idea of finding whoever it was she was following. I dont think she had ever aimed to, only she hadn't told him yet. I reckon this was the first time she had ever been further away from home than she could walk back before sundown in her life. And that she had got along all right this far, with folks taking good care of her. And so I think she had just made up her mind to travel a little further and see as much as she could, since I reckon she knew that when she settled down this time, it would likely be for the rest of her life. That's what I think. (479–80 / 558–59)

Well, if that is what he thinks, we can rest easy, for he has shown himself to be a sound judge of character, even in the face of some (may we say?) fishy appearances.[33] And since, as many have noted, this is the moment when Lena gets her man, it can be seen as the drawing in of nets.[34]

---

33. Using litotes, Brooks (73) says that the furniture dealer's "insights into the relations of man and woman, the nature of chivalry, and the connection of love with honor are not untouched by a certain wisdom."

34. See, for example, Straumann (146), who stresses Lena's desire for a man.

What was it in John that suggested to Faulkner the May Day ceremonies? The link is in the character of Byron-Adonis-Peter, all three of whom suffer the fate of the hanged god, for Peter will also be hanged, by his own choice, upside down. Thus, we find the May Day material from Frazer chosen because of Jesus' prediction: "When thou wast young, thou girdest thyself, and walkedst whither thou wouldest: but when thou shalt be old, thou shalt stretch forth thy hands, and another shall gird thee, and carry thee whither thou wouldest not. This spake he, signifying by what death he should glorify God." Now it could be that Faulkner is presenting simply the amusing parallel of Byron's being treated by Lena like a baby. But what I suspect is that by giving Byron Peter's role, Faulkner's final joke is that his marriage to Lena, even though it be to Mother Earth herself, sooner or later will represent the usual male crucifixion. At the very least, it may carry him "whither thou wouldest not."

That final hyperbole of John, which says that he could not begin to tell all that Jesus did, is compelling. Without equating Faulkner with Jesus, I share the awe of the recorder and perhaps the tendency to overstate. Others should correct and augment. The correspondences are there, and the impulse to look for meaning is right. Begin like Faulkner, with the word and the form, and we may (God help us) fill the world with books on the things that we find.

Appendixes
Bibliography
Index

APPENDIX A:

Divisions in Faulkner's Novels

Year	Work	Chapter no.	Divisions	Subdivisions
1926	Soldiers' Pay	9	CHAPTER I, CHAPTER II,	Yes
1927	Mosquitoes	6	Prologue, The First Day, The Second Day; Epilogue	Yes
1929	Sartoris	5	PART ONE, PART, TWO	Yes
1929	The Sound and the Fury	4	April 7, 1928; June 2, 1910; April 6, 1928; April 8, 1928	No
1930	As I Lay Dying	59	Darl (19), Vardaman (10), Tull (6), Cash (5), Dewey Dell (4), Cora and Anse (3 each), Peabody (2), Jewel, Samson, Addie, Whitfield, Armstid, Moseley, MacGowan (1 each)	No
1931	Sanctuary	31	ONE, TWO,	Yes
1932	Light in August	21	1, 2,	Yes
1935	Pylon	7	Dedication of an Airport; An Evening in New Valois; Night in the Vieux Carré; Tomorrow; And Tomorrow; Lovesong of J. A. Prufrock; The Scavengers	No
1936	Absalom, Absalom!	9	I, II,	No
1938	The Unvanquished	7	Ambuscade; Retreat; Raid; Riposte in Tertio; Vendee; Skirmish at Sartoris; An Odor of Verbena	Yes
1939	The Wild Palms	10	Wild Palms [alternating with] The Old Man	No
1940	The Hamlet	4	BOOK ONE: Flem; BOOK TWO: Eula; BOOK THREE: The Long Summer; BOOK FOUR: The Peasants	Yes

Year	Work	Chap-ter no.	Divisions	Sub-divisions
1942	Go Down, Moses	7	Was; The Fire and the Hearth; Pantaloon in Black; The Old People; The Bear; Delta Autumn; Go Down, Moses	Yes
1948	Intruder in the Dust	11	Chapter One, Chapter Two,	No
1951	Requiem for A Nun	3	The Courthouse (A Name for the City); The Golden Dome (Beginning Was the Word); The Jail (Nor Even Yet Quite Relinquish—)	Yes
1954	A Fable	10	Wednesday; Monday, Monday Night; Tuesday Night; Monday, Tuesday, Wednesday; Tuesday, Wednesday; Tuesday, Wednesday, Wednesday Night; Wednesday Night; Thursday, Thursday Night; Friday, Saturday, Sunday; Tomorrow	Yes
1957	The Town	24	ONE, TWO, with names: Charles Mallison (10), Gavin Stevens (8), V. K. Ratliff (6)	Yes
1959	The Mansion	3	Mink; Linda; Flem (or) 18 ONE, TWO	Yes
1962	The Reivers	13	Chapter 1, Chapter 2,	No

APPENDIX B:

The Primary Uses of *The Golden Bough* in *Light in August*

Faulkner chapter	Discussion in Frazer	Volume	Pages
1	Absence & Recall of the Soul	3	30–77
	Knots & Rings Tabooed	3	293–317
	Isis as Cow at the Festival of Sais	6	46–51
	Isis	6	115–19
2	The Myth of Osiris	6	3–23
	The Nature of Osiris	6	96–114
	Dionysus	7	1–34
	The Festivals of Fools & Innocents	9	313–45
	Water to Wine at the Easter Fires	10	120–46
3	Magicians as Kings	1	332–72
	The Burden of Royalty	3	1–25
	Taboos on Showing Face or Leaving House	3	120–26
4	Hippolytus	1	24–40
	Virbius & the Horse	8	40–47
	The External Soul	11	153–58
5 & 6	The Principles of Homeopathic Magic	1	52–147
5	Warriors, Hunters, & Fishers Tabooed	3	157–223
	Not to Step over Persons & Things	3	423–25
	Volcanic Religions	5	188–259
	Between Heaven & Earth	10	1–21
	Balder & the Mistletoe	11	76–94
	The Golden Bough	11	279–303
6	Contagious Magic	1	174–214
	Sacred Men & Women of the Temple	5	57–109
	Eating the God	8	48–108
	Homeopathic Magic of Flesh Diet	8	138–68
	Transmigration of Souls into Animals	8	285–309
7	Initiation Rites	11	225–78

Faulkner chapter	Discussion in Frazer	Volume	Pages
8	Women Tabooed	3	145–57
	Demeter & Persephone	7	35–91
	Transference to Stones and Sticks	9	8–30
	The Human Scapegoat	9	252–74
	Seclusion of Pubescent Girls	10	22–100
9	The Doctrine of Lunar Sympathy	6	140–50
	Dionysian Rites	7	22–34
	Expulsion of Embodied Evils	9	170–252
10	St. George the Shepherd	2	324–48
	Sacrifice to Stay a Cattle Plague	10	300–327
11 & 12	The King of the Wood	1	1–43
	Diana as a Goddess of Fertility	2	120–29
	Dianus & Diana	2	376–87
	Feasts of All Souls	6	51–83
	The Halloween Fires	10	222–46
11	The Worship of Trees	2	7–58
	The Influence of the Sexes on Vegetation	2	97–119
	The Marriage of the Gods	2	129–55
	The Succession to the Kingdom	2	266–323
12	Magical Control of Rain	1	247–311
	The Worship of the Oak	1	349–75
	The King as Jupiter	2	174–94
	The Corn Mother	7	113–305
13	Expulsion of Disembodied Evil	9	72–169
	The Roman Saturnalia	9	306–12
	The Need-fire	10	269–300
	The Fire Walk & Midsummer's Eve	11	1–20
14	Taboos on Intercourse with Strangers	3	101–16
	Mourners Tabooed	3	138–45
	Manslayers Tabooed	3	165–90
15	The Fire Sticks	2	207–26
	Sacrifice of First Fruits	8	109–37
	Killing the Divine Animal	8	169–273
	Processions with Sacred Animals	8	316–25
16	Carnival Death	4	205–71

Faulkner chapter	Discussion in Frazer	Volume	Pages
	Games in Primitive Agriculture	7	92–112
	Rites of Plough Monday	8	325–35
17	Incarnate Human Gods	1	373–421
18 & 19	The Dying God	4	1–195
19	Priestly Sacrifice	5	261–317
	The Crucifixion of Christ	9	412–23
20	The Magician's Progress	1	214–19
	The Public Magician	1	244–47
	The Omnipresence of Demons	9	72–108
21	Relics of Tree Worship	2	59–96
	Adonis	5	3–56
	The Ritual of Adonis	5	223–35
	The Gardens of Adonis	5	236–59

Bibliography

The Bible and Myth

Anchor Bible: *Gospel According to John.* 2 vols. Ed. Raymond E. Brown. Garden City, N.Y.: Doubleday, 1966.

Cambridge Bible: *The Gospel According to St. John.* Ed. A. Plummer. Cambridge: Cambridge Univ. Press, 1923.

Frazer, Sir James George. *The Golden Bough: A Study in Magic and Religion.* 3d Ed. New York: St. Martins. Vols. 1 & 2, *The Magic Art and the Evolution of Kings.* 1911. Vol. 3, *Taboo and the Perils of the Soul.* 1911. Vol. 4, *The Dying God. 1911.* Vols. 5 & 6, *Adonis, Attis, Osiris: Studies in the History of Oriental Religion.* 1914. Vols. 7 & 8, *Spirits of the Corn and of the Wild.* 1912. Vol. 9, *The Scapegoat.* 1913. Vols. 10 & 11, *Balder the Beautiful: The Fire-Festivals of Europe and the Doctrine of the External Soul.* 1913. Vol. 12, Bibliography and General Index. 1915.

International Bible: *A Critical and Exegetical Commentary on the Gospel According to St. John.* Ed. J. H. Bernard. 2 vols. New York: Scribner, 1929.

Ludwig, Emil. *The Son of Man: The Story of Jesus.* Trans. Eden & Cedar Paul. New York: Boni & Liveright, 1928.

Merrymount Press: *The Holy Bible Containing the Old and New Testaments and the Apocrypha.* Boston: R. H. Hinkley, n.d. 14 vols. (The Holy Bible Translated Out of the Original Tongues in the Year of Our Lord 1611.)

Moffatt Bible: *The Gospel of John.* Ed. G. H. C. MacGregor. New York & London: Harper, 1928.

Westcott, B. F. *The Gospel According to St. John.* London: John Murray, 1882.

Faulkner and His Works

Abel, Darrel. "Frozen Movement in *Light in August.*" *Boston University Studies in English* 3 (1957): 32–44.

Abrams, M. H. *The Mirror and the Lamp: Romantic Theory and the Critical Tradition.* New York: Oxford Univ. Press, 1953.

Adams, Robert Martin. *AfterJoyce.* New York: Oxford Univ. Press, 1977.

Asals, Frederick. "Faulkner's *Light in August.*" *The Explicator* 26 (1968): no. 74.

Baker, Carlos. "William Faulkner: The Doomed and the Damned." In *The Young Rebel in American Literature,* ed. Carl Bode, 143–69. New York: Praeger, 1960.

Baldanza, Frank. "The Structure of *Light in August.*" *Modern Fiction Studies* 13 (1967): 67–78.

Bassett, John Earl. *Faulkner: An Annotated Checklist of Recent Criticism.* Kent, Ohio: Kent State Univ. Press, 1983.

Benson, Carl. "Thematic Design in *Light in August.*" *South Atlantic Quarterly* 53 (1954): 540–55.

Blotner, Joseph L. *Faulkner: A Biography.* 2 vols. New York: Random House, 1974.

———. *William Faulkner's Library—A Catalogue.* Charlottesville: Univ. Press of Virginia, 1964.

Brooks, Cleanth. *William Faulkner: The Yoknapatawpha Country.* New Haven and London: Yale Univ. Press, 1963.

Brumm, Ursula. *American Thought and Religious Typology.* New Brunswick, N.J.: Rutgers Univ. Press, 1970.

Brylowski, Walter. *Faulkner's Olympian Laugh: Myth in the Novels.* Detroit: Wayne State Univ. Press, 1968.

Burroughs, Franklin G., Jr. "God the Father and Motherless Children: *Light in August.*" *Twentieth Century Literature* 19 (1973): 189–202.

Campbell, Harry Modean, and Ruel E. Foster. *William Faulkner: A Critical Appraisal.* Norman: Univ. of Oklahoma Press, 1951.

Capps, Jack L., ed. *Light in August: A Concordance to the Novel.* West Point: U.S. Military Academy, 1979.

Coindreau, Maurice. "Preface to *Light in August.*" *The Time of William Faulkner: A French View of Modern American Fiction: Essays by Maurice Edgar Coindreau.* Trans. George M. Reeves. Columbia: Univ. of South Carolina Press, 1971.

Collins, Carvel. Introduction. William Faulkner's *New Orleans Sketches*. New York: Grove Press, 1958.

———. "The Pairing of *The Sound and the Fury* and *As I Lay Dying*." *Princeton University Library Chronicle* 18 (1957): 114–23.

———. "Faulkner's *The Sound and the Fury*." *The American Novel from James Fenimore Cooper to William Faulkner*. New York: Basic Books, 1965. 219–28.

Collins, R. G. "The Game of Names: Characterization Devices in *Light in August*." *English Record* 21 (1970): 82–84.

———. "*Light in August*: Faulkner's Stained Glass Triptych." *Mosaic* 7 (1973): 97–157.

Cottrell, Beekman W. "Christian Symbols in *Light in August*." *Modern Fiction Studies* 2 (1956): 207–13.

Cowley, Malcolm. Introduction. *The Portable Faulkner*. Rev. ed. New York: Viking, 1967.

Cross, Barbara M. "*The Sound and the Fury*: The Pattern of Sacrifice." *Arizona Quarterly* 16 (1960): 5–16.

Culley, Margaret M. "Judgment in Yoknapatawpha Fiction." *Renascence* 28 (1976): 59–70.

Davis, Charles E. "William Faulkner's Joe Christmas: A Rage for Order." *Arizona Quarterly* 32 (1976): 61–73.

Dickerson, Mary Jane. "Some Sources of Faulkner's Myth in 'As I Lay Dying.'" *Mississippi Quarterly* 19 (1966): 132–42.

Douglas, Ellen. "Faulkner's Women." In *"A Cosmos of My Own": Faulkner and Yoknapatawpha 1980*, ed. Doreen Fowler & Ann J. Abadie, 149–67. Jackson: Univ. of Mississippi Press, 1981.

Douglas, Harold J., and Robert Daniel. "Faulkner's Southern Puritanism." In *Religious Perspectives in Faulkner's Fiction: Yoknapatawpha and Beyond*, ed. J. Robert Barth, 37–51. Notre Dame: Univ. of Notre Dame Press, 1972.

Doyle, Charles. "The Moral World of Faulkner." *Renascence* 19 (1966): 3–12.

Eliot, T. S. "*Ulysses*, Order and Myth." *The Dial* (Nov. 1923): 480–83.

Ellmann, Richard. *James Joyce*. London: Oxford Univ. Press, 1959.

Fadiman, Regina K. *Faulkner's* Light in August: *A Description and Interpretation of the Revisions*. Charlottesville: Univ. Press of Virginia, 1975.

Faulkner, William. *Absalom, Absalom!* New York: Random House, 1936.

———. *Light in August*. New York: Random House, 1959.

———. *Light in August: The Corrected Text*. New York: Random House, 1987.

———. "Light in August." Manuscript, 188 pp. Charlottesville: University of Virginia Library.

———. *Mosquitoes*. New York: Dell, 1927.

———. *Faulkner at Nagano*. Ed. Robert A. Jelliffe. Tokyo: Kenkyusha Press, 1956.

———. *Faulkner in the University: Class Conferences at the University of Virginia, 1957–1958*. Ed. Frederick L. Gwynn & Joseph L. Blotner. Charlottesville: Univ. Press of Virginia, 1959.

———. *Lion in the Garden: Interviews with William Faulkner, 1926–1962*. New York: Random House, 1968.

———. *Selected Letters of William Faulkner*. Ed. Joseph L. Blotner. New York: Random House, 1978.

Ficken, Carl F. "A Critical and Textual Study of William Faulkner's *Light in August*." Ph.D. diss., Univ. of South Carolina, 1973.

———. "The Christ Story in *A Fable*." *Mississippi Quarterly* 23 (1970) 251–64.

Fiedler, Leslie A. "William Faulkner: An American Dickens." *Commentary* 10 (1950): 384–87.

Fowler, Doreen. "The Ravished Daughter: Eleusinian Mysteries in *The Sound and the Fury*." In *Faulkner and Religion*, ed. Fowler & Ann J. Abadie. Jackson: Univ. of Mississippi Press. Forthcoming.

Frazier, David Lowell. "The Theme in Faulkner's *Light in August*: An Approach through Polarity." M.A. thesis, Indiana Univ., 1957.

Greer, Scott. "Joe Christmas and the Social Self." *Mississippi Quarterly* 11 (1958).

Gwynn, Frederick L. "Faulkner's Prufrock—and Other Observations." *Journal of English and Germanic Philology* 52 (1953): 63–70.

Hall, Constance Hill. *Incest in Faulkner: A Metaphor for the Fall*. Ann Arbor: UMI Research Press, 1986.

Hardy, John Edward. *Man in the Modern Novel*. Seattle: Univ. of Washington Press, 1964.

Hirshleifer, Phyllis. "As Whirlwinds in the South: An Analysis of *Light in August*." *Perspective* 2 (1949): 225–38.

Hlavsa, Virginia V. "The Levity of *Light in August*." In *Faulkner and Humor: Faulkner and Yoknapatawpha, 1984*, ed. Doreen Fowler & Ann J. Abadie, 47–56. Jackson: Univ. of Mississippi Press, 1986.

———. "The Mirror, the Lamp, and the Bed: Faulkner and the Modernists." *American Literature* 57 (1985): 23–43.

———. "The Vision of the Advocate in *Absalom, Absalom!*" *Novel* 8 (1974): 51–70.

———. "St. John and Frazer in *Light in August*: Biblical Form and Mythic Function." *Bulletin of Research in the Humanities* 83 (1980): 9–26.

Holman, C. Hugh. "The Unity of Faulkner's *Light in August*." *PMLA* 63 (1958): 155–66.

Inge, M. Thomas. "William Faulkner's *Light in August*: An Annotated Checklist of Criticism." *Resources for American Literary Study* 1 (1971): 30–57.

220 ° Bibliography

Irwin, John T. *Doubling and Incest, Repetition and Revenge.* Baltimore: Johns Hopkins Univ. Press, 1976.

Jacobs, Robert D. "Faulkner's Tragedy of Isolation." In *Southern Renascence: The Literature of the Modern South,* ed. Jacobs & Louis D. Rubin, Jr. Baltimore: Johns Hopkins Univ. Press, 1976.

Jenkins, Lee. *Faulkner and Black-White Relations: A Psychoanalytic Approach.* New York: Columbia Univ. Press, 1981. 61–105.

Kaplan, Harold. *The Passive Voice: An Approach to Modern Fiction.* Athens: Ohio Univ. Press, 1966. 111–30.

Kazin, Alfred. "The Stillness of *Light in August.*" *Partisan Review* 24 (1957): 519–38.

Kenner, Hugh. "Faulkner and the Avant Garde." In *Faulkner (New Perspectives),* ed. Richard H. Brodhead, 62–73. Englewood Cliffs, N.J.: Prentice-Hall, 1983.

Kerr, Elizabeth. *William Faulkner's Gothic Domain.* Port Washington, N.Y.: Kennakat, 1979.

Kohler, Dayton. "*A Fable:* The Novel as Myth." *College English* 16 (1955): 471–78.

Kreiswirth, Martin. "Plots and Counterplots." In *New Essays on* Light in August, ed. Michael Millgate, 55–79. Cambridge: Cambridge Univ. Press, 1987.

Krieger, Murray. *The Classic Vision: The Retreat from Extremity in Modern Literature.* Baltimore: Johns Hopkins Univ. Press, 1971.

Kunkel, Francis L. "Christ Symbolism in Faulkner: Prevalence of the Human." *Renascence* 17 (1965): 148–56.

Lamont, William. "The Chronology of *Light in August.*" *Modern Fiction Studies* 3 (1957): 360–61.

Langston, Beach. "The Meaning of Lena Grove and Gail Hightower in *Light in August.*" *Boston University Studies in English* 5 (1961): 46–63.

Leavis, F. R. "Dostoevsky or Dickens?" *Scrutiny* 2 (1933): 91–92.

Longley, John L., Jr. "Joe Christmas: The Hero in the Modern World." *Virginia Quarterly Review* 33 (1957): 233–49.

McCamy, Edward. "Byron Bunch." *Shenandoah* 3 (1952): 8–12.

McHaney, Thomas L. "*Sanctuary* and Frazer's Slain Kings." *Mississippi Quarterly* 24 (1971): 223–45.

———. *William Faulkner: A Reference Guide.* Boston: G. K. Hall, 1976.

———. *William Faulkner's* The Wild Palms: *A Study.* Jackson: Univ. of Mississippi Press, 1975.

Meeter, Glenn. "Quentin as Redactor: Biblical Analogy in Faulkner's *Absalom, Absalom!*" In *Faulkner and Religion,* ed. Doreen Fowler & Ann J. Abadie. Jackson: Univ. of Mississippi Press. Forthcoming.

Meriwether, James. *The Literary Career of William Faulkner: A Bibliographical Study.* Princeton: Princeton Univ. Press, 1971.

Millgate, Michael. *The Achievement of William Faulkner.* Lincoln: Univ. of Nebraska Press, 1963. 124–37.

Minter, David L. *William Faulkner: His Life and Work.* Baltimore: Johns Hopkins Univ. Press, 1980.

Morrisseu, Thomas J. "Food Imagery in Faulkner's *Light in August.*" *Nassau Review* 3 (1978): 41–49.

Mortimer, Gail. *Faulkner's Rhetoric of Loss: A Study in Perception and Meaning.* Austin: Univ. of Texas Press, 1963. 135–51.

Moseley, Edwin M. "Christ as Social Scapegoat: Faulkner's *Light in August.*" *Pseudonyms of Christ in the Modern Novel: Motifs and Methods.* Pittsburgh: Univ. of Pittsburgh Press, 1962. 246–59.

Murphy, Denis M. "*The Sound and the Fury* and Dante's *Inferno:* Fire and Ice." *Markam Review* 4 (1974): 71–78.

Naples, Diane C. "Eliot's Tradition and *The Sound and the Fury.*" *Modern Fiction Studies* 20 (1974): 214–17.

Nemerov, Howard. *Poetry and Fiction: Essays.* New Brunswick, N.J.: Rutgers Univ. Press, 1963.

O'Dea, Richard J. "Faulkner's Vestigial Christianity." *Renascence* 21 (1968): 44–54.

Ohashi, Kenzaburo. "*Light in August:* The Spell of the 'Window' and the Tragedy of the 'Earth.'" In *Faulkner Studies in Japan,* ed. Thomas McHaney, 116–47. Athens: Univ. of Georgia Press, 1985.

Parker, Robert Dale. *Faulkner and the Novelistic Imagination.* Urbana & Chicago: Univ. of Illinois Press, 1985.

Peterson, Richard F. "Faulkner's *Light in August.*" *Explicator* 30 (1971): item 35.

Pitavy, François L. *Faulkner's* Light in August. Bloomington & London: Indiana Univ. Press, 1973.

Porter, Carolyn. "The Problem of Time in *Light in August.*" *Rice University Studies* 61 (1975): 107–25.

Reed, Joseph, Jr. *Faulkner's Narrative.* New Haven: Yale Univ. Press, 1973.

Rice, Julian C. "Orpheus and the Hellish Unity in *Light in August.*" *Centennial Review* 19 (1975): 380–96.

Roberts, James L. "The Individual and the Community: Faulkner's *Light in August.*" *Studies in American Literature,* ed. Waldo McNeir & Leo B. Levy, 132–53. Baton Rouge: Louisiana State Univ. Press, 1960.

Rose, Maxine. "From Genesis to Revelation: The Grand Design of Faulkner's *Absalom, Absalom!*" Ph.D. diss., Univ. of Alabama, 1973.

Rosenzwig, Paul J. "Faulkner's Motif of Food in *Light in August.*" *American Imago* 37 (1980): 93–112.

Rovere, Richard H. Introduction. *Light in August.* New York: Modern Library, 1950.

Rubel, Warren Gunther. "The Structural Function of the Christ Figure in the Fiction of William Faulkner." Ph.D. diss., Univ. of Arkansas, 1964. 96–146.

Schlepper, Wolfgang. "Knowledge and Experience in Faulkner's *Light in August*." *Jahrbuch für Amerikastudien* 18 (1973): 182–94.

Schoenberg, Estelle. *Old Tales and Talking: Quentin Compson in William Faulkner's* Absalom, Absalom! *and Related Works.* Jackson: Univ. of Mississippi Press, 1977.

Singleton, Marvin K. "Personae at Law and Equity: The Unity of Faulkner's *Absalom, Absalom!*" *Papers on Language and Literature* 3 (Fall): 354–70.

Slabey, Robert M. "Faulkner's *Mosquitoes* and Joyce's *Ulysses*." *Revue des Langues Vivantes* 28 (1962): 435–37.

———. "Myth and Ritual in *Light in August*." *Texas Studies in Literature and Language* 2 (1960): 328–49.

Slatoff, Walter J. *Quest for Failure: A Study of William Faulkner.* Ithaca: Cornell Univ. Press, 1960.

Smith, Don Noel. "The Design of Faukner's *Light in August*." Ph.D. diss., Univ. of Michigan, 1970.

Smith, Julian. "A Source for Faulkner's *A Fable*." *American Literature* 40 (1968): 394–97.

Solomon, Robert H. "Classical Myth in the Novels of William Faulkner." Ph.D. diss., Pennsylvania State Univ., 1976.

Straumann, Heinrich. *William Faulkner.* Frankfort: Athenaum Verlag, 1968.

Sundquist, Eric J. *Faulkner: The House Divided.* Baltimore: Johns Hopkins Univ. Press, 1983. 64–95.

Taylor, Carole Anne. "*Light in August:* The Epistemology of Tragic Paradox." *Texas Studies in Language and Literature* 22 (1980): 48–68.

Taylor, Walter. *Faulkner's Search for a South.* Urbana: Univ. of Illinois Press, 1983.

Thompson, Deborah. "*Light in August:* A Manuscript Fragment." *Mississippi Quarterly* 32 (1979): 477–80.

Thompson, Lawrance. *William Faulkner: An Introduction and Interpretation.* New York. Barnes & Noble, 1963.

Vickery, Olga. *The Novels of William Faulkner: A Critical Interpretation.* Baton Rouge: Louisiana State Univ. Press, 1959.

Waggoner, Hyatt H. *William Faulkner: From Jefferson to the World.* Lexington: Univ. of Kentucky Press, 1959.

Watkins, Floyd C. "William Faulkner in His Own Country." *Emory University Quarterly* 15 (1959): 237.

Yonce, Margaret. "Faulkner's 'Atthis' and 'Attis': Some Sources of Myth." *Mississippi Quarterly* 23 (1970): 289–98.

Yorks, Samuel A. "Faulkner's Woman: The Peril of Mankind." *Arizona Quarterly* 17 (1961): 119–29.

Index